Crowood Travel Guides are the essential starting point for a holiday to remember – and they'll be the signpost to enjoyment every step of the way. Easy-to-follow, practical advice, combined with a warmth and enthusiasm for the peoples and cultures of the world, mean that they'll be turned to again and again for direction and inspiration.

The Dordogne

First published in 1991 by
The Crowood Press Ltd
Gipsy Lane, Swindon
Wiltshire SN2 6DQ
© The Crowood Press Ltd. 1991

British Library Cataloguing in Publication Data
Marriott, Michael, *1928 –*
   The Dordogne. – (Crowood travel guides)
   I. Title
   914.47204839

   ISBN 1–85223–461–X

All photographs by the author except pages 36, 41, 42–43, 58, 63,
64, 70, 90, 92, 110–111, 116, 126, 132–133, 142–143, 167, 175,
232–233, 241, 264–265, 271, 274, 276–277, 285(top), 312
by Tony Oliver with thanks to Sealink.

Maps by Taurus Graphics
Typesetting and page layouts by Visual Image
Printed and bound by Times Publishing Group, Singapore

The Dordogne
Crowood Travel Guide

Michael Marriott

The Crowood Press

The Dordogne

Contents

The Dordogne of the Midi-Pyrénées region – early mist over the river near Martel in the *département* of Lot

Introduction High in the north-eastern Auvergne on a flank of the jagged Puy de Sancy, the river Dore rises from its volcanic bedrock. From a neighbouring peak, the Puy de Cacodogne, the river Dogne bubbles up from its source and flows down to join the Dore. At the confluence, these two streams become the Dordogne – one of the most beautiful and certainly one of the most dramatic water-courses in France.

Dordogne - Périgord: Le pays de l'Homme

Once a thunderous torrent along the upper reaches, the river has been tamed by extensive and elaborate barraging, so that where there was foaming whitewater, there is now placid and regulated calm. But the work of man in taming the waters is, geologically speaking, very recent and the landscape between Clermont-Ferrand and Bordeaux is marked with the spectacular effects of thousands of years of the river scouring and sculpting the limestone strata of the river valley. Along the upper and central reaches of the main river and its neighbours, the Cère and the Vézère, the river has created gorges and ravines of great splendour – a landscape of grandeur through which the upper Dordogne flows with restrained power.

Lower down, the river flows more quietly through the gentle landscape of western Aquitaine, where grapevines, soft fruit and cereal crops patchwork the river valley flanks, and completes its journey spilling into the Atlantic Ocean via the Gironde estuary, after tracing a route of almost three hundred miles.

The Dordogne river, like so many other waterways in France, also lends its name to a regional *département* which spreads wide to the north of the central river area. The *préfecture* of the Dordogne *département* is Périgueux, the ancient capital city of Périgord, some 35 kilometres north of the river. Here there are still vestigial

The spectacular scenery of ancient France yet with every traveller comfort and convenience - La Roque - Gageac, south of Sarlat

remains of second- to fourth-century ramparts and a splendid twelfth-century cathedral magnificently restored in Byzantine style during the nineteenth century.

Sarlat-la-Canéda too, a cluster of medieval France around a twelfth-century cathedral, is also distant from the Dordogne banks, but in the Dordogne *département,* as is Les Eyzies-de-Tayac,

fount of pre-history and arguably the most significant crucible of early *Homo-sapiens* on the continent of Europe.

This is rich and diverse country offering much to a visitor in search of traditional France. As well as the famous attractions of Rocamadour and the Lascaux cave paintings, there are many lesser-known features like Château de Val, a fifteenth-century

11

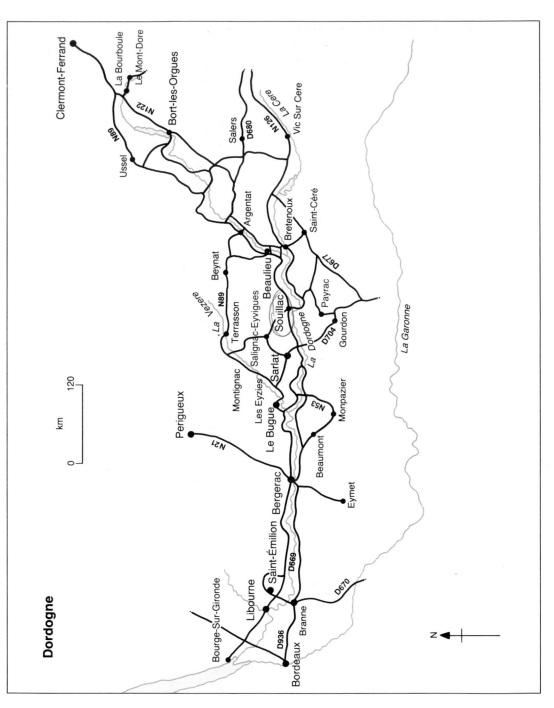

Dordogne

fairy-tale structure near Bort-les-Orgues, and the cliff dwellings of venerable La Roque-Gageac on the Dordogne river south of Sarlat. But, above all, the region attracts the visitor because of its peaceful, rolling countryside. There are no crowded beaches, no major conurbations, and no motorways in the Dordogne. There is only one sizeable town, Bergerac, actually on the Dordogne river, and predominantly life revolves around the small villages, market towns and farming communities. The people live a relatively simple way of life and are courteous and welcoming to visitors. The farms and vineyards of the Dordogne yield some of the best produce and wine to be found in all France. The cuisine of the area, dispensed mainly from family-owned restaurants and country hotels, is also outstanding. Périgueux is the regional centre of the *foie-gras* production and at nearby Sorges there is a museum devoted to the history of truffles!

The vineyards around the lower reaches of the river from Bergerac to the Gironde estuary are famed for the quality and variety of Bordeaux vintages, while around the upper reaches of the mighty river the piquant Auvergne cheeses are produced. Crops of chestnuts, apples, strawberries and walnuts come from Périgord, and Limousin beef, from animals that graze in the open air all year round, is much admired.

For those in search of more active holidays, the Dordogne has much to offer too. Gentle, easy-stage walking holidays, utilizing small hotels, cycle-touring or backpacking, overnighting at *gîtes* or camp grounds, or more strenuous climbing or white-water canoeing are all available and horse-riders and anglers are well provided for too.

Within the Dordogne region is encompassed a wide variety of landscape, a wealth of historic interest, a bountiful cuisine and scope for every kind of sporting and outdoor activity. Between May and October it basks beneath bright blue skies and offers the visitor its timeless appeal – an invitation to traditional France.

Part One: **Pre-Planning**

**The Dordogne at its most
tranquil and atmospheric
under early morning mist at
Beaulieu**

Pre-Planning

When to Go The traditional holiday period – June to September – is, in some ways, an ideal time to visit. The days are long, the nights are short, the sun shines, and the facilities and amenities are open and operating fully. The French Ministry of Tourism publishes a nationwide list of resorts, both coastal and inland, recommended as long-stay holiday bases. There are some 300 in all, called *Stations de Longue Durée*. This list is freely available (with map) from most main French tourist offices, and includes details of an exceptional variety of diverse holiday activities and facilities where tariffs are quoted as 'advantageous'. Of the Dordogne centres, it recommends Ste-Foy-la-Grande, Sarlat, Les-Eyzies, Rocamadour and Le Mont Dore.

At the peak period of August, however, the whole of the Republic seems to be *en vacances,* together with the vast crowds of foreign visitors, and France can seem to be intolerably crowded. Although this is less true of the Dordogne than of the Riviera or the Atlantic coast between Brest and Bayonne, given freedom of choice, there are better months to visit the region even though the holiday amenities may not be quite so comprehensive. Le Mont Dore, for example, in the Puy-de-Dôme *département* of Auvergne, is a four-season resort, with Super-Besse, a few kilometres southwards, increasingly popular with skiers.

Late October, especially to the south-west of the region away from the mountains, is often a time of warm, golden days that are perfect for hillwalking, horse-riding, cycling or simply exploring the great river in uncrowded peace and seclusion.

Earlier in the year, in the spring months of April and May, the Dordogne is at its most radiant, and while it may be cool in the higher areas, it is often warm and sunny at the western end of the region beyond Bergerac and towards the Gironde estuary.

The mean annual sunshine average of the Dordogne is between 1,800 and 2,000 hours, while the average summertime temperature is 20–22°C (a couple of degrees less in the Auvergne mountain region). In winter, while the air temperature at the western end of the river in the Bordeaux area seldom varies from 6–8°C, in the Mont Dore area where the Puy de Sancy towers to 1,886 metres above sea-level, the winter temperature is often below zero, with frequent snowfalls. Average rainfall here is over 1,000mm annually, while at the western end it is approximately 800mm.

Travel Documents To visit France you need a valid passport. Keep it as safe as possible. Caravanners and campers can also apply for an International Camping Carnet, acceptable at all French touring parks and campsites in lieu of the more valuable documents. It is available from the Caravan Club, East Grinstead House, East Grinstead, West Sussex RE19 1UA (for members only), or the Camping and Caravanning Club, 11 Grosvenor Place, London SW1 0EY, or the AA or RAC. A modest fee is charged for this document, which bears an insurance stamp giving third party insurance cover in respect of camping equipment. It also entitles the holder to slightly reduced camp fees at some sites.

British drivers must have a full driving licence, third-party insurance indemnity against injury to other persons, the vehicle registration document and a GB sticker affixed to the rear of their vehicle. A Green Card is no longer obligatory for residents within the EEC although it is the document most readily accepted in the case of accidents, and offers cover against damage to another vehicle.

Health There are few infection sources to worry about in France. Indeed, some would claim that the drinking water, for example, is much better than in other countries. There is a seasonal surfeit of mosquitoes in low-lying areas like the Carmargue, or the marshy Solonge area. The Dordogne is not overly plagued by insects, either fliers or crawlers, compared to the hotter regions of the south, but if you are particularly susceptible to stings or bites, pack a suitable insect repellent for a high summer visit. Unless you have a cast-iron constitution, think carefully about eating shellfish anywhere inland and never drink hotel tap water (one of the most frequent causes of serious stomach upset). Enjoy the Dordogne sunshine but be reasonable about sudden, lengthy exposure. Those rays are appreciably stronger than the British variety.

Rabies Never forget that rabies is endemic throughout most of the European mainland. *Never* go to the assistance of a sick animal, no matter how distressing the case; don't attract the attention of any stray dog, seek immediate medical advice, no matter how superficial the bite may appear. The government is currently investing vast sums in a programme of wildlife vaccination, with tasty edible baits (often distributed by air-drops) giving animals immunity for a year or more. According to the medical authorities, France should become virtually rabies-free within five years. Rabies is rare, but it definitely pays to be aware and circumspect.

Medical expenses, in case of injury or illness, can be high. British visitors should obtain Form E11 from any Department of Health office, which entitles the holder to free (or reduced) emergency treatment under an EEC reciprocal agreement. The document is permanently valid as long as the holder continues to live in Britain and gives detailed information about procedure abroad in case of injury or illness. It does not necessarily cover all medical expenses and it never covers the cost of bringing a person back to the UK in the event of serious illness. In France, you can expect to be refunded about 75 per cent of medical fees, and for more comprehensive coverage you should take out a personal insurance policy.

Emergency Services:
Le Mont Dore

Medical centre, 2 Rue du Capitaine Chazotte (Tel: 73 65 22 22). Chemist: M. Camus, Pharmacie du Parc (Tel: 73 65 05 53), 24 hrs. Doctor: J. P. Baud, 6 Allée Georges Sand (Tel: 73 65 00 80 or 46 47 59 21).

Dentist: J. F. Dubourg, 45 Place de la République (Tel: 73 65 07 87).

Police or fire (Tel: 73 65 01 70). Ambulance: 9 Avenue de la Libération (Tel: 73 65 05 63).

La Bourboule

Medical service: Dr M. Barjaud, Villa les Elfes, Avenue d'Angleterre (Tel: 73 81 06 15).

Chemist: M. Petiot, Pharmacie des Establissements Boulevard Clémenceau (Tel: 73 81 06 09).

Dentist: G Ferreyrolles, Résidence Ambassadeurs, Boulevard Clémenceau (Tel: 73 81 04 36).

Police: (Tel: 73 81 03 71).

Ambulance: M. Lionel, Boulevard Louis Choussy (Tel: 73 81 12 60).

Clermont-Ferrand

Emergency medical help (Secours Medical d'Urgence) including anti-poison centre (Tel: 73 27 33 33).

Police: (Tel: 73 92 10 70).

Bort-les-Orgues

Local hospital: (Tel: 55 96 02 51).

Ambulance: Mme Doutreluigne, 105 Rue de Paris (Tel: 55 96 86 58).

Police: Avenue Jean-Jaurés (Tel: 55 96 00 17).

Doctor: Dr Boutarel, Avenue de la Gare (Tel: 55 96 08 24).

Dentist: Dr A. Dupont (Dental surgeon), Boulevard Voltaire (Tel: 55 96 76 30).

Chemist: Pharmacie Casero, Place Marmontel (Tel: 55 96 00 72).

Beaulieu

Several medical doctors in town (médecins): Dr Blavoux, Rue General de Gaulle (Tel: 55 91 00 12) and Dr Bouchetoux, Rue de la République (Tel: 55 91 20 67) are two of them.

Souillac

Ambulance: Taxi-ambulance Richard – 24 hour service (Tel: 65 37 06 13).

Doctor: Doctors Jallais & Machemy, Les 2 Pigeonniers (Tel: 65 32 78 43).

Dental surgeon: F. Joffroy, 34 Boulevard L. J. Malvy (Tel: 65 37 03 14).

Chemist: Pharmacie Bourdet, 25 Boulevard L. J. Malvy (Tel: 65 32 79 48).

Police: Route de Sarlat (Tel: 65 32 78 17).

Fire station: (Tel: 65 37 82 18 or 65 32 78 17).

Bergerac

Hospital Mixte et Hospice, Avenue Calmotte (Tel: 53 57 77 77).

Gendarmerie: (Tel: 53 57 00 17).

Libourne

Hospital: 112 Rue de la Marne – general hospital (Tel: 57 51 22 22).

Police: 76 Cours Tourny (Tel: 57 51 11 22).

Fire Station: 20 Cours Tourny (Tel: 57 51 05 94).

Bordeaux

Doctors: (SOS) (Tel: 56 44 74 74).

Chemists: all night service (Tel: 56 90 92 75).

Hospital: (Tel: 56 96 83 83).

Anti-poison centre: (Tel: 56 96 40 80).

British Consul: 353 Boulevard President Wilson (Tel: 56 42 34 13).

How to Get There

Airports: Bordeaux, Clermont-Ferrand (via Paris or Lyon).

Main SNCF stations:
Ste-Foy-la-Grande, Bergerac, Sarlat, Souillac, Perigueux, Bordeaux, Clermont-Ferrand.

Roads from Britain: A26, A1, A10 to Bordeaux (about 877km).

By Plane Although outside the principal area covered by this guide, Bordeaux is the most convenient point for any lower Dordogne visit if you prefer to use local transport. The major international airport is 10km to the west of the city, with good rail connections to all the principal towns and places of interest along the lower and central reaches of the river and the *département* of Dordogne. British Airways have daily scheduled flights to Bordeaux from London Heathrow, Birmingham, Manchester, Newcastle, Glasgow, Edinburgh and Belfast (flight reservations: 071-897 4000). Try to reserve your seat as far in advance as possible (especially in high summer), bearing in mind that passengers with hand luggage only are generally subjected to shorter check-in times than those with cumbersome excess.

For the upper Dordogne, Clermont-Ferrand is the nearest major airport and Air France operate two scheduled flights from Britain every day to this destination – London Heathrow to Paris, then Paris to Clermont; and London to Lyon, then Lyon to Clermont. Rail connections from Clermont are excellent, via a scenic line which winds its way in a huge semi-circular loop around the Monts Dômes high country to Le Mont Dore terminus, below the Puy de Sancy. Air France also run flights from a number of regional British airports, including Birmingham, Manchester and Southampton.

France, almost hexagonal in shape, and approximately 600 miles wide and 600 miles long, is crossed in just about an hour by plane – as long as you suffer no delays. These afflict charter companies more than scheduled airlines as a general rule, but it is possible to gain considerable financial concessions if you have no

**Train tickets must be
'compostése' (stamped) in the
waiting room machine**

objection to travelling with the former. You need to decide on
your priorities.

By Train The French SNCF (Société Nationale des Chemins
de Fer) is acknowledged to be one of the best in the world; it is
certainly one of the most extensive and innovative. Any SNCF
office will provide full information about local and other travel,
and where no trains run at all, as in the mountainous areas of the
Midi, there are organized rail-road links with coach or bus
companies.

In Britain you can book through any travel centre to any of
the Dordogne towns of note, including Ste-Foy-la-Grande,
Bergerac, Sarlat, Souillac and Périgueux. The route is via
Bordeaux for the western Dordogne, or Clermont-Ferrand for
the north-east. Fares include the ferry crossing of the Channel
and senior citizens can claim an appreciable deduction if they
hold a British Rail pass as can students (*see* details on travel
concession cards).

In the Dordogne region itself, the rail system extends eastwards
alongside the river (with branch lines south to the towns of
Gourdon and Rocamadour and northwards to Périgueux),
terminating with the high country of the Dordogne gorges to the
north of Castelnau. There is another excellent link between
Clermont and Le Mont Dore. Fast and efficient as the French rail

service may be, the super-speed TGV has not yet reached the Dordogne valley, and is not likely to for some years to come.

In France, every principal railway station is an excellent source of travel information, while visitors staying a while in Paris can call the English-language train information service on 45 82 08 41. Finally, there is a first-rate Air France – SNCF link service. You can fly direct to Paris from Gatwick, Stansted, Bristol or Southampton then transfer to rail for a five-and-a-half-hour journey to Bergerac for a very competitive inclusive return fare. For further details write to French Railways House, 179 Piccadilly, London W1V 0BA, requesting general information on rail travel in France (Tel: 071-493 9731).

By Coach The most competitively-priced of the transport services, the inter-European coach schedules, have now reached a high level of sophistication, speed, comfort and safety. European coach operators such as National Express operate services to over 190 destinations, including Bordeaux and Clermont-Ferrand (coach/train). There are daily departures throughout the year from all principal British cities and most return tickets are valid for up to 6 months. Victoria Coach Station, in London, is the main departure terminal for Europe and, once aboard the coach, passengers stay with the vehicle to their final destination in most cases. There are financial concessions for students and senior citizens. For more information call National Express on (London) 071-730 8235 (Birmingham) 021-622 4225, or (Manchester) 061-236 2120.

By Car France is still the supreme country of western Europe for leisure motorists, despite the horrendous crush of traffic on major routes on some high days and holidays. There is the prospect of discovering a still largely pastoral country for those prepared to explore minor-road France *en route* to the Dordogne region.

Drivers with limited time who want to use the speedy motorways should take the A26 from just outside Calais, then the A1 to join the Paris *péripherique,* then the A10 direct to the northern outskirts of Bordeaux via Orléans, Tours and Poitiers. It is *péage* all the way (save for the capital ring-road) – about half as much again as the amount spent on fuel. The distance from Calais to Bordeaux by the most direct route is approximately 877km.

For a more leisurely trip to the Dordogne area, the following route passes through beautiful and historical parts of France: south-west to Rouen, south to Chartres, Vendôme, Blois, Loches, Chateaureaux, Limoges and on to Périgueux.

In France seat belts must be worn, and young children must be back-seat passengers. A red triangle is compulsory in case of a breakdown or an accident, unless the vehicle is fitted with hazard warning lights. It is probably advisable to take both in a country where driving is rather robust. Speed limits are: *autoroutes* 130kmph (80mph); dual carriageways 110kmph (68mph); other roads 90kmph (56mph); and built-up areas 60kmph (37mph), or as directed. Yellow headlights are not necessary, though adjustment of the dipping system should be made.

Ensure that the vehicle is thoroughly serviced before leaving; particularly the tyres, brakes, clutch and radiator hoses, which may be affected by the heat. At the peak of summer, it may pay to install a summer-grade thermostat in the radiator.

Driving on the right swiftly becomes second nature, but be wary first thing in the morning especially if the road is not busy.

Ferry Services Even the most apprehensive of sea voyagers should not be troubled by crossing from England to France on one of the new generation of super-ferries. Meeting the challenge of the charmless Chunnel, these are bigger and better than ever, sophisticated, and stable enough to smooth even the choppiest waters. Sailing times are around 75 minutes on the Dover to Calais run, slightly longer on the Folkestone to Boulogne route, and only 30 minutes on the Dover to Calais Hoverspeed 'flight'.

It *is* possible to arrive at Dover Eastern Dock, pay, board and be off driving in France within a couple of hours, but you should book in advance for peak periods: P&O European Ferries, 0304 214422; Sealink British Ferries, 0233 47033; Sally Ferries, 0843 595522. Brochures detailing all routes and services, timetables and fare structures, can be obtained from P&O European Ferries, Channel House, Channel View Road, Dover, Kent CT17 9TJ; Sealink Holidays, Charter House, Park Street, Ashford, Kent TN24 8EX; Sally Ferries, Sally Holidays, 81 Piccadilly, London W1V 9HF. Sally Line operate between Ramsgate and Dunkerque, P&O between Portsmouth and Cherbourg or Le Havre, and Sealink between Weymouth and Cherbourg (summer only).

All the ferry companies offer a range of special inducements for motorists; the more off-season you travel, on sailings at 'unsociable hours' the greater the fare reductions.

Independent foot passengers should try the acknowledged Channel crossing route between Folkestone and Boulogne on the Sealink twins, Hengist and Horsa, which cater specially for car-less travellers.

Travel Concession Cards The French have long held in high regard those members of its society at either end of the age range. Students and senior citizens benefit widely as travellers and concessions are now extended to other members of the European Community. Students carrying a valid International Student Identity Card are entitled to discounts of up to 50 per cent on train and other travel fares and on museum, theatre and cinema tickets. All foreign tourists are entitled to a *France Vacances* Rail Pass and its bonuses, while senior citizens over 60 can buy an RES card (*Rail Europ Senior*), at a modest cost. This entitles the holder to up to 50 per cent reduction on rail travel in France, provided a BR Senior Citizen Railcard is already held. For students under 26 there is similar provision under the *Carré Jeune/Carte Jeune* system. These rail passes must be ordered through a travel agency in Great Britain.

Getting About

Walking Perhaps the best and most revealing way of seeing the Dordogne is on foot; this is quite a compact region with something or somewhere of interest at regular and not too distant intervals. Ideal are the *Sentiers de Grande Randonnée,* splendid long-distance footpaths which criss-cross the length and breadth of France.

In the Dordogne the GR6 and GR46 meander throughout the western and central areas, largely within the Périgueux–Sarlat–Bergerac triangle; while the GR44 and GR641 traverse the upper river area on the Limousin/Auvergne borders. These major long-distance trails are supplemented by many local footpath routes, linking selected towns and villages of scenic interest, or circular in configuration. Such pedestrian ventures can be greatly rewarding. For those wishing to stride out with map and compass, the *Topo-Guides,* produced by the *Fédération Française de la Rondonnée Pédestre,* are indispensible companions. These pocket

Pastoral France is well served by a splendid network of long-distance and local footpaths, like this forest route in Aquitaine

Bicycle touring is very popular, though parts of central and upper Dordogne are quite hilly

booklets describe the routes, with IGN map reproductions, plus refreshment points and lodging addresses *en route,* local transport information, environmental features and other useful information. The volumes for the Dordogne can be found at Robertson McCarta, 122 Kings Cross Road, London WC1X 9DS. They operate an efficient postal service, and their telephone number is 071-278 8276.

Cycling Cycling as a method of leisure travel involves two quite distinct pursuits – touring and using pedal-power to get about locally.

Touring is very popular with visitors to the Dordogne for, although the region is distinctly hilly in parts, there are no real mountains (except at the extreme north-eastern end. The best way of arriving in the touring area with your own machine is to travel by air. Cycles are included as baggage allowance on most scheduled flights, while camping kit in saddlebags or panniers is classified as hand baggage. You may be required to remove the front wheel and pedals, so carry suitable spanners and arrive at least an hour earlier than the stipulated time, to avoid any hitches. The logical destination for Dordogne-bound cycle-tourists is Bordeaux.

Cycles are rated as hand baggage on French trains, as in Britain, although there is no guarantee that you and your bike will arrive simultaneously. Allow at least two days (sometimes longer) for the bike to catch you up. An alternative, for train travellers, is to take advantage of the *train-plus-vélo* service operated by the SNCF. Cycles are available for hire on a daily basis from some 250 railway stations throughout France, and special cycle hire centres are also located in all major holiday towns and in many inland resorts. Travel as lightweight as possible (even if cycle camping), in the interests of safety, mobility and enjoyment; and don't be too ambitious about daily mileages. Cycling through this part of France should be as serene and deeply pleasurable as the countryside itself. For comprehensive advice on all aspects of cycle-touring in France, contact the Cyclists Touring Club, a much-respected organization which has been looking after cyclists' interests since 1897. Their national headquarters are at Cotterell House, 69 Meadrow, Godalming, Surrey GU7 3HS (Tel: 048 68 7217).

Car Hire Car hire is possible in France at all major airports and at many of the domestic terminals. Hire is usually on a weekend or weekly basis, and may or may not include unlimited mileage. Hiring a car is not cheap, but it does give you valuable independent mobility. Avis have a reservation centre in Boulogne (Tel: 4 609 92 12), where operators are bilingual; for Hertz ring Paris (Tel: 4 574 59 33). The SNCF also runs a car-hire service known as SCETA for rail passengers, who can arrive at one of about 200 train stations throughout France and find a car ready and waiting (for information Tel: 0 505 05 11).

For those who don't object to the open air (no hardship in summertime Dordogne), moped hire is an economical alternative to hiring a car. Most sizeable towns have hire centres, usually run in conjunction with cycle hire. You must be over 21, and have held a full driving licence for more than a year to comply with the law.

Taxis, Buses and Local Trains Taxi ranks will be found in all French towns of any size, certainly at mainline railway stations and often prominently lined up in the town centre.

Smaller towns are also efficiently served, and you can usually conjure a cab by enquiring at the railway station, the *Syndicat d'Initiative,* the *Mairie* (town hall), or the ubiquitous café. These same sources of information are equally reliable about bus services within the *département.* Country bus services *do* run regularly between strategic towns and villages, but may not always be immediately apparent to the stranger.

Visitors to the Dordogne who want to get around western and central parts of the region by train are particularly well served, for the railway network serves all the principal riverside towns of the Dordogne *département,* as well as outlying resorts like Le Bugue on the Vézère river to the north, and Gourdon to the south, below the vast Gramat plateau.

Driving French drivers pay no road fund tax, just extra for their petrol, so the car owner pays according to kilometres covered. Premium petrol is *super,* lower octane is *essence* and lead-free fuel is *sans plomb.* Diesel is appreciably cheaper than in Britain. Try to buy fuel from supermarket or hypermarket pumps if you can, especially if you are filling a near-empty tank (but bear in mind that this service is usually suspended between midday and 2pm, sometimes 3pm.

French drivers seldom cruise, but hustle along on all roads. If you wish to admire a view or whatever, pull up and park, but never on a main road as this is illegal. If you enjoy pottering, take to the country routes (not at all difficult in the Dordogne), where, more often than not (especially outside the peak summer season), you will frequently seem to have the whole of France to yourself. If you dislike legions of TIRs, restrict your travel to Saturdays and Sundays when the heavies are virtually silent.

Drive steadily, neither too fast nor too slow, and never make an erratic move if you happen to lose the way. Be extra careful when overtaking, for obvious reasons, and respect the law. There are swingeing fines and possible jail for drunken driving, and on-the-spot fines for not wearing seat belts, crossing a double white line, exceeding the speed limit, and so on. That can make a big dent in your holiday budget!

Driving around France is not difficult. Not long ago the roads were primitive, dangerously cambered, potholed, interspersed with crude *pavé,* and only sporadically signposted, but within three decades the system has graduated from the worst to the very best. Parking can sometimes be a problem, but only in major cities and larger town centres. Parking meters and double yellow lines are, as yet, scarcely seen in rural France; and that applies to much of the Dordogne. Exceptions are obvious tourist attractions like Rocamadour and Sarlat-la-Canéda.

France now boasts more than 6,000 kilometres of *autoroute*, most of which is toll road (*péage*), except, for example, crossing cities like Lille and around the Paris *péripherique*. If you aren't in too much of a hurry, the prettier, less-used *Bison Futé* routes are there for your pleasure and convenience, usually signposted simply as *Bis*.

While that erstwhile heart-stopper, *priorité à droite* has all but disappeared from the open road with the advent of the international stop sign, and the traffic roundabout, it still pays to be wary about traffic entering the mainstream from the right when city driving.

If you are stopped by the police you *must* be able to produce your driving licence, insurance certificate (and Green Card if you have one), and the vehicle registration document.

The Disabled Visitor France extends a helping hand where possible to the disabled, for whom using certain forms of transport, negotiating historic public buildings and grounds, or locating suitable accommodation, often requires disproportionate effort. Helpful travel hints for the handicapped are contained within a pamphlet available from the French Tourist Office in London. Hotels with facilities for the disabled are listed regionally, usually available locally though tourist offices or the *Syndicat d'Initiative*. For the most comprehensive information on holiday planning and travel abroad, the recognized source in Britain is RADAR (the Royal Association for Disability and Rehabilitation), at 25 Mortimer Street, London W1N (Tel: 071-637 5400).

Accommodation

Hotels France provides an extraordinary diversity of traveller accommodation, from the palatial luxury of the Ritz in Paris and the Negresco in Nice, to the camp ground in a natural setting that is no less appealing to the outdoor lover. Between these two extremes, there is a wealth of choice to suit every preference and every pocket.

France offers accommodation to suit every pocket, from the luxury hotels to simple campsites. This is a middle-bracket sign with appeal for tourists seeking a rural base

In France hotels are graded by the Ministry of Tourism from one-star to four-star luxurious. In the Dordogne – with one or two notable exceptions – the average hotel is comfortable and homely rather than sumptuous, and the average two-star room will be reasonably priced. Rates quoted are normally per night for two persons, with Continental breakfast (*café* and croissants), usually extra. The rates must, by law, be posted on the back of the door of the room.

Very few single rooms are available, although a third bed for a child will seldom cost more than a third of the room rate, while many hotel chains offer a free extra bed for a child under 12 years of age. Hotels with their own restaurants may expect you to take dinner when staying the night. Room and all meals – full board or *pension* – will usually be offered for a stay of three nights or longer. Half board – *demi-pension* – comprising bed, breakfast and a main meal, is often available outside the peak holiday period, and increasingly during the high season too, in recognized resort areas.

There are over seventeen thousand *hôtels de tourisme* throughout France and they generally reflect an overall high standard for their respective star ratings. In the *département* of Dordogne, there are 60 towns and villages with hotel accommodation listed in the *Michelin Red Guide,* as well as countless alternatives, including self-catering holiday units. There are none of those impersonal chain hotels though. The Dordogne is devoted to the traditional idea of good service in comfortable country establishments. Many are family managed, with the emphasis on highly efficient, low-profile value for money. For this kind of accommodation, coupled with renowned regional cooking, there are many examples of the famous *Logis de France* in the region (over 5,000 nationwide, mostly of one- to two-star category). For a free guide and a full list of the addresses of *Logis et Auberges de France,* write to the French Government Tourist Office, 178 Piccadilly, London W1V 0AL. Write early in the year and enclose stamps for postage.

Advance booking is advisable in July and August almost anywhere in France, while in the Dordogne it is almost obligatory.

Gîtes de France There are now more than 20,000 of these reasonably-priced self-catering units in France, usually located inland, within or near small country villages. *Gîtes d'Étape* which

A welcome indicator for the holidaymaker. There are numerous 'B & B' boards like this throughout the region

may be small country cottages, village houses, flat extensions or parts of farm outbuildings, while *Gîtes Ruraux* offer simple accommodation in farms, cottages or similar. Sometimes food supplies are available, or cooked meals are served, depending on the location and the season of the year. There is now also a growing number of 'second-generation' *gîtes*, purpose-built, and often beautifully appointed. These are usually located in areas of dramatic visual impact and their rates reflect their quality. For details send a stamped addressed envelope to *Gîtes de France* at the French Government Tourist Office, 178 Piccadilly, London W1V OAL.

An extension of the *gîte* concept is the farmhouse holiday, now increasingly sought by visitors in certain areas of France. The Dordogne is one of the regions most in demand. Visitors live in, taking meals with the resident family. The rates are reasonable and for those wanting to sample true country life (and perhaps improve their French), the farmhouse holiday is excellent.

Youth Hostels *Auberges de la Jeunesse* constitute a non-profit-making organization, founded in 1930, to help young people travel the world, take part in different activities organized in the hostels, and meet young people from other countries and different backgrounds. Length of stay at French hostels is usually limited to three or four nights during the peak season. Dormitory sleeping arrangements and communal catering routines are the

A welcoming but no-frills youth hostel, opposite the Chapel of penitents in old Beaulieu

norm. For full information in Britain about youth hostelling in France, contact the YHA, 14 Southampton Street, London WC2E 7HY (Tel: 071-836 8541).

Caravanning and Camping France is an excellent country for the touring fraternity and outdoor enthusiasts. The summer climate along with an enormous diversity of terrain make it an ideal holiday destination for the caravanner and the camper.

Every city and town in France boasts at least one municipal camp ground, and many villages do too. You can park your van or pitch your tent in an almost endless variety of settings, ranging from the gracious grounds of medieval *châteaux* (using the long-established *Castels Camping et Caravaning* chain), and architect-designed and landscaped leisure parks providing super-modern amenities, to simple farm sites (*camping à la ferme*), or *Aire Naturel* paddocks, with their provision of basic traveller needs.

The Dordogne has its fair share of touring parks and camping sites. As in the rest of France, some are superb, some are mediocre, while a few are only tolerable for the briefest of visits.

Good examples will be indicated here for each area. Probably the most widely used camp ground guide is the *Michelin Green Guide*, available in most good bookshops.

Currency The *franc* is the currency of France and it is divided into one hundred *centimes*. When changing money don't be afraid to ask the cashier for smaller notes if they might be more useful. Two hundred and five hundred *franc* notes are quicker for the teller, but you may find it hard to change them later.

Banks are open in France from Monday to Friday in major cities and some larger towns and holiday resorts, and often from Tuesday to Saturday in provincial towns. In rural villages they are sometimes only open on market days. There are no standard business hours for banks; between 9am and 12 noon and between 2.30pm and 4pm are the best times to try. France has eleven national bank holidays every year, so don't get caught out! Always use a bank to exchange money if you can; although hotels and exchange agencies may be useful in an emergency, their rate will certainly be lower than the official one. Roughly, you can consider ten *francs* to equal £1.

For caravanning and camping France is arguably the best country in the world, but you must be gregarious to enjoy family sites

Credit Cards Out of courtesy, always ask before offering plastic as payment, especially off the beaten tourist track. Increasingly, cards are acceptable in recognized resort areas and this includes most of the Dordogne region. Hotels, restaurants, fashionable shops and so on will accept Visa cards, American Express and Diners Club, but may be considerably less enthusiastic about others. Visa cards are the most widely accepted of all, with over six million outlets around the world.

Cheques Travellers cheques are still the most widely favoured and safest traveller currency; when the cheques are exhausted you know the holiday is over! Rapidly gaining in popularity, however, is the Eurocard, issued by banks and used in conjunction with special Eurocheques. With a Eurocard you can withdraw a fixed maximum of local currency at any foreign bank and your current account is then debited. They may be even more attractive than travellers cheques, especially since the exact amount of francs demanded at the French bank will be delivered.

Eurocheques are popular with travellers

Security Everyone is more security-conscious today than was necessary a couple of decades ago, especially when travelling abroad. France is perhaps less plagued by opportunist thieves than most other western European countries, but this should not lead to complacent behaviour on the part of the visitor. France has its black spots – the fun-strips of the Riviera and cities like Marseille – but there are no such areas in the Dordogne. None the less, if you must take high-value items like jewellery, don't flaunt them. Leave valuables in hotel safes, and never leave anything precious in a hotel room.

Thieves can spot a quality handbag and a bulging wallet as swiftly as they can snatch it, so keep a low profile by dressing down. Carry cash in a money-belt and, if you must carry something in your hand, make it a dreary-looking carrier bag. Appear just a little less affluent than you really are.

Gratuities On the other hand, tip according to your true worth to gain full Gallic approval from hotel staff, taxi drivers, waiters and (always customary in France), cinema and theatre usherettes. Generally, a service charge is included in hotel and restaurant bills, provided it is *service compris,* and there is no obligation to pay a *centime* more unless you want to. Small change can be a token of appreciation and often the only way of relieving yourself of escalating piles of coins; a saucer is frequently displayed with prominence on café counters. In public toilets that are staffed there is a small set fee which, if paid to the exact *centime,* will often raise a reproving glance rather than a farewell smile.

If your hotel or restaurant bill does not display the words *service compris,* you should add on around 15 per cent of the total. If you are in doubt, or if funds are dwindling, always enquire beforehand about prices. Never be shy as financial prudence is always appreciated, indeed admired, by the majority of French people.

Restaurants France is traditionally the gastronomic centre of the western world, although the French are no longer the only nationals who live to eat. In some of the busier cities, too, the fast food habit is on the increase. None the less, in general the choice, preparation and presentation of meals in *most* French hotels and restaurants is of an enviably high standard. However, don't expect culinary wizardry at every eating place – you won't find it just because you are in France.

Dining out is one of the greatest pleasures of being in France

It pays to shop around when you are looking for a restaurant. Evening strolling in search of somewhere nice to eat is practised just as much by the natives as it is by visitors and there can be no more pleasant way of honing the appetite than a ramble combined with a casual sightseeing tour of a medieval town in the cool of a summer evening. If there is already healthy patronage of a potential meal-stop, with cars (especially if they have French number-plates) jostling for parking space, the place will definitely be worth a visit.

36

On the other hand, if only the proprietor is visible, and there is no alternative, order frugally and stick to simple fare.

If you do find that full car park, you will discover that dining out in a well-run family hotel is one of the great pleasures of being in France. In the Dordogne region you can eat in restaurants noted for their *haute cuisine*, but tucking in with trencherman gusto in a cosy bistro alcove, perhaps adjacent to a busy bar, will be equally satisfying. The bistro scene may also

37

reward you with revealing glimpses of everyday French café life, adding richness and variety to your travel.

Dining out begins between 7.30 and 8pm (although the majority of French people take their main meal at midday). Restaurants specializing in *déjeuner* (lunch) may put on a restricted menu for *dîner* (dinner), but this is not always the case; look carefully at the menus displayed at restaurant entrances. You may choose an *à la carte* meal, where you select what you fancy, or the fixed-price dinner *un menu*. A *menu touristique* indicates a choice of various dishes for each course, served for a fixed price.

Bars When the sun is high in the sky, a priority for the traveller is liquid refreshment. Happily, in France you will never be far away from one of those ubiquitous little bars. Some are dull, impersonal and staffed by minders all but hostile to casual trade, but most are cosy, atmospheric and welcoming. Many of them serve simple snacks like the *Croque Monsieur* (toasted cheese sandwich), or *frites,* which hit the spot well, especially when accompanied by a *bière à la pression.*

Picnics Many of the French are still *paysans* at heart, never happier than when they are out of doors, *le pique-nique* is universally

For fun shopping and the best of really fresh fruit and vegetables the village and town markets are always the best bet in France

popular. Roadside picnic areas abound throughout France, often complete with tables and bench seating. Enjoy sitting under a shady chestnut tree on the banks of the Dordogne, with a freshly-baked *baguette,* regional cheese, fruit and a bottle of the local *Vin Rouge* – literally 'dining out'. This is the cheapest way of taking lunch almost anywhere in western Europe, and of course one of the most popular among both French and foreign motorists in transit.

Village Shops and Open Markets In almost any market town or village in France all the ingredients for a bumper picnic lunch can be collected within a hundred metres or so. First to the *boulangerie* for your fresh bread (white, brown or wholemeal nowadays), then to the *épicerie* for cheese, the *charcuterie* for pâté or a wide choice of cooked meats, often with dishes of prepared salads, and finally to the general grocery store (*alimentation*) for wine, soft drinks or bottled water.

Despite fierce competition from supermarkets and hypermarkets on the outskirts of almost every large town, the small shopkeeper retains a great deal of customer loyalty in rural France. For the French, life without the little shops, in country towns and in virtually every village, would be considered quite intolerable. Outside the big cities, the pace of life remains sanely steady, and it is important to exchange courtesies with, and glean the latest news and views from the local shopkeeper. This local communication is pleasing to see and experience and also infectious; it soon becomes a habit to say *bonjour* as you enter a shop and *au revoir* when you leave.

The traditional open market, which transforms a small town or village square into a bustle of colourful activity once (or more times) a week, is often a treasure-house of local produce, or specialized items of decorative or practical value. It is fun browsing and people-watching, and perhaps picking up a memento or two, but not really for serious shopping, unless you are fluent in French and know a real bargain when you see one. Exceptions are fresh fruit, preserves, honey, and other products for which the region is renowned.

Sunday morning is the ritual time to visit the *patisserie,* and this is almost a religious experience for many French families. The boxed and beribboned examples of the cake-maker's art are very expensive, but most visitors should be tempted at least once during their holiday.

The French telephone service is excellent. Car kiosks are well distributed and the cards themselves are available through numerous outlets

Supermarkets For all self-catering foreign visitors the supermarket is obviously the main food source, if only because of its convenience and because you need to know scarcely a word of French. Supermarket shopping is almost identical the world over, and not a stimulating experience. In France, patronize the supermarket rather than the hypermarket if food is your prime consideration – the latter does not always dispense top-quality edible produce – and do your shopping at any time other than Friday evening or Saturday morning if you can. Finally, don't be surprised to find that supermarkets (along with many other establishments), are closed on Mondays.

Food prices, whether at supermarkets or village stores, are comparable to those in Britain. The cost of the whole shopping basket may be a bit less if wine and beer are included. This applies to basic food stuffs only, not to exotic treats like the *patisserie* creations.

The Paper Shop The *Maison de la Presse* is the place for newspapers, magazines, postcards, local maps and guide booklets to surrounding attractions, sometimes available in English-language editions. English-language newspapers are usually available in larger towns or recognized holiday resorts, coastal or inland, but they will of course cost more than at home, and will often be at least one day out of date. French paper shops may also sell photographic film (and be a processing depot), and in some smaller towns the paper shop may stand in for the tourist office or *Syndicat d'Initiative* when it is closed, by keeping hand-out publicity material about the town and its environs.

The Pharmacie Although the French now have a health service, they have, until quite recently, had to be self-reliant in remedying ills. For any petty malady they make not for the local doctor (ie *médecin*), but for the chemist, who is usually highly skilled at diagnosing and dispensing for minor complaints, particularly those apt to affect the holiday visitor, like sunburn, diarrhoea, constipation, and minor injuries. Every town, even the smallest, boasts a *pharmacie* supplying a wide range of effective panaceas. Opening hours vary regionally, but it is common to find dispensaries open until 7.30pm or a little later.

Post and Telephone In France the post office (*Poste Téléphone Télégraphe*) is advertised by the initials *PTT*. Post-boxes are yellow, and stamps may be bought not only at post offices, but from tobacco shops, kiosks and cafés displaying the *Tabac* sign. Post offices are open from Monday to Friday, from 8 till 12 noon, and from 2 till 4pm. Saturday morning opening is from 8 till 12 noon. A *poste restante* service is available at most main post offices.

Part Two: **Local Colour**

Puy de Dômes

Local Colour

The French People The Frenchman, small of stature, moustachioed under a black beret, wine glass in one hand and *Gauloise sans filtre* in the other, is the conceptual archetype gone for ever. None the less, there are elements of truth in every well-observed cartoon, and the French *do* have certain specific characteristics. While generalizing is largely valueless, it is always fascinating.

Physically the French *are* slightly smaller, lighter of build and darker-complexioned than northern Europeans. They have piercing dark eyes, aquiline noses, and employ exaggerated gestures when conversing, inherited features and behavioural traits of their Celtic ancestors, an Indo-European race who migrated originally from the east. These, I suppose, might be considered to be their national characteristics. Regionally, there are wide ethnic gulfs. The stolid and pragmatic Normandy farmer and the factory worker from Lille are totally different from the mercurial and hedonistic southerner, who basks under the *Provençal* sun. The *Basques* and the *Bretons* of the western seaboard consider themselves nationals in their own right, as do the mountain people of the high Auvergne; while the cosmopolitan and urbane *Parisian* views all provincials with disdain.

Yet there is a curious, powerful bond that welds them irresistibly into a complete and cohesive whole. It was started by Charlemagne, largely achieved by Napoleon Bonaparte, and perpetuated by Charles de Gaulle. The symbol of nationhood, the blue, white and red *Tricolor,* is universally respected, and flies above every *Mairie,* from the Alps to the Atlantic and from Calais to Cannes.

National pride is instilled early; children quickly learn how privileged they are to have been born French. Those disciplined and well-behaved crocodiles of infants, shepherded by dedicated teachers are being taught according to a national curriculum which places importance not only on the three Rs, but also on decent social behaviour.

Later on, all a schoolchild's energies will be devoted to passing the *baccalauréat,* the passport to university and the *Grandes Écoles.* Students are politically prickly, hell-raising and ever on the edge of delinquency or revolt, but their early training means that they rarely take out their youthful frustrations through vandalism, and they are almost never overtly hostile to the older generation. Three-quarters of all students reach university standard.

You will encounter awkwardness, rudeness and even verbal aggression on occasion in France (particularly if you are travelling by car), but it will rarely be entirely gratuitous. You may have broken a code of surprisingly rigid behaviour laid down very early in life, and this will very swiftly bring forth a stream of Gallic invective.

The French *are* very different from the Anglo-Saxons with distinctly Gallic priorities and aspirations. Those visitors with entrenched prejudices often deride them, but for those for whom the reason to travel is exactly that difference between cultures, the French are a source of endless fascination. They are one of the most complex and colourful races on earth, in turn captivating, infuriating, intelligent and stupid, effusive and sullen, friendly and brusque. They will certainly make their mark on you somehow; no visitor to France can be indifferent to them.

France, in the final analysis, is made by its people and frequent visitors will discover that it is one of the most tolerant and liberal of countries. You can do what you like (within lawful reason), wear what you fancy, be as eccentric as you wish, and no one will really give a second glance. There is an atmosphere of freedom for all those who pay their dues promptly, respect the law and don't impinge on the lives of others.

The French at Work and Play The day of the average French family, whether urban or rural, starts early. The journey to school or workplace is often made in the dark, while most of the important shops, especially the *boulangerie,* are open before it is light. Any impression that life is spent café-lounging during a

45

For most French people leisure is synonymous with the great outdoors – the countless barrage lakes created nationwide during the twentieth century are all heavily used

protracted lunch hour is inaccurate. The French work as hard – and play as hard – as any other race, with an undisputed inventiveness and sense of design. A nation that can create high-tech wonders like the Concorde and the deadly Exocet missile, as well as low-tech wizardry like the Citroen 2CV, must be peopled by a super-mix of artist and artisan.

The French are the fourth-largest producers of motor cars in the world, while their expertise in building nuclear power stations, immense river barrages, and commercial and domestic housing projects on a grand scale, is only surpassed by their flair in agriculture, and especially wine growing. France is the second-largest exporter of agricultural products in the world, after America.

This success is the result of determined industry and application, and the French are now firmly within the premier league of the western world. The French life-style has consequently changed out of all recognition since World War II, and new wealth has brought increased leisure opportunities.

46

Superbly-appointed sports complexes abound, with athletic tracks, swimming pools, football and rugby pitches, and top-quality tennis courts, all patronized enthusiastically all year round.

France is still a nation of individualists, and you will still see plenty of recognizable Frenchmen of the old school, *bons viveurs* who throng the river banks with their fishing rods and ensure the continued existence of countless cafés. Their wives, shrewd of intellect and among the best cooks in the world, are key figures at the market stalls.

By contrast, their daughters probably shop at the supermarket, work full- or part-time, look after a home and children, and still find time for leisure activity in the evenings and most certainly at weekends. As is the case with other European countries, France is people by two generations – oldsters born into a world when the motor car was an innovation, and their children and grandchildren who take technology for granted.

Fortunately, the ancient ways of bygone France are not being allowed to disappear entirely, so that old-world habits continue to survive alongside modernity. The French may travel between Paris and Lyon at 270km per hour on their *train à grande vitesse,* but they still have to have their bread baked daily; they drive like *grand prix* racers to the café, yet still spend an inordinate time when they get there over an *aperitif;* and it is still the case that no French person will use one word when a thousand will do!

Visitors have been known to level accusations of rudeness, closeness and arrogant self-interest. There *is* a national characteristic which reflects an ostensible indifference to the rest of the world and a Frenchman's consuming interest and concern is for himself and his nearest and dearest. It may make hackles rise, but it is an honest attitude. Learn at least a few words of French, and you are more likely to enjoy friendly acceptance.

History Most of the Dordogne land-mass falls within the boundaries of Aquitaine, itself one of the largest designated regions in France, encompassing all the countryside both north and south of the Dordogne river and its neighbouring watercourses, from the Atlantic Ocean to a line just west of Souillac. To appreciate the fascinating evolution of the Dordogne area – and the close ties between the Celts (or Gauls) and the Anglo-Saxons which exist to this day – it is necessary to consider Aquitaine history.

Although it now forms part of the largest afforested area of western Europe, in the early Middle Ages Aquitaine was largely treeless – a vast wilderness of swamp and sandy heath. The forest now covering the great prairie of the Landes *département* took centuries to create, through the skill and determination of generations of French foresters. At one time much of the Aquitaine must have been forbidding away from the coastal settlements like Bordeaux or the navigable watercourses of the Garonne or the Dordogne.

The rivers flowing through the fertile valleys provided natural military and trading routes when roads were rudimentary and often impassable. The Dordogne river played a principal part in the formation and development of the region, following a route of turbulent and colourful history.

Around 30BC the Romans subdued the territory between the Pyrénées and the Gironde estuary, and called it Aquitania. The region was extended, then, after the fall of the Roman Empire, the Visigoths moved in, only to be usurped in turn by the Franks, under their leader Clovis, in the sixth century. The indigenous Celtic people did not welcome the rule of the Germanic Franks. (Their sense of individuality born at this time, even though they did not enjoy independence, exists to this day.) Charles Martel, also admiringly known as 'The Hammer', was the great eighth-century hero of Aquitaine. The grandfather of Charlemagne, he imposed a crushing defeat upon the Moors at Poitiers in AD732, resisting their threat to southern France. Eventually Charlemagne, as emperor, bestowed Aquitaine upon *his* son, and in the ninth century the region underwent a period of irreversible Frankish domination.

The most important event of regional history was the marriage of 30-year-old Queen Eleanor (after divorcing King Louis VII), to 18-year-old Henry II of France who succeeded to the throne of England in 1154. Eleanor's wedding dowry was the region of Aquitaine, inherited by her new young husband. From then on, Aquitaine was allied to Anglo-Saxon fortunes right up to the end of the Hundred Years War in 1453, which effectively marked the end of English occupation of most of France.

Present-day Aquitaine is large, but it seems positively diminutive when compared to the size of the territory which came under the crown of England in the twelfth century. The English king's sovereignty extended all the way from the Pyrénées to the Loire valley, representing about one-third of France. The region of Aquitaine bequeathed to medieval England encompassed all the land to the south-west of contemporary Pays de la Loire, as well as Poitou–Charentes, Limousin and the Auvergne. Thus, almost the whole of the Dordogne area was, temporarily at least, under English rule.

That royal alliance with England was crucially important at a time when the acquisition of territory represented the strength and prowess of medieval nation states. However advantageous this dynastic alliance was, Louis VII of France refused to acknowledge the take-over, and so provoked an armed struggle and bitter enmity between the two nations which lasted, intermittently, for centuries. In 1189, Richard the Lionheart (son of Henry and Eleanor), succeeded his father; in 1199 he was mortally wounded at Chalus in a minor skirmish of the protracted war that was being fought to retain Aquitaine for England. Louis VII reclaimed the region for France in 1202, but the area was given back to England under the Treaty of Paris, signed in 1259.

From 1337, the start of the Hundred Years War, there were countless clashes between rival dukedoms, constant warring between religious factions and, of course, war on the grand scale between England and French France. Significant events of that dark age were the defeat of the élite French army by the English at Agincourt (1415), and Joan of Arc's inspired crusade to expel the English (1429).

During this period, the south-west of France saw much change and modernization, with a population increase, and the introduction of largely English-inspired *bastides,* or fortress townships. These walled towns at once ensured vastly improved security against surprise attack and pillage, providing a stable environment in which trade could flourish. The new climate of social well-being allowed a burgeoning of artistic and meditative expression, heavily overlaid with religious fervour, and mighty new cathedrals were created, at Clermont-Ferrand near the north-eastern end of the Dordogne valley, near the south-western end at Bordeaux (the cathedral of St André – only slightly smaller than Notre-Dame de Paris), and at Périgueux,

Joan of Arc, the national heroine of France, has a sculpture above her birth village of Domrémy-la-Pucelle in Lorraine

then the capital of old Périgord, where the remarkable Cathedral of St Front was built.

The great age of enlightenment came at the end of the fifteenth century, with the Renaissance, when a revival of artistic creativity heralded the transition from the Middle Ages to the modern world. Gradually, the great feudal lords submitted to the crown and French became the official language. Artistic expression flourished, and a string of glittering *châteaux* were built along the Loire valley, as much for aesthetic reasons as for practical ones, since the threat of attack – constant during the Dark Ages – had by now largely diminished. Patrons of immense wealth (and bright intellect), like King François I, began wooing artists of enormous talent. Leonardo da Vinci was one who was tempted, leaving Italy for ever, and bringing with him to France his most famous painting, the *Mona Lisa*.

Against this background of progress however, was the savage persecution of the French Protestants (the Huguenots), which escalated into the Protestant Wars, and afflicted much of the Dordogne region, causing bitter enmity and creating widespread hardship and poverty. The struggle ended temporarily in 1598 through the Edict of Nantes, which granted Protestants freedom of worship. The assassination in 1610 of Henry IV (once the Protestant Henry of Navarre, before Catholic conversion), effectively signalled the end of the glorious Renaissance and in

50

1685 the Edict of Nantes was revoked, and Protestantism was outlawed once more throughout France, bringing more social upheaval and brutal repression.

The seventeenth century was notable for literary and intellectual giants like Molière, Pascal, Racine and Descartes, and for power titans like Cardinal Richelieu, Minister of State to Louis XIII, Sebastien Vauban, military architect to Louis XIV, and the Vicomte de Turenne, Marshal of France. These key figures may have had fabulous wealth, but for the peasantry of the Dordogne life was harsh and usually short. Abject poverty was exacerbated by outbreaks of plague, disastrous floods, when the untamed river burst its banks with a terrifying ferocity, starvation and the constant threat of pillage and massacre by warring groups. Punitive taxation, imposed by nobles through their powerful bourgeois collectors, was the final catalyst for the seventeenth-century peasant revolt. A century later the national revolution exploded. The Dordogne was not affected as much as other parts of France, but Périgueux, for example, did not entirely escape 'The Terror' which followed the events of 1789.

. . . and Pre-History

The Dordogne is richly endowed with tangible evidence of pre-history, revealing itself as crucible of early *Homo sapiens* existence. The region holds a unique place, not only in the annals of recorded European history, but also in terms of global antiquity.

Recorded history tells us that the early inhabitants of south-west France were the *Petrocorii* (the Celtic tribes subdued first by the Romans and later by the Franks). These people, however, were comparative latecomers to the region in the chronology of *Homo sapiens;* especially around the central area of the Dordogne valley within the great triangle formed by the Dordogne and Vézère rivers. This, according to the evidence of cave archaeology, is the birthplace of European Man.

In Britain evidence has been found (lately supported by carbon dating), of occupation by *Homo sapiens* during the Pleistocene epoch, around one million years ago, while in Germany, remains were discovered in 1856 to establish the existence of Neanderthal Man. As far apart as Java and Belgium, other examples support the theory that Neanderthal Man is probably the oldest known

51

humanoid species, around between one and two million years ago. He may have been ape like in build and features, but he would ritually bury his dead, revealing a spiritualism that could only be human.

Much of the indisputable evidence of early man is found in the central Dordogne region, concentrated within a small area of the Dordogne valley, and centring on Les Eyzies and the caves of Lascaux and Bara-Bahau near Le Bugue on the river Vézère. Beside rich hordes of primitive bone, antler and flint technology, there are breathtaking cave paintings and limestone carvings, depicting human and animal figures.

Paul Broca, the eminent nineteenth-century anthropologist born at Ste-Foy-la-Grande in 1824, coined the name 'Cro-Magnon' for the early Stone Age skulls unearthed at Les Eyzies in 1868. An extremely important figure in cranial study, Broca was awarded the *Légion d'Honneur* for his services to medicine, but his lasting fame is as a brilliant archaeologist. The Broca theory, now widely accepted, is that Cro-Magnon Man drifted westwards from Siberia, following the great mammals which he hunted, to escape the increasing cold of the Pleistocene epoch, which began around a million years ago. Whatever the motive for the congregation of early mankind along the Dordogne river, it is a compelling reason to visit the area. Nothing puts mundane life into true perspective better than to approach a little closer to ancestors of such infinite antiquity.

Religion The religion of the French is, in the main, Roman Catholicism, although there are still pockets of Protestantism in certain areas of Languedoc-Roussillon, the lower Rhône valley and elsewhere, including the Dordogne valley. However, although the average contemporary French family may be Catholic, they are unlikely to be any more devout than the average Church of England British family.

Having said that, religion, although drastically relegated in the second half of the twentieth century, still plays an important role in the marking of life's milestones. Church weddings are still almost obligatory nationwide, lavish and quaintly old-fashioned. But Sunday is also fun day, when leisure is pursued even more fervently than it is on Saturday, and commerce thrives in many towns and villages more than it does on Monday.

Mainly Catholic, partly Protestant, the French are far less fervent than their ancestors, although evidence of a turbulent religious history is widespread

The legacy of an important religious past, however, is evident in every settlement in France, from the greatest cities to the smallest back-country villages. There is a richness and diversity of cathedrals, churches and chapels, now appreciated by all who are aware that such enduring masterpieces in stone will never be created again. A programme of restoration and preservation is under way to arrest the deterioration of centuries, and billions of francs are made available through a state-assisted scheme for this urgent task.

These architectural gems are now little used for worship. One telling statistic says that eight out of ten French children are still baptized, but not more than two out of ten will grow up to be practising Catholics. Of course, the strength of faith varies from region to region, and while attendance at mass may be desultory within most *départements* of the Republic, the Church is still strong, very influential and, surprisingly, beginning slowly to attract the younger generation back in others.

Politics Politically, the Dordogne and the Auvergne have been much affected by the drift from pastoral to urban life. The allure of city living has taken its toll on the population, which has

53

decreased alarmingly since the end of World War II. The importance of tourism has ensured a wide programme of preservation and restoration, which in turn has created problems of second-home ownership, and summertime crowding, but the region *has* benefitted from its new service-industry economy. Pastoral Dordogne has been changed by relentless rescuing, tidying and prettying-up of farmhouses, *châteaux,* villages and even entire town centres, but the restoration work is politically expedient, keeping the majority happy and the municipal coffers healthy.

The experience of the Dordogne has been the experience of the whole of France, where the much-vaunted 'Second Renaissance' has totally transformed the country from a predominantly agrarian society to one of high-tech affluence. Four decades have done nothing short of miraculous. During the late 1940s and early 1950s France was a shambles, and a holiday there was an adventure fraught with hazards and uncertainty. It was a colourful but crumbling country, with governments coming and going almost on a weekly basis, exhausted by two world wars, listless, lacklustre and disillusioned. That France has now been erased utterly and permanently.

The Republic is now a close-knit and confident country in good heart. The 21 regions that comprise metropolitan France have never been so unanimously in accord under the beloved tricolour. Much of this national solidarity has come about with a realization of the national value of younger people. Their enthusiasm, vitality and determination are seen to have been the ingredients of national success. The planning of major development projects across France – the road system, the harnessing of nuclear power, and the colossal barraging and hydro-electric schemes on the major French rivers – owe much to the ambition of the new, younger middle class.

The 'deluge' after General de Gaulle was not that which he had envisaged, but rather it was the surge of the younger, liberated generation. In 1967 the French electorate was the oldest on record; by the next presidential election in 1972 (following the serious student unrest), it was the youngest. Successful generals do not necessarily make good politicians.

Perhaps the most significant of the recent drastic changes in France has been the decentralization of government – a logical, if long overdue, process. If each community is dominated by a young, vital electorate, who are also diligent, intelligent and reasonably honest, success is almost guaranteed. The proof of that success is plain to see.

Every *préfecture, département,* and governing *région* strives to achieve what the French consider to be *really* important – personal fulfilment through culture, leisure pursuits and educated appreciation of civilized living via cuisine, fashion and animated conversation. During the *ancien régime* all roads led to Paris, but now radiation from the *Ile de France* national hub is definitely *out*wards. Parliamentary elections are held every seven years, the President being elected for the same period, and the country is governed by two houses – the National Assembly and the Senate. Despite decentralization, Paris is still the head and the heart of the nation. But the vibrations of its influence now reach the most distant pastoral hamlets where, through the *Mairie,* a certain conformity and continuity are ensured.

The fact that the quiet revolution is working well is quickly apparent to the traveller using the roads, the telephones, the train service, the hotel or campsite network, the supermarkets and hypermarkets. And as far as the natural, cultural and historic treasures are concerned, no country has a finer record of presentation or accessibility. This state of affairs owes much to the contented political stability which now (by and large) prevails throughout France. Politics, generally, are centre-of-the-road socialist, with definite conservative leanings, and this has been confirmed in the polling booths over successive post-war decades. No extreme party of either left or right has made any real headway since the Communist Party came close to power immediately after the war. Personal advancement is a major objective, and the French know that this is only possible with collective effort in a climate of continued social stability.

Economics So, in four decades, France has transformed herself from one of the most backward countries in western Europe, to one of super-modern and dynamic independence. Much of the energy for this transformation came from the traumatic experience of World War II. Consciously or otherwise, the country was determined to eradicate that era, and therefore threw itself headlong into the post-war industrial, technical age with a fierce will to work, and an innovative Gallic flair. French technological know-how in every field of modern commercial endeavour became much acclaimed, while their award-winning designs were in demand world-wide. Cities expanded rapidly through building programmes of massive ambition, incorporating factory and housing complexes completed, in many cases, at break-neck speed.

This accelerating pace of change has had other effects. The bland conformity of modern city living, the advance of transatlantic traits, and the increasingly exhausting way of life in built-up conurbations have led to a new yearning for country-life simplicity. Hence the great escape *en masse* of city people at every opportunity, and the institution of *le weekend*. Families will frequently travel up to 150 kilometres from the urban concrete to indulge in leisure pursuits.

The countryside they visit has, for economic reasons, changed immeasurably. Hundreds of thousands of small farms have disappeared nationwide, along with the postage-stamp holdings created through the ancient French laws of inheritance which divided property equally among children. Now, there are only

Tending a vineyard near Beaune which could well be more valuable than the adjacent house and garden

tens of thousands and even these are diminishing steadily in an age of agri-business conceived on a mega-scale.

Happily, the landscape of the Dordogne does not lend itself readily to grand-scale farming, and many of its regional specialities (*foie gras,* truffles, walnuts and chestnuts) are best produced from small, family-run enterprises. Much of the region has escaped the scars of the 'economic miracle' too. Certainly, Clermont-Ferrand, Bordeaux, Périgueux and Sarlat have suffered, but most of the rest of the area (apart from the taming of the upper Dordogne river from the source to Argentat), remains green and rural of aspect, with towns and villages that have not spread unduly beyond their pre-war bounds.

This is not to say that the region has been bypassed by the great economic advance. The advance in its quality of life has been gained through tourism, exploiting its incomparable landscape. Natural and historic features are displayed with shrewdness to maximum effect, so that every high spot has its full share of visitor throughput and therefore currency. Modern roads, railways, internal airlines, hotels and a wide choice of alternative accommodation, all ensure easy access, and in this way the French have applied their talents to 'the holiday', with remarkable success.

Geography and Geology France, with its triple shore-line totalling nearly 3,000km (2,000 miles), is representative geophysically of all of Europe. It is possible to find scenery and climate closely akin to both northern Norway and southern Spain in certain pockets while other patches are as gentle as southern England or as harsh as the Russian steppes. Overall, however, France is blessed with a temperate climate, with a surprisingly narrow fluctuation band, although extreme contrasts do occur where mountain ranges are of sufficient size. Once away from the coastal swathes, particularly in the *comparatively* isolated lofty regions like the *massif central* or the Juras, summer and winter temperatures rise and fall more dramatically.

South-west France, and the Dordogne region in particular, enjoys a very comfortable average summer warmth of about 20 – 22°C (except in the high Auvergne, where the temperature could be a couple of degrees or so lower). Much of the overall south-western French ambience is created by the influence of the

57

exceptionally wide Garonne basin, which is relatively low-lying and sufficiently distant from the Pyrénées to be unaffected by the frequent cloud-base and rainfall levels the more southern but higher country attracts. Where old Périgord merges geographically with loftier Limousin the sunshine hours per year fall just slightly, although paradoxically this inland part of the Dordogne is warmer than the coast.

This benign, fertile, pleasant place to live is geographically stimulating too. There is great diversity within the region, from the low-lying forest and wine-growing country to the west, and the splendid rolling farmland (and forest) which cover much of Dordogne *département,* to the deep-cut limestone river valleys and magnificent canyons of dramatic configuration to the north-east. From the gloriously wooded valleys of the Limousin, to the stern and visually exciting *causse* plateaux of ancient Quercy province south-east of Sarlat, the area represents a France that retains much of its ancient, natural allure.

Physically France is divided into four principal river basins – of the Seine, the Loire, the Rhône and the Garonne. The Garonne river basin covers almost all of the south-west corner of the country, a huge area, stretching from the Pyrénées to the upper Limousin, and encompassing cities as far apart as Toulouse and Bordeaux. Where it spills eventually into the Gironde estuary, the Garonne river is joined by the Dordogne, which itself flows for a major part of its navigable length through the Garonne basin and the gently undulating countryside renowned for magnificent vineyards. The rest of the great basin is a rich source of soft fruit, with crops flourishing readily in a fertile alluvial soil, nurtured by a favourable semi-Mediterranean climate.

North-east of Sarlat-la-Canéda, the landscape has been formed by drastic volcanic upheaval, and is very different from the plains to the west, which, during the Jurassic period (around 150 million years ago), were submerged under the sea. (Indeed, during this epoch all of France was under water, except the *massif central,* Brittany and the Ardennes.) Only during the Miocene period, around 25 million years ago, when the seas had retreated, did some of the greatest volcanic disturbances occur on France's central plateau. The evidence of these may be seen to this day in the Parc des Volcans just to the south-west of Clermont-Ferrand.

**Opposite
The landscape of Dordogne**

59

Régions: Aquitaine, Midi-Pyrénées, Limousin, Auvergne

Départments: Gironde, Dordogne, Lot, Carreze, Cautal, Puy-de-Dome

We know already that *Homo sapiens* chose to settle in the Dordogne valley, and with good reason. Here was a perfect climate and an abundance of game to be hunted, and a terrain whose structure made the area irresistible to hunter-gatherer groups. The fast-flowing rivers, bountiful with game fish, had scoured the predominant limestone over millions of years, creating countless caves and overhangs, ideal for shelter and defence. Such cave complexes may be seen today on the Quercy and Périgord *causses,* notably the Gouffre de Padirac, an astounding underworld of stalactites and stalagmites, the most celebrated in the land. The great underground chambers were interspersed with smaller ones, either natural or with man-made modification, and these safe 'houses' were obviously incentive enough to detain early Man, despite his strong nomadic instinct.

Régions and Départements Climatically closer to the Mediterranean than to northern France, yet subject to severe winter weather at its north-eastern extremity, the Dordogne river descends from the heights of the *massif central* to the wide fertile basin around Bordeaux, where it joins the Garonne river, some 75km from the Atlantic. Below its confluence with the Vézère, the river carries considerable navigation, once wholly commercial, now predominantly leisure craft. There is in excess of 160km of navigable water. The Dordogne is one of France's mightier water courses, and forms the central strand of this guide, but it *is* only a strand. Riverside high spots are not the only places to visit, and there are features worth seeing from Clermont-Ferrand to Bordeaux and from Nontron to Vic-sur-Cère.

The *régions* covered here are Aquitaine, Midi-Pyrénées, Limousin and Auvergne. The *départements* within these *régions* are, from west to east: Gironde, Dordogne, Lot, Corrèze, Cantal and Puy de Dôme. Of these, Dordogne is the principal. Created from old Périgord province in 1790, following the Revolution, it covers over 5,600 square kilometres (3,500 square miles) of the *massif central* western slopes, with high plateaux descending westwards to pine-forested country intersected by majestic valleys. Millions of years of creative scouring by the Dordogne, the Vézère, the Dronne and the Isle have left a remarkable landscape.

Périgueux (erstwhile capital of Périgord Noir), is the *préfecture,* while Sarlat, Bergerac and Brantôme are the principal towns. The

**Opposite
The medieval jewel of
Carennac**

département is largely agricultural in the south and south-west, particularly along the Dordogne and Isle river valleys, while grapes and tobacco are grown around Bergerac. The forest areas are mainly of pine, oak and chestnut, which flourish in a climate inclining towards humidity.

The Gironde *département*, although within the same *région* of Aquitaine, is very different from Dordogne. Much of it is part of Laudes, a vast sandy plain, planted so intensively over the past two centuries that it now forms the greatest forested area in western Europe. Eastern Gironde is not quite so sandy, nor so hot and featureless. Along the river Dordogne, and at its confluence with the river Isle, is one of the world's most important wine-growing centres, with the towns of Saint Emilion and Libourne, wine capitals since the Middle Ages. Significant towns are Castillon-la-Bataille, closely connected with English history, and Ste-Foy-la-Grande, a thirteenth-century *bastide,* centre of Protestantism and still reminiscent in part of a medieval fortified township.

The *département* of Lot is within the *région* of Midi-Pyrénées. Its northern tip contains the fabulous man-made treasure of Rocamadour, and the natural landscape of stern, wild beauty known as the *causses,* rugged limestone plateaux which are breathtakingly dramatic in places.

Corrèze, in the *région* of Limousin, has much to interest the visitor, especially Beaulieu-sur-Dordogne and Bort-les-Orgues. Corrèze is a hilly tableland, intersected by many fertile rivercourses. Its south-eastern part, watered by the Dordogne, has a variable climate, often with high winter rainfall (or snow), and long cold spells between autumn and spring. The *département* is primarily agricultural in the south-west, and more industrial around Brive and Tulle to the north.

Cantal, named after its mountains, lies at the heart of the Republic's central plateau, most famous for its volcanic peaks of Plomb-du-Cantal and Puy Mary. Lush cattle country predominates in the west, below the lofty hill ridges, with wide horizons and a sparse population. Cantal is richly watered by the Lot and the Allier tributaries of the Dordogne. High-country Cantal enjoys hot summers and its winters are often dominated by violent winds and extreme cold. The area is renowned for tangy Roquefort cheese.

**Opposite
Breténoux, in the
département of Lot**

Bort-les-Orgues

The *département* of Puy-de-Dôme, in the Auvergne, is distinguished by a strange landscape, the focal point of which is the Puy de Sancy. This is not only the birthplace of the Dordogne river, but also the highest point in central France. The fascinating configuration of the Parc des Volcans (the largest *parc naturel* in France) is the most important feature for any visitor. Between the Puy de Dôme, towering over Clermont-Ferrand, and the Puy Mary to the south in Cantal, lies an almost unique volcanic legacy, with strange rock cones, craters, eroded valleys, basalt outcrops and weird geological formations.

The Dordogne river is scarcely formed in Puy-de-Dôme, where it flows past Mont Dore and La Bourboule, and through the deep valley which divides this *département* from Corrèze. The climate of this volcanic area is frequently one of marked contrast; very hot during the height of summer, icy-cold during winters that can last quite a long time.

Towns and their Market Days These are the principal towns and villages in this area with their *départements*, population totals (approximate), and market days where applicable. The letter E denotes exceptional interest.

The Upper Dordogne

Argentat (Corrèze) 4,000 – 1st and 3rd Thursday monthly

Beaulieu (Corrèze) 1,700 E – Market Day Wednesday and Saturday

Beynat (Corrèze) 1,200

Bort-les-Orgues (Corrèze) 6,000 – 2nd and 4th Tuesday monthly and every Saturday

La Bourboule (Puy-de-Dôme) 2,500 – every weekday

Bretenoux-Castelnau (Lot) 1,100

Carennac (Lot) E

Clermont-Ferrand (Puy-de-Dôme) 155,000 – every weekday

Collonges-la-Rouge (Corrèze) E

Condat (Cantal) 1,600

Gramat (Lot) 4,000

Besse-en-Chandesse (Puy-de-Dôme) 1,500 – Monday

La-Roche-Canillac (Corrèze)

Laroquebrou (Cantal)

Martel (Lot) E

Maurillac (Cantal) 4,500

Le Mont Dore (Puy-de-Dôme) 1,100 – Friday

Murol (Puy-de-Dôme) – Wednesday

Rocamadour (Lot) E

Salers (Cantal) E

Turenne (Corrèze) E

Central Dordogne

Belves (Dordogne) 1,700 – Saturday

Biron (Dordogne)

Brantôme (Dordogne) E 2,000 – Tuesday

Champagnac (Dordogne)

Domme (Dordogne) E – Thursday

Excideuil (Dordogne) 2,000 – 1st Thursday every month

Gourdon (Lot) 5,000 – Tuesday

Grolejac (Dordogne)

Hautefort (Dordogne) 1,000 – 1st Monday each month

Jumilhac-le-Grand (Dordogne) 1,500 – 2nd and last Wednesdays every month

Don't miss: Beaulieu, Collonges-la-Rouge, Martel, Rocamadour, Salers, Brantôme, Daume, La Roque-Gageac, Les Eyzies, Monpazier, Sarlat, Perigueux, Saint Emilion.

La-Roque-Gageac (Dordogne) E
Le Bugue (Dordogne) 2,800 – Tuesday and Saturday
Les Eyzies (Dordogne) E
Les Milandes (Dordogne)
Limeuil (Dordogne) E
Mareuil (Dordogne)
Monpazier (Dordogne) E – 3rd Thursday each month
Montignac (Dordogne) 3,000 – Wednesday
Nontron (Dordogne) 4,000 – Wednesday and Saturday
Rouffignac (Dordogne) – 2nd and last Monday each month
Saint Cyprien (Dordogne) 3,700 – Sunday and 2nd Tuesday in month
Sarlat (Dordogne) E 11,000 – Saturday
Siorac (Dordogne) – Wednesday
Sorges (Dordogne) – Friday
Souillac (Lot) 4,000 – Friday plus Market-Fair 1st and 3rd Friday monthly
Terrasson (Dordogne) – Thursday
Thiviers (Dordogne) – Saturday
Tremolat (Dordogne)

Lower Dordogne
Beaumont (Dordogne) 1,500 – 2nd Tuesday in month
Bergerac (Dordogne) 29,000 – Wednesday and Saturday
Bordeaux (Gironde) 618,000 – Daily
Bourg-sur-Gironde (Gironde)
Carsac (Dordogne)
Castillon-la-Bataille (Gironde) 3,000
Eymet (Dordogne) 3,000 – Thursday
Lalinde (Dordogne) 3,000 – 2nd Tuesday monthly
Le Fleix (Dordogne)
Libourne (Gironde) 23,000 – Tuesday, Friday and Sunday
Monbazillac (Dordogne)
Montcaret (Gironde)
Périgueux (Dordogne) E 35,000 – Wednesday and Saturday
Riberac (Dordogne) 4,500 – Friday
Saint-André-de-Cubzac (Gironde) 5,000
Saint Emilion (Gironde) E 3,500 – Sunday morning
Ste-Foy-la-Grande (Gironde) 3,600 – Saturday
Velines (Dordogne) – Wednesday

Fairs and Festivals

Argentat – Antique and flea market fair July

Beaulieu – Classical music concerts July and August. Fête 1st Sunday in September. Fairs 1st and 3rd Friday each month

Belves – Antique fair (*brocante*) July and August

Biron – Dance festival July and August

Bordeaux – Music festival May; international show-jumping, December

Bort-les-Orgues – Summer folklore festivals

Brantôme – Midsummer dance festival

Cenac (near Domme) – Wine festival, August

Champagnac – Sheep fair and market last Sunday in August

Clermont-Ferrand – National fair September; biannual carnival

Collonges-la-Rouge – Floodlight display during July and August

Gourdon – Harvest festival 1st weekend in August

Hautefort – Basket weaving exhibitions throughout summer

La Bourboule – Folk festival, July; concerts June, July, August

La mothe-Montravel – Antique and bric-à-brac fairs July and August

La Tour d'Auvergne – Cheese fair, July

Libourne – Palm Sunday fair

Le Mont Dore – Thermal spa festivals, June, July and August

Murol – Medieval 'Theatre in Action' daily, July and August

Montignac – Folklore festival, July

Nontron – Annual fête, mid-August

Périgueux – Festival of mime, August; *foie gras* markets, November to February (Annual Fair 1st week in September)

Rocamadour – Pilgrimage week, September; *son et lumière* spectaculars July and August

Rouffignac – Garlic fair (biannual) end of July. Annual fair August

Souillac – Jazz concerts July and August

Tours de Merle – *Son et lumière* shows daily, July and August

Turenne – Classical music concerts, July and August

Ste-Foy-la-Grande – Annual fairs, March and November

Le Bugue – Annual fairs, August and September

St Emilion – Grand fête, September

Travel Tips For anyone in serious trouble the UK embassy may be a final resort. The address is 35 Rue du Faubourg-St-Honore, 75383 Paris. Tel: 42 66 91 42.

There are also consulate-general offices in Bordeaux, Lille, Lyon and Marseille, plus consulate offices in Cherbourg, Nantes, Toulouse, Nice, Perpignan, Calais, Boulogne, Dunkerque, Le Havre, St Malo, Dinard and Montpellier.

Public Holidays

New Year's Day	January 1
Easter Sunday	
Easter Monday	
Labour Day	May 1
Ascension Day	May 28
Whitsun Sunday	
Whitsun Monday	
National Holiday	July 14
Assumption	August 15
All Saint's Day	November 1
Armistice Day	November 11
Xmas Day	December 25
Boxing Day (Alsace/Lorraine only)	December 26

Official holidays which fall near the beginning or towards the end of any week, are usually extended to ensure a long weekend, a practice known as 'le pont' (the bridge).

France is now a very healthy country. For example, any water supply not safe to drink must, by law, be marked 'eau non potable'. However, as an elementary precaution against respiratory infection (like Legionnaire's disease), it is advisable always to run any hotel shower for a few minutes before stepping under.

If you have to take regular medication, ensure any supply will last for the holiday period in France: and if you wear dentures, consider taking an emergency repair kit.

Addicts of the British national drink might consider taking a supply of their favourite tea, for in France there are no infusions that will produce a 'powerful' cup.

In most parts of the Dordogne it is possible to receive BBC sound radio programmes on car radios, provided they have a decent aerial. The other alternative is a short-wave receiver, especially in the mountainous eastern region.

Standard European two-pin electrical plugs are employed for most small appliances. Larger devices are often fitted with three-pin round plugs. The British standard pattern is of no use. Modify any appliance accordingly or take a special plug-adaptor.

A useful information source is the French post office. Almost all main post offices in the Republic operate a Minitel system covering most service information requirements. Dial for information and the answer comes up on a visual display screen, concerning required local needs.

Part Three: **Upper Dordogne**

Beaulieu

The Upper Dordogne Where the Dordogne river springs into existence is exciting terrain. This is the high country of the Auvergne, a *région* which covers much of the mighty *massif central,* and has within its boundaries the extraordinary and impressive Parc Naturel Régional des Volcans. Two of the three Auvergne départements fall in the area of the upper Dordogne – Puy de Dôme to the north, and Cantal to the south. The Monts Dore mountains straddle the central part of the Parc des Volcans, matched scenically by the Monts Dômes group, just to the west of Clermont-Ferrand (the *préfecture* of Puy de Dôme), while the Monts du Cantal, graced by the Puy Mary, rise to the north-east of Aurillac (the *préfecture* of Cantal).

The *massif central* is the third most elevated region in France after the Alps and the Pyrénées, and one of the most distinctive earthscapes in western Europe. It has a moon like surface in places, of basalt lava rock, formed many millions of years ago by cataclysmic volcanic upheavals. The result is an extensive sweep of strange thrusting peaks, some jagged and saw-toothed, others rounded by erosion into plump puddings, interspersed with massive crater lakes of extraordinarily blue water.

When the sun is shining and the air is warm, this is a wonderful place, but when the clouds are low it can be a desolate and even depressing grey-black landscape. It is a fiercely savage country in some ways, still largely untamed, where, not so long ago, shepherds and cowherds eked out a Spartan existence along with their animals, enduring winters of constant gales and bitter cold among the bare plateaux.

Of course, changes have been made for the benefit of the contemporary visitor; parts of the mountainous country would

have been unrecognizable to us at the end of World War II. Road-builders and ever-more sophisticated technology have seen to this. Heavy winter snowfalls are now seen as nothing more than a commercial virtue for ski resorts such as Super-Besse in the Monts Dore and Super-Lioran in the Monts du Cantal. In summer, the hot Auvergne weather (caused in part by the subterranean strata which are still abnormally warm), is welcomed by the locals, who now earn their living largely through tourism.

The facilities and leisure amenities offered by this former mountain wilderness are so varied that there really is something for everyone, of every age group and inclination. There are custom-built children's leisure playgrounds with special crèches for the very young, as well as almost every athletic or adventurous activity, from swimming and tennis, golf, fishing and horse-riding, to mountain climbing and hillwalking, hang-gliding and parascending. Cable-car ski lifts operate during the summer to offer spectacular summit views, a sight-seeing coach does full- and

The jagged profile of the Puy de Sancy, the highest peak in the Auvergne and source of the Dordogne

half-day tours of scenic high spots. Indoors, time might be enjoyable spent in a spa Jacuzzi, sauna or solarium, and in the evening there is salon music or disco dancing, cinemas and casinos complete with bridge-club facilities.

The choice of accommodation in the Parc des Volcans is really quite wide, from the plushiest of three-star hotels, retaining outward and inward signs of Edwardian charm and elegance, through every conceivable form of self-catering unit, from farmhouse annexes to holiday-village chalets, to havens for touring caravanners and campers. Your base can be within strolling distance of the bright lights, or in pastoral tranquillity (frequently with marvellous high-level vistas as a bonus).

Le Mont Dore and La Bourboule All these facilities are found in abundance, alongside glorious natural country, in the area where the Dordogne springs to life on the flank of the Puy de Sancy – in and around the thermal spas and Auvergne mountain resorts of Le Mont Dore and La Bourboule. These two townships, transformed and greatly extended after World War II, nestle in the steep-sided, lushly-wooded valley at the source of the Dordogne river, and are year-round resorts. Not only are there the thermal cure centres, but also the winter snows, which make both places highly attractive to the skiing fraternity. Whether you are ailing with rheumatic or respiratory troubles, or super-fit and athletic, there is something for you all the year round.

Both towns are entirely dependent on tourism in one form or another. One statistic reveals that Le Mont Dore has an indigenous population of around 1,100 and visitor accommodation totals 1,400 places. They are first-rate examples of their type. Historically, however, there is little to interest the visitor; there remains hardly any vestige of Roman Mont Dore, or of any buildings constructed before the *Belle Epoque* (when Le Mont Dore was called Le Mont Dore les Bains – the old name still on the post office). The spa has attracted some interesting people in the past, including George Sand, the nineteenth-century novelist. She first visited in 1827, felt the 'letter devil' lying within her and came back every year until her death in 1876.

The street layout and architectural features of both resorts are mainly functionally bland or brightly ornate; quite suitable for their purpose. As mountain resorts, Le Mont Dore and La

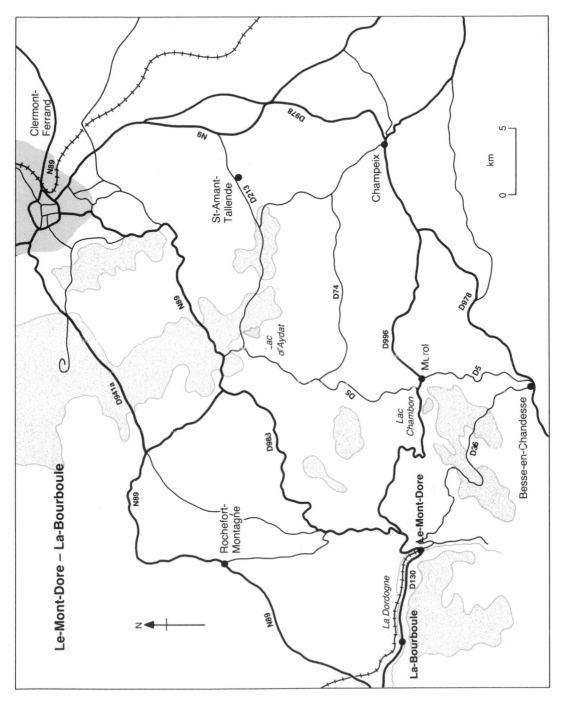

Le-Mont-Dore – La-Bourboule

Clermont-Ferrand

N89

N9

D978

St-Amant-Tallende

D213

Champeix

D74

D978

N89

D996

Mt rol

D5

Lac d'Aydat

D5

Lac Chambon

D36

Besse-en-Chandesse

D941B

D983

N89

Rochefort-Montagné

Le-Mont-Dore

La Dordogne

D130

La-Bourboule

N89

N

km

5

0

Bourboule are highly commended, but they really excel as a base for wider exploration of the dramatic volcano park.

This valley is about 450km from Paris by road, and 340km from Bordeaux. Access is also by an excellent railway service, and there is an airport link at Clermont-Ferrand (Aulnat), 50km away.

Route by Car To reach this high and handsome valley by plane, train or coach is simple (*see* pages 20-22). To get there by road, avoiding the traffic problems which afflict the areas of Clermont-Ferrand at times, leave the N9 or N144 main approach roads from the north at Riom, and turn west then south to skirt the huge national park. Mountain drives for more relaxed exploration can be made in due course. This route is scenic enough, the traffic is much lighter, and there are interesting places, such as Volvic (for bottled water), Pontgibaud and Rocheforte-Montanne, along the N89, before you branch on to the D922 for La Bourboule.

Le Mont Dore Le Mont Dore is the 'senior' thermal spa, first discovered by the Celts, then sophisticated by the Romans, who were familiar with the therapeutic qualities of the mineral water geysering from a volcanic crust. For centuries after the Roman departure, the hot springs were treated simply as a natural phenomenon, until the era of the 'Grand Tour' towards the

The green and gracious centre of Le Mont Dore, one of France's foremost all-season mountain resorts

middle of the nineteenth century, when remedial use of the waters became fashionable once again. During the opulent *Belle Epoque*, the value of the thermal springs was fully appreciated, and exploited, particularly with the coming of the railway which made the cure accessible to the affluent.

The architecture of this small town displays a grandeur perhaps more appropriate to Vichy, or parts of Paris. Tall, ornate buildings predominate around the centre, and even the central post office emulates the dignified contours of the Grand Hotel almost opposite. The Greco-Roman-style thermal palace holds pride of place.

Le Mont Dore lies at an altitude of 1,050 metres, although new development has gradually crept up the valley towards the peak of the Puy de Sancy, and the tourist office can now quote a second altitude of 1,886 metres. It has an old funicular railway, installed in 1898, which is worth a ride. A designated *Zone de Silence* envelops the town, in deference to the health-seeking clientele, and it remains peaceful at all seasons of the year. Despite a high-profile fun image, and the consequent influx of the younger generation, the insistence on decorum is effective, extending to a ban on motorists using their horns within the town precincts. Often the loudest noise after midnight is the babble of the Dordogne flowing fast through the town centre, although it is scarcely wider than a brook at this point.

As with all high-altitude settlements, the configuration of Le Mont Dore is longish and narrow, with maximum use being made of the valley floor. The ingenious street layout incorporates four main thoroughfares, with numerous lateral links. Tall buildings predominate, and, for the most part, progress is either uphill or down. Grading has been cunningly executed, so that the ups and downs, at least within the centre, are not noticeably acute.

The thermal establishment, Le Panthéon, is the hub of the town. Entry is via an ornate public concourse, invariably thronged during opening hours. Once inside, in a steamy and oppressive atmosphere, you make your way to the many and various curative annexes depending on whether your particular ailment is nasal, abdominal or muscular. White-coated ladies, serious of countenance, relieve you of your *francs* in return for treatment tickets. It's rather like a religious experience. At peak

The diminuitive watercourse of the Dordogne through the centre of Le Mont Dore

hours, especially in the mornings, you will see hosts of health-seekers enter the hallowed halls with earnest compulsion and leave (no doubt revived, if only psychologically), swathed in overcoats and scarves, even though the outdoor temperature may be in the upper 70s. Outside the imposing shrine, amid the numerous cafés, flower gardens and hotel-lined streets, invalids mix with climbers, joggers, backpackers and cyclists, many clad in nothing more than singlet and shorts. It all makes for fascinating people-watching over a drink at one of the pavement tables.

Le Mont Dore's outdoor-leisure spread is the Parc des Léchades, just off the Route du Sancy, with a whole variety of up-to-the-minute fun equipment like sophisticated water slides, carousels, bumper-cars, junior assault courses and an Apache fort. For older visitors there is tennis, horse-riding and more green space below the big mountain. There is also a second sporting venue beside the town's cultural centre – a bowling alley in summer, an ice-skating rink in winter – and a 9-hole golf course laid out at 1,250 metres.

Claiming, with some justification, to be a four-season resort, Le Mont Dore suffers a commercial paradox. While half the place is enjoying economic success, the other half is in the midst of a seasonal depression. As a result, furry yeti boots often share a window with bikinis, and snow-chains with water-wings. The permanently successful enterprises are of course those not affected by the time of year, like food shops, of which Le Mont Dore has a reasonable number. There is a colourful covered market at the older, higher end of the town, in the Place de la République, and, just off here, a king-sized *fromagerie* which dispenses most known brands of French cheese, including the local *Auvergne Nectaire*. There are one or two *alimentation* stores for self-catering visitors, but the Suma supermarket (off the D996 on the western fringe of the town) is the main venue for routine food shopping.

In the old part of town, faint traces of yesteryear have not quite been eliminated, reminders of a harsher era when life for the indigenous people was really difficult. Today opulence predominates, although Le Mont Dore inevitably shows some visible signs of year-round visitors.

On the whole, however, the town manages to keep invitingly burnished, especially around the three main assembly areas: the

Place Charles de Gaulle, featuring the imposing post office, an ornamental pond and an unremarkable neo-Gothic church; the cultural and conference centre, graced by flower gardens and tree-shaded lawns through which the Dordogne flows; and the Place de la République the café and restaurant location favoured by the younger set in the evenings. These are the main focal points of a compact yet surprisingly comprehensive mountain resort. Staggered-level subsidiary roads, above, below and around the centre, give the impression that Le Mont Dore is quite large, but it is really little more than an overgrown village.

La Bourboule La Bourboule is considerably larger than its upper-valley neighbour, lying at a height of 850 metres where the valley is wider and where building development is consequently easier. It also claims to be a four-season fun resort, while it outdoes the spa of Le Mont Dore by having two thermal baths. Its original, mock-Byzantine version is called the *Grands Thermes*. The town is dominated by its thermal baths, but the imposing casino is also quite impressive, stylish and elegant in its flamboyance.

La Bourboule - childrens' transport in front of the ornate Grands Thermes, pragmatically used by local residents as a town runabout during the low season

La Bourboule maintains its bright image as a leading spa and holiday resort by emulating its rival Le Mont Dore, and going one better where it can. New arrivals are invited every Monday evening (in season) to a tourist office 'welcome drink' reception, where information is given about all the local activities on offer. This is a friendly gesture and a very useful overture to any holiday stay. Among other attractions is the shopping in the town, especially intriguing selections of polished volcanic stone. These make excellent souvenirs, since they are timeless mineral rocks and fossils and genuinely local to the region.

La Bourboule also has an elevated beauty area – the Charlannes Plateau, at 1,150 metres and reached via the *téléphérique* which whisks passengers aloft from the terminus located in the splendid Fenestre Park. This is a municipal playground of grand design, with many imaginative children's amusements, including a miniature train, a giant slide, crawler tunnels and climbing frames. It occupies a small area of magnificent lawn sweeps bordered by beautifully-tended flower beds, shrubs and tall Sequoia pines which have thrived for over a century. This is a very popular strolling area on summer evenings – a green cloister just five minutes' walk from the busy centre.

Taking the Waters For those interested in taking the therapeutic waters, the natural temperature of the thermal outflow varies between 100 and 120°F, while constituent trace elements of the water are – among others   bicarbonate of soda, chloride of sodium, iron, arsenic, strontium and zinc; plus fizzy gases like krypton, argon, neon and helium. Both spas specialize in the treatment of respiratory troubles. La Bourboule also has a name for dermatology, while Le Mont Dore is favoured for the alleviation of rheumatism. Le Mont Dore also has the distinction of being one of the oldest thermal stations in France.

The thermal bath season at Le Mont Dore is from 15 May to 30 September, while the season at La Bourboule opens a little earlier on 25 March.

Walking in the Area There is a wealth of walking within easy distance of either of these town centres. From Le Mont Dore, just by the tourist office, there is the *Chemin des Mille Gouttes* ('Path of 1,000 Sweat Drops'), which ascends fiercely and directly at first, through beech woods alongside the funicular railway to the Salon du Capuçin, a rest-and-refreshment centre on a high mountain meadow. Rack-railway passengers and walkers have a choice of marked trails to explore around here. Consider, too, the cable-car which will transport you to a neighbouring peak of the Puy de Sancy, from where there are glorious views via adjacent footpaths, across mighty mountain tops above the Val d'Enfer ('Hell's Valley').

From La Bourboule, you can drive up to the celebrated Plateau de Charlannes, or take the *télécabine* from the Parc Fenestre. At an altitude of 1,150 metres there is splendid pine wood and mountain pasture to explore from a choice of waymarked paths. There is nice walking too around the distinctive Roche-Vendeix (stronghold of brigands during the Hundred Years War), reached via a short and scenic drive from town. For sparkling waterfalls, consider (among several in the area) La Bourboule's Cascade des Vernière, about 30 minutes' walk from Camping Cascades, off the D130; or the Grande Cascade, above the southern end of Le Mont Dore, off the D983. Between the two resorts, just off the old Bourboule road and well signposted, is a creation of ancient Dordogne water flow, the grotto of the petrified fountain. There are some 14 waymarked local footpaths to suit all aptitudes and age groups. Detailed information is available from either town centre tourist office.

La Bourboule has two large hotels – the Parc Hilton near to the casino alongside the Dordogne river, and the three-star Iles Brittaniques on the Quai Gambetta, which reflects a long-gone era. There is also a wide selection of smaller hotels and *pensions,* as well as numerous restaurants and cafés, and spaciously elegant and welcoming brasseries.

Both resorts have a good choice of caravan and camping parks, all of which are signposted. La Bourboule municipal ground is perhaps better than the one at Le Mont Dore, which is heavily used and consistently crowded (open eleven months of the year).

Le Mont Dore's three-star hotel is the Carlina in the Rue René Cassin. It is quite imposing, high-rise to an extent, but dwarfed by the famous old funicular which climbs from the adjacent ground station. One attraction of this particular hotel setting is its proximity to the Puy de Sancy.

Le Mont Dore – Useful Information

Tourist Office: Avenue de la Libération BP 96 63240 Le Mont Dore, Puy de Dôme, Auvergne (Tel: 73 65 20 21 Hotel reservations Tel: 73 65 09 00).

70 hotels – 400 furnished apartments – 4 caravan and camping sites (one within town precinct) – youth hostel on Route de Sancy – holiday villages (3) – Maisons d'Enfants (3).

Suggested hotels. 3-star Hotel Carlina (Tel: 73 65 04 22). 2-star Le Paris, Place du Pantheon (Tel: 73 65 01 79). 1-star Royal Hotel, Rue Rigny (Tel: 73 65 01 26). Tourist hotel, Hostellerie Saint-Hubert, Rue Lavialle (Tel: 73 65 01 92).

Leisure Amenities. Horse-riding centre, tennis courts (8), 9-hole golf course, crazy golf, casino, 2 cinemas, 3 discoteques, 10-pin bowling. Specialized guided walks organized from tourist office throughout summer for those interested in botany, wild life, geology, or volcanology. Bicycle hire in town (sports shop), or from railway station.

Winter amenities – Mont Dore is the main ski resort in the Auvergne for both downhill and cross-country sport established 1912. There are 70 kilometres of downhill pistes on the Puy de Sancy and 400 kilometres of cross-country tracks, maintained daily on the Massif. Special ski-plus accommodation packages are available and accompanied cross-country tours are organized daily.

The tourist office is open every day from 9 to 12.30 and from 2pm to 6.30pm. Sundays and bank holidays from 10am to 12 noon and from 4pm to 6.30pm.

La-Bourboule – Useful Information

Tourist Office, *Syndicat d'Initiative*, BP 80 63150, La-Bourboule, Puy de Dôme, Auvergne. Tel: 73 81 07 99.

28 hotels within town environs – 100 furnished apartments – 3 caravan and camping sites (one within town precinct) – 20 Maison d'Enfants (holiday homes for children).

Suggested hotels: 3-star Iles Britanniques, Quai Gambetta (Tel: 73 65 52 39). 2-star Hotel Regina, Avenue Alsace Lorraine (Tel: 73 81 09 22). 1-star Hotel Les Baigneurs, Quai de la Liberation (Tel: 73 81 07 66). Tourist hotel, Dordogne, Rue de Pologne (Tel: 73 81 04 56).

Leisure Amenities – Heated municipal swimming pool (covered and open). Horse-riding centre, bicycle hire SNCF, casino, fitness centre (including Jacuzzi, sauna and gymnasium), tennis courts, cinema, two night clubs (baby-sitter list at tourist office).

Winter season – Covered swimming pool and tennis courts open. Cross-country ski centre with tuition facilities and 254 kilometres of marked trails. Sight-seeing coach services (Tourisme Verney or Volcatours) reservation offices in Mont Dore and Bourboule.

An active day in or on the mountains hereabouts will certainly raise the appetite which any of a dozen restaurants, or half-a-dozen snack bars in Mont Dore will be happy to assuage. For farmhouse speciality regional dishes, try l'Auberge des Mancelles, 1 kilometre from centre on the Route de Sancy. In Bourboule, all the hotels offer a good table, and there are also three restaurants, plus six pizzerias and creperies.

Clermont-Ferrand and the Monts Dômes One of the great delights of touring France in general, and the Dordogne in particular, is the prospect of exploring your surroundings from a comfortable base. Le Mont Dore and La Bourboule are both ideally located for the Puy-de-Dôme *département,* the northern gateway to Auvergne and the *massif central.* The Chaîne des Puys is made up of some 80 volcanoes, all about 10,000 years old. From the summit of Puy de Dôme (1,465 metres), easily accessible by car, the panorama includes some fine examples of craters (the *Puy de Pariou*), jagged cones (the *Puy de la Vache*), and natural crater lakes (the *Gour de Tazenat*). This range of mountains is a little to the north-west of Clermont-Ferrand, and it is worth taking in the Auvergne capital city too.

From the Puy de Sancy to the Puy de Dôme Leave the valley at the foot of the Puy de Sancy, and take the winding D983 road north-east, right through the central part of the *parc naturel.* This fine ridge route affords views of strange outcrops – in total there are over a thousand volcanic peaks in this area. First you will see the enormous twin pillars of *La Roche Tuilerie* and *La Roche Sanadoire,* which stand above the lower country to the west, at the boundary of the Parc des Volcans. There is easy parking at the viewing *belvédère,* between the tiny volcanic lakes of Guéry and Servière; the latter, below the Puy de L'ouire, is almost perfectly circular in outline.

The great Gothic Cathedral of
Clermont-Ferrand. From this
prominent medieval centre,
Pope Urban II exhorted the
First Crusade to recapture
Jerusalem and the Holy Land
in 1095

Carry onwards and upwards, crossing the rock-strewn plateau which precedes the hamlet of Randanne, and join the N89. Continue straight across (on to the D5) to visit the central Maison du Parc, at the Château Montlosier. Back on the N89, veer east beneath the Puy de Charmont, and make the long descent through a landscape that becomes softer, greener and more lushly wooded, but is always dominated by the Puy de Dôme to the north-west.

At Ceyrat, a semi-suburb of Clermont, take the D941C fork north towards Royat and then the D68 west for the tarmac ascent of the mountain which lends its name to the *département*. Royat is a spa town, developed by the Romans on the banks of the river Tiretaine. There is a host of hotels, a municipal casino, landscaped parks and a 7-acre camp ground with 200 units. The old hillside village, clustered around an eleventh-century fortified church stands above the contemporary development, which includes the famous Charade motor racing circuit.

The Puy de Dôme is 6km west of Royat. Once it dominated Clermont-Ferrand, but now urbanization of the volcano is just about total, all dating from the birth of the motor car. Housing developments have crept along fresh-cut terracing of the black basalt, and reach ever higher from the enormous sprawl of Clermont below the eastern mountain flank. On the summit, a Roman temple once stood, there is an observatory, a restaurant and a TV mast. Although there is still much scenic landscape in the area, and a number of delightful waymarked pedestrian trails on the mountain, the influence of Clermont is overwhelming. Don't expect the Puy de Dôme to be unspoiled. Most of the city's industry is devoted to keeping the world's wheels turning, and any mewing of buzzards has long been drowned out by the squeal of tyres on the Michelin test track to the north of Clermont.

Clermont Clermont-Ferrand, at just 400 metres above sea-level is not, strictly speaking, part of 'the Dordogne' but it provides an interesting and lively diversion. Not so long ago, Clermont and Montferrand were two feudal enclaves, more often than not at daggers drawn, and only incorporated into one city in the mid-seventeenth century. The original Clermont *bastide,* its name derived from the Latin for 'bright mountain', was a much

Place de Jaude, the vibrant heart of Clermont and the home of the famous theatre

assaulted stronghold throughout the Dark and early Middle Ages. Its rich past is evident in parts of the old town, which boasts intriguing alleys, old houses and medieval arches. Despite its historical aspects, however, the city is as modern as any other in most respects. Sometimes called 'Michelinville', since its major revenue comes from tyre production, Clermont is also a fun place. The ancient centre-piece of Clermont is a thirteenth-century cathedral with incredibly tall and pencil-slim spires. Massively Gothic, and rather overpowering, it is built of black basalt stone. The other impressive religious landmark is the twelfth-century Basilica of Notre Dame du Port, not far from the cathedral. Its hewn, Volvic stones, quarried from a region of

87

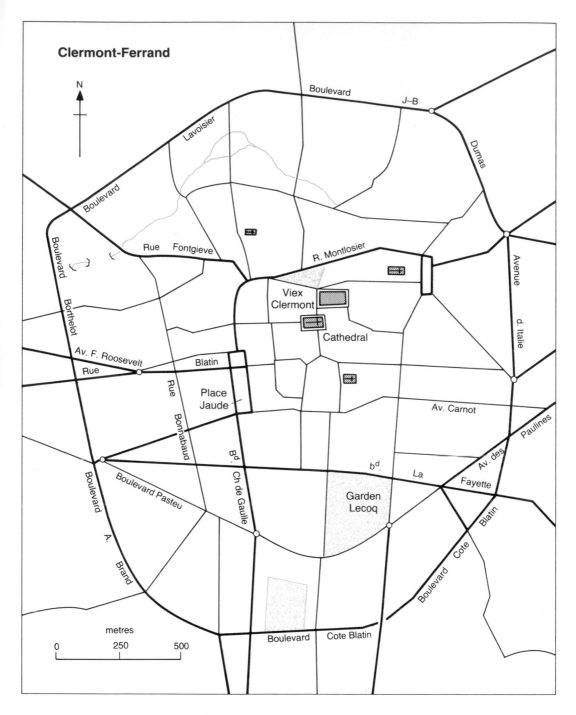

Clermont-Ferrand

extinct craters and basalt seams, give the city its other nickname of 'Clermont the Black'.

The other part of the old city is a couple of kilometres to the north-east, at Montferrand. See the fifteenth-century Maison de l'Apothicaire in the Rue de la Rodade, the oddly named Maison de l'Eléphant in the Rue Kléber, and the fourteenth-century church of Notre Dame de la Prospérité. But the real heart of Clermont is the Place de Jaude, a vibrant patch of urban France that represents the link between the old and new Clermont.

Approaching the city by car on the N89, it is virtually a straight road into the centre (follow the Place de Jaude signposts). Here you should find a parking space. The Place de Jaude is a curious square of massive proportions, very modern in parts and only recently much restored. There are impressive reminders of a more ancient France too, especially around the cathedral, the imposing theatre building and the statue of heroic Vercingetorix, the Gaulish warlord who defeated an army of Julius Caesar on the outskirts of the city in 53BC. The battleground, on the Plateau de Gergovie (near the suburb of Romagnat), is a celebrated archaeological site, and many Roman remains were also discovered during the modernizing of the Place de Jaude, once the site of a Roman temple. Poor Vercingetorix was eventually captured and executed, but his exploits were heroic enough to allow him to be re-created by Bartholdi (the sculptor responsible for the Statue of Liberty) at the beginning of the twentieth century.

Don't miss: Cathedral; Basilica of Notre Dame du Port; Maison de l'Apothicaire; Maison de l'Eléphant; Notre Dame de la Prospérité church; Place de Jaude

For homesick Britons there is a British club, with deep leather armchairs and footrests. Le Sheldon, as it is called, in the Place Allord in Royat suburb, has a high reputation of many years' standing plus a fine selection of Scotch whiskies. For more lively entertainment after dark there is a variety of nightclubs and bars. The Rabelais is in the Place de Jaude. The Opéra Municipal, in the Boulevard Desaix, presents slick productions of classics like *My Fair Lady*. For other types of music there are half a dozen discos within the city, devoted to every modern enthusiasm, from hard rock to acid house, as well as cabaret and jazz clubs like Le Dauphin and Le Montmartre. Full details of evening entertainment are available from the tourist office at 69 Boulevard Gergovia, or the pavilion annexe in the Place de

Jaude. Both are open every day during the summer season.

For shopping, the Rue de Port is recognized as one of the best streets, while the alleyways off it are often thronged with antique hunters. When you tire of the thronging commercial centre, make for Jardin Lecoq, to the south of the Place de Jaude, a spacious park with an ornate lake. Nearby is the Lecoq natural history museum, close to a number of university buildings. This area was no doubt one of the haunts of the city's most famous literary son, Blaise Pascal. One of the universities is named after the writer, and the other is devoted to modern science.

Perhaps because Clermont is one of the major tyre production centres of the western world, cars are tolerated with a strange reverence. However, there are more restful – and revealing – ways of exploring the city centre: on foot, by local transport, by taxi or by bicycle. The tourist information office will advise on the bus services, which operate within two areas – Zone One for the inner city, Zone Two for a wider circle. For single journeys you pay as you board. Taxis are usually in abundance around the city centre, the station and the airport at Aulnat on the eastern boundary. The taxi service telephone number is 78 90 75 75, the SNCF (information) 73 92 50 50 and Aulnat airport 73 91 71 00. Bicycles may be hired for half or full days, from Mazeyrat Sport, 3 Boulevard Gergovia.

In the Boulevard Gergovia is one of Clermont's three-star hotels, the Frantal (at 82), together with its recommended restaurant, La Retirade (Tel: 73 93 05 75). A second three-star choice is the Lyon, at 16 Place de Jaude, also with a restaurant of high reputation (Tel: 73 93 32 55). A popular two-star hotel (among about half a dozen), is the Midi, at 39 Avenue de l'Union Soviétique; its restaurant is closed on Mondays (Tel: 73 92 26 39).

Clermont to the Puy de Sancy Between Clermont and the valley of the Puy de Sancy there is a lovely scenic route. Leave Clermont via the southbound N9, fork westwards along the D978 through picturesque Champeix, and fork again on to the D996 for St Nectaire and Murol. St Nectaire, once famous for its cheese market, is now a health spa clustered around a twelfth-century church; Murol, in the heart of volcanic cone country, has a spectacular *château* ruin perched on a mound just to the north of the village. This thirteenth-century red-stone

**Opposite
Clermont-Ferrand**

91

Bort-les-Orgues

Worth a visit: Chambon-sur-Lac;
Besse; Orcival; Messeix.

fortress, dominating its surroundings, is brought to medieval life each summer by the 'Theatre of Action'.

There is a choice of routes from Murol. Either continue west on the D996 alongside the pretty lake of Chambon, through fine hill country and over the Col de la Croix Morand (1,400 metres), around the shoulder of the Puy de la Tache and so down to Mont Dore, or continue south from Murol along the D5 wooded valley road to Besse-en-Chandesse.

Chambon-sur-Lac village has remained relatively undeveloped and picturesque, a small hill-country settlement surrounding a twelfth-century church of Romanesque simplicity. The lake is a popular spot in high summer, with a bathing beach backed by woodland and distant views across impressive terrain. There is a choice of small hotels, a youth hostel and four camping grounds. Chambon's celebrated beauty spot is the Saut de la Pucelle ('Maiden's Leap'), a towering remnant cliff of an extinct volcanic rim, inevitably the subject of a legendary tale of passion and tragedy.

Besse is a beautiful medieval village. Perched high above the valley, it is a black lava-rock eyrie of fifteenth- and sixteenth-century houses lining narrow twisting streets, with tiny squares and a lovely old church. Another superbly preserved country market town, Besse has been particularly renowned for St Nectaire cheese since the Middle Ages. Explore on foot to make the most of any visit using the allocated parking space on the village fringe. Super-Besse winter resort, with indoor swimming pool and ski-lifts, lies some 7km westwards at an altitude of 1,400 metres.

From Besse to the valley of the Puy de Sancy the D36 offers an invigorating drive (immediately north, then west), over the Col de la Croix St Robert. Open between April and November, this road tops an altitude of 1,450 metres, and is the high Auvergne at its most rugged. There are some fine views of the Mont Dore on the final descent.

This northern area of the Parc des Volcans offers both natural and man-made riches, and is surprisingly uncrowded. If you have time, visit the village of Orcival, a few kilometres north of Le Mont Dore; it is blessed with one of the most perfectly proportioned (and preserved) twelfth-century churches in the Auvergne. Worth seeing, too, are the individual crater-lakes or peaks which grace the vicinity of the Puy de Sancy.

Bort-les-Orgues is not far from La Bourboule, but the difference in environment is profound. Bort is a working town, tainted with a degree of industrial drabness, which conceded nothing to tourism until a few years ago. It is ugly in parts, though not depressingly so, but it can also make you feel fond of it. Familiarity breeds an affection for the place – warts and all – for in and around the old town there are some intriguingly high spots. Consider it, perhaps, as a base for seeing rural France. Bort is reached by the D922 but this reveals nothing of the Dordogne river. If you have enough time, there is a more interesting route from La Bourboule. Turn south momentarily on to the D922 then, beyond Bourboule, west along the signposted D601, just south of St-Sauves-d'Auvergne. This is the start of the meandering Gorges d'Avèze route, which follows a steeply twisting road descending gradually to the fast-flowing Dordogne, at the base of a beautifully quiet and richly wooded valley. There is easy parking here and a pleasant picnic area beside the scenic river bridge.

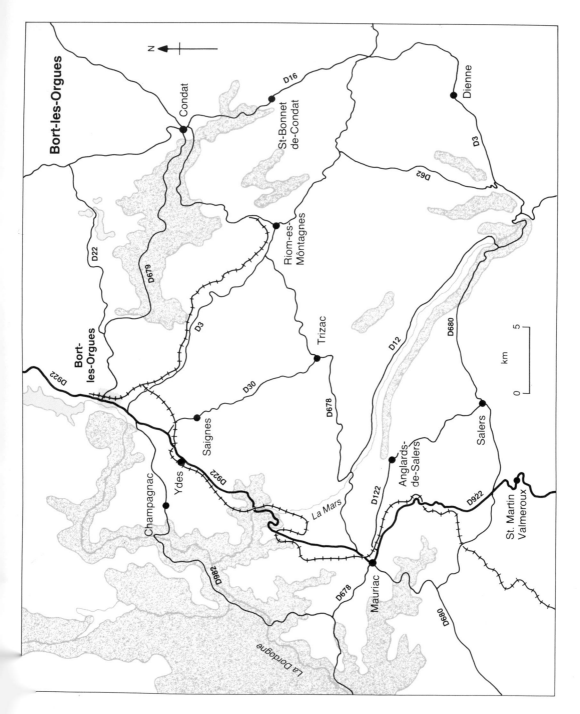

The subsequent climb up to Messeix is beautiful. Messeix is a charming hill village, with faint echoes of *Clochemerle,* especially around the tiny central square, with its sprinkling of essential shops and prominent town hall. South along the D78, where the road once more comes close to the river, there is a simple but well-appointed camping ground. The landscape becomes less wooded and more arable, with cattle grazing lush hills between forest swathes.

There are several access roads around here to secret parts of the Dordogne, as well as a couple of secluded touring caravan sites. Below the picturesque hamlet of Singles, on the outskirts of Larodde, a signposted minor road leads to the northern extremity of the great Bort barrage lake, some 18km. This artificial inland sea is one of the biggest in France, and carries a cruise ferry. This end is seemingly remote, while the southern end bustles with activity.

Don't miss: Chateau Val; Bort barrage lake; the Orgues; Mauriac.

At the end of this back route from Bourboule is Château Val, a fairy-tale castle that is the pride of the western Auvergne. It is most romantically approached from the minor road westward from Trémouille-St-Loup hamlet, rather than via the direct turn-off from the D922 at Lanobre village.

Only *just* in Auvergne – Limousin lies across the water – Château Val is a perfectly proportioned cluster of elegant towers and stout ramparts. During the Middle Ages it commanded the fast-flowing and turbulent river, perched on the rim of a regal Dordogne gorge. When the valley was flooded Château Val's location was changed out of all recognition. It is now in the care of Bort municipal authority.

This dramatic transformation of aspect has not really detracted from the beauty of this architectural masterpiece. Below the slender, fifteenth-century turrets, summer art exhibitions are held, while from a specially constructed causeway jetty, sightseeing cruisers come and go among smaller, privately-owned craft. There is a strip of pleasure beach and a popular *relais* restaurant adjacent, while just up the road, on the way to Bort along the D922, there is the Musée de la Radio et du Phonographe. This is an interesting and celebrated centre of early sound.

Bort-les-Orgues on the Limousin side of the regional boundary is divided into two distinct halves by the shallow,

95

Château Val was once high over the Dordogne. Now at water level, it is still dramatic to behold

reduced Dordogne water, which descends from the lake above the town, below the Artense plateau. Much of riverside Bort is indifferent, alongside a frequently dusty and noisy road. Across the river bridge, on the north bank of the Dordogne around and above the Place Marmontel (the *Syndicat d'Initiative* is located here), the old town is far cosier and much more atmospheric. There are good shopping facilities, notably in the steep and narrow Rue de Paris, a nice twelfth-century church and some ancient alleys around the town hall.

There are fourteen hotels in town, nine of which have restaurants, as well as a number of eating houses including *creperies* and pizzerias. There is a spacious municipal camping ground on the western edge of town, and another about 3km away on the same road. The latter is scenically located beside a sweeping bend of the Dordogne. Both are efficiently signposted. For self-catering visitors, there is a choice of supermarkets – an Intermarché by the post office, and a Suma (open on Sundays) at the opposite end of town.

Bort-les-Orgues is a good base, retaining its essential – and very ancient – working-town honesty and vigour, but also enjoying its relatively new fame as a tourist attraction. The town's history reaches back to a very misty past. The word *bort,* in Gallic, means 'bridge' or 'house', although, according to the town hall archives, the word may be a corruption of *bord* (bank); perhaps this is more likely for a riverside settlement. The *Orgues* part of the name has an obvious origin; the mighty rock outcrop which looms on the skyline to the north-west, dominating the town even more than the massive barrage, resembles a row of giant organ pipes.

This curious configuration of nature has drawn visitors for over two centuries, although not as many as the great lake which the dam created in 1951 does. The Bort barrage is one of the largest and most sophisticated hydro-electric schemes in Europe, an engineering masterpiece embracing all the expertise of modern technology. The hydro-control centre for the entire Dordogne river is now located here, and EDF (Electricité de France), in co-operation with Bort *Syndicat d'Initiative,* have helped to give the complex a high profile. The lake provides comprehensive water sports facilities, while a visitor circuit around the dam gives an insight into the fascinating business of creating hydro-electric power on a gigantic scale.

The strangely shaped Orgues represent the principal attraction for climbers, geologists and other visitors fascinated by the quirkiness of nature. The serried rows of petrified volcanic pillars were formed by terrifying forces of creation millions of years ago. The towering wall is sternly impressive (and almost menacing on a dull day) and fills the horizon above the little town. Access is via a narrow road, and the view from the summit over the town is as near to aerial as you could get with your feet still on the ground. Until recently, a public footpath encircled the skyscraper rocks, but this is closed because much of the surrounding land is now in private hands.

A number of local footpaths still network the Bort terrain however. The *Syndicat d'Initiative* dispenses free guide pamphlets on waymarked routes. Consider route numbers 4 and 5. Number 5 takes about one and a half hours of gentle walking and begins with a street and then lane ascent through the old town to a Notre Dame statue on a hill flank. You pause for a deep breath here, then continue for another half-kilometre before turning sharp right just past a farm, off the tarmac and along a foot path slightly higher than the obvious farm track. A low stone wall is then followed through the woods along the hill flank for some fine panoramas, not only of the town, but also of the distant Dore mountains.

Route number 4 is slightly longer, to the neighbouring hamlet of Puy Morel to the south-east of the town, over the Dordogne (hence back into the Auvergne). There is an obvious footpath (green-arrowed) which takes over at the end of a narrow tarmac lane, to traverse a rock-studded plateau of meadow and woodland, before descending to the gates of a special education centre (CAT) and then returning to town via a railway line. Both these routes offer some lovely high-level views (including the ever-dominant *Orgues*), as well as a sight of a country town that was once just a backwater tannery, with small hat- and clog-making industries supplementing the leather production.

As well as walks, water sports and other sporting activities, there are numerous half- and full-day scenic drives from Bort, also detailed in the tourist office. One of the best is the round route which visits the Parc des Volcans, and takes in some splendid places in the Auvergne, as well as two high spots of Cantal *département* – Salers and Puy Mary.

Bort-les-Orgues – Useful Information

Office de Tourisme: Pavilion, Place Marmontel 19110 Bort-les-Orgues, Correze, Limousin (Tel: 55 96 02 49). Open all year; plus a *Syndicat d'Initiative* (July and August only), at the Base Nautique des Aubazines off the Ussel/Limoges road. Hotel reservations best obtained from the main office.

Forty hotels (9 with restaurants in town), some 80 hotels in the town and vicinity categorized as 'comfortable' and some 30 chambres d'hotes and other furnished accommodation; many of these are located around the huge man-made lake in scenic surroundings. The top hotel in Bort is the 2-star Central, at 65 Avenue de la Gare. There are 25 rooms here, a restaurant of reputation (Tel: 55 96 74 82).

Leisure Amenities: Individual or conducted tours around the great Bort barrage, all forms of water sport from some eight water access points around the lake; boat cruises (roughly one hour duration), from the Base de Val just north of town. Car park and visitor circuit (signposted), around the Bort Barrage (off CD92 road), just east of tanneries. Quickest and most direct route to the Orgues *belvédère* is north-west of town centre via the Rue de Paris and then the Route des Orgues. An 8-mile circuit drive to the top of this scenic plateau which lies at an elevation of 789 metres.

There are 5 banks in Bort, an efficient taxi service and car-hire service, while bicycles may be hired from the SNCF railway station. Shopping facilities for self-catering visitors is very good and there is a covered market specializing in fruit and cheese regional products. Good souvenir buys of local leather products and a wide selection of atmospheric cafes and restaurants, notably in the Rue de Paris.

Don't miss: the ramparts; Maison de Bargue; Place d'Armes; Maison de Betrandy; Grande Place; Maison de Ronade.

About 30km south of Bort, via the D922, is Mauriac, the first celebrated historic remnant on this excursion route. At the very heart of this ancient market town is an imposing black-stone twelfth-century church, Notre Dame des Miracles, with a tympanum of remarkable carved ascension scenes that is revered as one of the best Romanesque entrance arches in the *massif central*. See it on a good day if you can – the lava stone is rather sombre. The old town is still active as a cattle dealing centre, as it has been for centuries, but it is gradually becoming less impressive as building expansion threatens to overwhelm the ancient and picturesque heart. The centre around the church is already disproportionately tiny. The tourist information office is in the Place Georges Pompidou.

Salers East from Mauriac on the D122, through a landscape that becomes increasingly dramatic as the boundary of the Parc des Volcans is crossed, is Anglards-de-Salers, at the head of the lovely valée de Falgoux. South from this back-country village, on the D22, is a visual treat – the once-fortified town of Salers, designated one of the five finest historic villages in France.

Salers was much-defended redoubt during the Middle Ages, sacked (and occupied) by English troops during the Hundred Years War, and battled over again during the Wars of Religions (when it was all but overwhelmed by Protestant forces). Somehow it has survived almost intact, with the majority of the old buildings, the ramparts and the quaint narrow streets retaining a genuine patina

La Place, Salers, this is one of the most striking ancient villages of France

of age. The medieval atmosphere makes it a delightful place to visit, and this is enhanced by its setting at 950 metres among green fields against an exquisite backdrop of Cantal hills.

Salers is seemingly timeless hewn from volcanic stone, with elegant towers of original medieval perfection. Charming cobbled alleyways, little squares and splendidly-proportioned archways offer an architectural feast. Salers slumbers, fully aware of its heritage value, but a hotel has been built into the old ramparts, and there are a number of modern shops (including a self-service grocery), as well as cafés, bars and outlets for Auvergne cheeses, famous dried hams and local wines.

For a fine view of Saler's beautiful surroundings, take the tortuous D35 road just to the east of town for a couple of kilometres. Within the walls, don't miss the dwellings around the

Place d'Armes, the Grande Place, the Maisons de Barque, Bertrandy and Ronade. These houses are much as they were in 1586 when Protestant soldiers attacked the town during the Wars of Religion. Agressive behaviour was by no means one-sided, however. History records that there was great Catholic apprehension in Salers at times, when, over the urgent tolling of the church bells, there rose the fearful cry of *Huguenots! Huguenots!* The attackers in 1586 were eventually repulsed, although not before a heavy price had been paid on the part of the Catholic inhabitants. The rampart walls (only erected during the latter part of the fourteenth century following pillage and plunder raids by English soldiery) saved the town. After this episode, Salers prospered, particularly during the sixteenth century, when it became a favoured residential town of privileged *bourgeoisie*.

The nineteenth century saw another downturn in its fortunes, as the Auvergne suffered depopulation, with serious migration from this hard country, where the topsoil is meagre and agricultural labour only grudgingly repaid. Such an environment breeds a toughness and self-sufficiency, and the fiercest of the *Maquis* resistance during World War II came from these resilient people. The historic photos in the Salers bookshop show life five or six decades ago a record of rural existence at subsistence level. Contemporary life is markedly easier.

There is spacious car parking at the foot of the village, close to two good hotels – the two-star Bailliage and the one-star Remparts. Both are well situated, with restaurants that are worth trying. On the fringe of town, attractively landscaped, is modern Camping le Mouriol. Excellent facilities are provided and entry is reserved for genuine touring visitors.

Another scintillating minor-road drive, via the D680, around Puy Violent and high above the Falgoux Valley, leads to the third peak of the Parc des Volcans, Puy Mary. Alluring and seductive of contour, it looms tall and green in a wonderful Cantal landscape about 20km south-east of Salers. It is 1,787 metres high.

The massive, semi-circular ridge is, of course, very popular with walkers and climbers. There is good access to the ridge, even for those who are not keen or experienced, while car parking, souvenirs and refreshments are found a couple of kilometres

The majestic Puy Mary. Some of the best hillwalking in the Volcans national park is hereabouts

north-east of the Pas de Peyrol. For an immediate short ascent, park at the summit pass and make the easy climb to the crown of the great mountain. For more extended walking (perhaps from Salers as a base) there are the GR4 and GR400 long-distance hiking trails, where you might almost imagine yourself in Scotland. Along the D680 the high pastures are virtually devoid of trees, while the dark scree and snow-patched corries of the Plomb-du-Cantal form a sweeping backdrop for long-horned cattle. If you penetrate more deeply into the gigantic Auvergne rifts, however, a completely unique landscape is revealed.

Condat and the Gorges de la Rhue North-east from Puy Mary, on the D680 just past Dienne hamlet, and after forking north off the Murat road on the D3, you will find Condat. Condat has charm and character. Its location, in a deep and richly-wooded valley, makes it a retirement-home enclave. Fortunately, the proliferation of holiday villas on the valley flanks have not yet spoiled the original attraction of the setting.

Just to the north of Condat is, the tiny village of Montboudif in its Spartan setting. There is not much in the way of lush woodland here, but it does have a claim to fame as the birthplace of Georges Pompidou, the son of a local schoolmaster and President of France from 1969 to 1974. This isolated rock-girt hill village no doubt bred a certain grit and determination in the man which made him leader of his country.

Worth a visit: Champagnac-les-Mines; Auriac; Tours de Merle.

There is nothing Spartan about the view from the D679, which winds its way westwards from Condat along the beautiful valley of the river Rhue. This river also feeds the huge Bort lake, through a massive and lengthy tunnel which carries the supplementary water supply some 12km. This engineering wonder is less impressive though, than the natural, thickly-wooded ravines of the Georges de la Rhue, about 25km from Bort-les-Orgues. They are spectacular.

The Dordogne Barrages Following the Dordogne river faithfully south of Bort-les-Orgues is another fascinating cross-country route of natural beauty. Take the D922 southwards and soon turn west on signposted minor roads for Champagnac-les-Mines; look back on this hill road for some fine views of the Orgues. Champagnac is the first of several atmospheric villages, with a stout Romanesque church and a miner's museum. Continue to Serandon village (on the outskirts see the signposted road for the scenic Route des Ajustants). Note the isolated fortified farm of ancient vintage, the Château de la Charlanne, on the right between Serandon and the impressive viewpoint high above the river, the Belvédère de Gratte-Bruyère.

From here, the Dordogne seems to be a string of man-made lakes linked by feeder trickles, so tamed and multi-barraged have the upper reaches of the river become. In the interest of progress, with the important motives of water conservation and the creation of vast hydro-electric projects, the near-total subjugation

View of the tamed Dordogne, below the Barrage de l'Aigle

of the watercourse was imperative. In the past the powerful Dordogne waters would periodically flood the agricultural plains too, with disastrous effects resulting in widespread famine, sometimes more than 150km from the river itself. Any risk of serious flooding is now much less.

After the *belvédère*, continue along a lake-shore road, then take the Mauriac road south to the village of La Besse, and then the Tulle road (D678) to another massive dam. This, the Barrage de l'Aigle (Eagle Dam), is only slightly less impressive than the lake at Bort. A glance downwards from the concrete balustrade will reveal the valley below, and the quiet, restricted trickle dissecting the V-shaped landscape where there were once foaming waters.

Descend a series of sharp hairpin bends to this near-dry valley floor, then continue to Auriac, a pretty backwater village with a sixteenth-century church and an attractive lake-side touring

caravan site and restaurant. Between here and St Privat, make time to detour to the secluded Chapelle du Puy du Bassin, signposted just off the D111. This is a perfect pine-tree clearing for a picnic lunch, with finely preserved religious history; the chapel door is permanently open to visitors.

Drive south now for 10km to one of the gems of the Dordogne. The Tours de Merle, impossibly perched on a natural bluff rising from the waters of the river Maronne (a Dordogne tributary and the same water that serves Salers), are genuine medieval ruins, thought to have been completed in the twelfth century. They remain virtually untouched by restorers since the walls first crumbled several centuries ago. Visually stunning these ruins are still a testimony to the skills of the military architects of the past. Twin strongholds of the Middle Ages, their impregnability was only threatened with the coming of artillery,

105

since when they have slowly and gently crumbled through he centuries to blend into the Maronne valley landscape. Son et lumière spectaculars are held here during high summer.

The Tours de Merle stand in another half-secret region of the *massif central*, known as La Xaintrie. To see more of this area, retrace your route north-west (perhaps stopping at the Auberge des Ruines de Merle for lunch) to the charming village of St-Cirques-la-Loutres on the D13. From here it is not far to the plateau village of Servières-le-Château, perhaps your next objective.

The Servières Plateau Much less visited than the upper Dordogne to the north-east (and downriver from Argentat), La Xaintrie, in the Corrèze *département* of Limousin, is one of the prettiest areas of the whole *massif central*. It is the triangle of terrain formed by the Dordogne gorges north-east of Argentat and the snaking Maronne tributary to the south, high country richly endowed with forests, fast-flowing feeder streams and a number of barraged lakes. One of these is Lac de Feyt, close to the little village of Servières.

The stunnigly evocative ruins of the Tours-de-Merle, successfully defended against several English assaults during The Hundred Years War

The hill town of Servières is majestically dominated by a mighty *château* and some gigantic rock crags which thrust upwards and outwards from almost sheer valley walls. The approach from St Privat is pleasant, but that via the minor roads south-east of Tulle is dramatic. From the pretty village of St-Martin-la-Meanne, follow the D29 to the huge Barrage du Chastang, then ascend the skyscraping valley ridge to Servières.

The château has a long and interesting history going back to the tenth century, although the present building dates only from the seventeenth century. During World War I it was used to house German prisoners of war and today it is a hospital for the mentally handicapped.

The village of Servières is colourful. There are two hotels with restaurants and a good local bus service to St Privat and Argentat. For walking, there is a precipitous medieval path which winds down from the high plateau settlement to the neighbouring village of Gleny, on the banks of the Dordogne far below. More leisurely (and more level), is the footpath circumnavigation of nearby Lac de Feyt. Surrounded by mixed woodland and with just the odd weekend chalet, the lake is about 6km in circumference and takes about three hours to walk around. The going is easy, with some feeder streams to negotiate. There is a very good touring caravan site on the lake shore, clean and quiet and, at the altitude of some 500 metres, with pine-laden air. There is a sailing school, and a tiny aqua sports centre hires out pedalo craft and offers refreshment to the lake-shore walker.

A few kilometres to the north-west, St-Martin-la-Meanne's neighbour is La-Roche-Canillac, an ancient and atmospheric village, with a tucked-away municipal camp ground that has chalet huts for hire and adjacent tennis courts. There is fine walking around here in beautiful deep wooded combes along lanes and forestry tracks, especially to the south of the village. Along the banks of the narrow river Doustre consider two distinctly picturesque footpaths to Roche-Haute, with its striking Gothic church, and the footpath to Roche-Basse, where a cluster of very ancient houses surrounds a Gothic fountain.

This area has close association with the twelfth-century Dordogne troubadour Bernart de Ventadour, one of La Xaintrie's most celebrated sons. The imposing tower ruins of Ventadour

Château, his birthplace (around 1122), can be seen at Egletons, just off the N89 to the north of La-Roche-Canillac, between Ussel and Tulle.

Troubadours played an important part in intellectual and artistic life during the Middle Ages. Poets and musicians, often of princely origin and feckless and ardent, they wandered freely around southern Europe, especially in France and the Dordogne region. Their role, which was to entertain and amuse, gave them an immunity; they would blatantly importune high-born ladies, and recite barbed poems or sing ballads directed against their peers. They could be dangerously audacious, and usually (although not always) got away with it.

Bernart de Ventadour was no poetic princeling but the son of a lowly serf in the service of Vicomte de Ventadour. This erudite nobleman apparently encouraged the lad's natural gifts, but the budding poet rewarded him by falling in love with his wife. Apparently she was in love with him too, and from this passionate alliance came a string of lyrical poems, some of the best from medieval times. When the affair was discovered Bernart fled to the protection of Henry II of England, and it is said that he was one of the king's entourage during a visit to London. The love-lorn troubadour lived to a ripe old age and died eventually in Poitou-Charentes.

The Barrage du Chastang Leave Servières in a south-westerly direction on the D129 for a marvellously stimulating route, a rapid, twisting swoop down from the high plateau. A series of wooded ravines and escarpments mark the gradual termination of Dordogne gorge country, scoured by the wild water over millions of years. The precipitous road drops from the great skyline *château* between thickly-wooded hills. At one point a grandstand view over the massive Barrage du Chastang is revealed. From the *belvédère*, where there is a technical data board, you can rapidly assess the sheer size and complexity of the project which has created an elongated lake between here and the L'Aigle barrage 30km away.

Another switchback descent to the south leads to the charming hamlet of Gleny. Here there is irrefutable evidence of the strength of the river when it flowed at its natural pace – the bankside medieval church beside the narrow road, once robust and sturdy has been all but swept away by past flood waters. Now only the Romanesque apse remains, protected by a defensive belfry walls which seals the remnant building against the elements. The Dordogne no longer represents a danger. The one-time church is now a miniature chapel, oddly appealing for its stubborn survival.

Argentat The Dordogne below Chastang dam runs swift, wide and deep to Argentat despite another small dam just to the north-east of the town, where the Doustre tributary joins the main water. South-west from this point, the towering gorges give way to more gentle country. A quite distinct change in character and aspect occurs. The Dordogne banks, instead of being steeply sheer in places and thinly populated, take on a much more stable and gentle appearance, with level or faintly sloping water-meadow margins instead of sheer-sided cliffs.

To either side of the watercourse there are still pockets of fine forest and the hills still rise to impressive heights, but in between expansive and fertile meadows support an increasing number of dairy farms, cereal crops and a proliferation of fruit and nut trees (especially walnut)

Argentat is the first impressive historic site to be found astride the river, an ancient town which once played a significant part in the story of river travel. In Latin Argentoratum, the town was fortified around the church in the tenth century and from the eleventh century was a bustling inland river port on a major communication route of south-west France. From Argentat all sorts of goods were transported – leather, wine casks, cheeses and timber – downriver to Bergerac, Libourne and, eventually (via the Garonne) to Bordeaux. All this trade was carried out in distinctive, flat-bottomed boats called *gabares*, made and sailed by intrepid boatmen called *gabariers*. They navigated frequently unpredictable waters, and were particularly in danger in the Gironde estuary. A trip might take months to complete, and it was a common practice at the end for the boatmen to sell not only their wares and produce, but also the boats, which were invariably broken up for their timber. How these merchant adventurers made their way home again is not recorded.

The visitor can still capture a taste of the derring-do of the *gabariers* by wandering around old Argentat near the splendidly preserved quayside, where replica *gabares* are displayed and,

Argentat

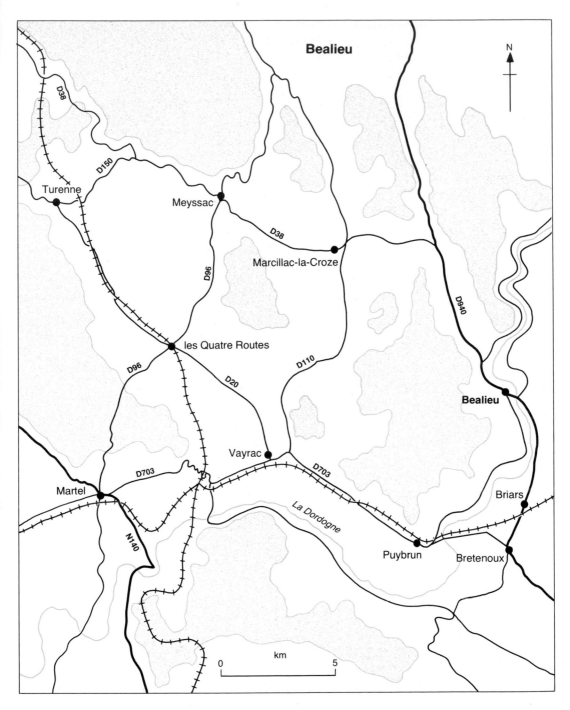

indeed, still used. During the summer, regular cruise boats leave Argentat and, further upriver, Spontour (where the traditional craft were constructed), and also the Bridge of Chambon in the centre of deep gorge country.

Argentat, in its southern Corrèze setting, has been awarded *Station Verte* status. Only the busy N120, which slices right through the heart of the old town, represents a black spot; park on the northern perimeter of the town, around the *parc des sports* and adjacent to the municipal camping ground.

From this safe parking place it is just a short stroll back to the quayside, which lies immediately below the N120 river bridge. The buildings in this locality have the glowing *lauze* roofs, with their patina of age, which are seen on many old buildings in the Dordogne region. Despite the traffic there is a serenity about this town, reflected not only by the delightful old houses, but also by the unhurried pace of daily life to be found alongside the Quai Lestourgie, also a pedestrian walk. Here towers and spires dominate the scene, and the Auberge des Gabariers is a popular eating place. Visit, too the medieval hub, centred on the Place de l'Eglise.

Don't miss: Quai Lestourgie; Place de l'Eglise.

There are four hotels in Argentat, three Logis de France, and one, the Nouvel Hôtel Gilbert in Avenue Joseph Gilbert, two-star rated. The tourist office is in Avenue Pasteur. The town is a good base, lying on the threshold of two quite distinctive tracts of Dordogne terrain. Its popularity is reflected by the number of self-catering accommodation units – 14 hotels, 8 caravan and camping sites, nearly 100 bed and breakfast houses, and some 25 *gîtes ruraux*. There is good supermarket shopping here, as well as some attractive specialist stores around the old town centre. Gastronomic treats are river trout and Limousin beef. For those who enjoy walking, there is a 9-km circular walk, the Circuit des Crêtes Marcel Bossoutrot, which begins form the Barrage du Sablier, just to the north-east of the town centre, off the Route de Longour.

Beaulieu Follow the widening Dordogne south-west from Argentat for the short and scenic journey to Beaulieu. Minor roads on either side of the sparkling river give access to several touring caravan and camping locations. On the southern side, the D116 provides wide scenic sweeps across the wooded valley

The market place and celebrated Romanesque church portal, Beaulieu

Don't miss: Abbey church; Place des Peres; Chapelle de Pénitents; Maison Renaissance; Quais de la Dordogne; Collouges-la-Rouge.

with the fine hills beyond, while the D12 on the northern side is slightly busier and less revealing.

Beaulieu, the 'beautiful place', is arguably the grandest medieval cluster along the Dordogne river. An old market town with an important heritage, contained within an almost circular perimeter road, it is centred upon the exquisitely preserved twelfth-century church which dominates a lively and colourful market place. The abbey church boasts one of the most famous of carved tympanums in France, depicting a terrifying vision of Hell. All around, the dwellings off the Place des Pères reflect an aura of the Middle Ages, above cobbled streets and gated courtyards.

This town centre must really be explored on foot, and this is wonderfully easy, since the whole of Beaulieu is compact. Don't miss the market place, the Chapelle des Pénitents, the Maison

114

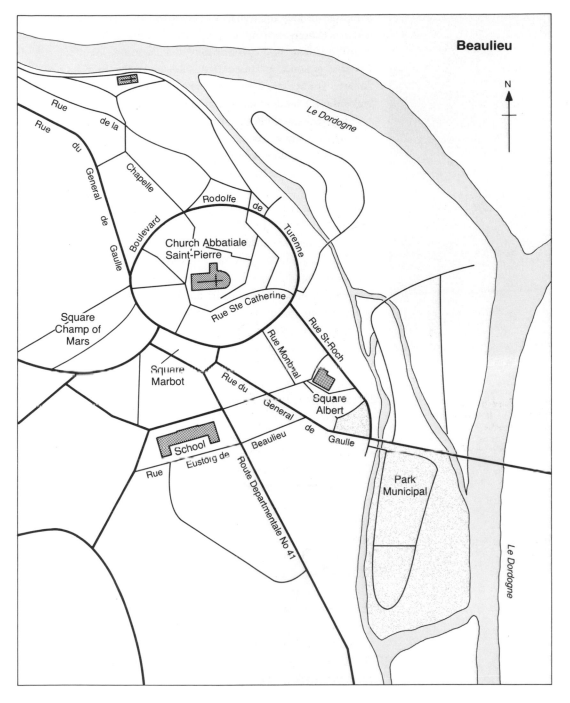

Beaulieu

N

Rue de la Chapelle
Rue du General de Gaulle
Boulevard
Rodolfe de Turenne
Le Dordogne
Church Abbatiale Saint-Pierre
Rue Ste Catherine
Rue St-Roch
Square Champ of Mars
Rue Monbnal
Square Marbot
Square Albert
Rue du General de Gaulle
School
Rue Eustorg de Beaulieu
Route Departmentale No 41
Park Municipal
Le Dordogne

Beaulieu

Renaissance and the Quais de la Dordogne. The old town has many buildings worthy of exploration, some dating back to the ninth century, when Rodolphe de Turenne, Archbishop of Bourges, named the place Bellus Locus at the founding of the Abbey. Today this little town is the epitome of France's past, beyond price because of its near-perfect state of preservation.

There is a good choice of hotels within the town confines – Le Turenne has three stars and is in a very attractive setting – as well as two touring sites, and a youth hostel within a fine old house opposite the ancient Chapelle des Pénitents. The *Syndicat d'Initiative* is well stocked with local information, and found in the Place Marbot, where there is generally car parking.

This reach of the Dordogne is sometimes known as the 'Limousin Riviera', with its favourable micro-climate and lush vegetation. There are a number of walks through the surrounding woods, alongside the water, where there is also canoeing. Canoe-hire and tuition centres are in the vicinity and Beaulieu boasts a fine swimming pool. Cycle hire is available from the youth hostel.

This old market town and its environs hold strong appeal for British visitors, and a number have settled permanently in the area. The Nicholls family are now the owners of a hill top farmhouse about ten minutes' drive from Beaulieu, and provide comfortable bed and breakfast accommodation. Their location, at the hamlet of La Poujade, between the Dordogne and the Cère, offers fine views across the Cère valley. Overnighting here is comfortable, and reasonable, and there is a vine-shaded terrace. Telephone Mrs Nicholls on 55 91 18 56.

Beaulieu – Useful Information *Syndicat d'Initiative:* Place Marbot, (Tel: 55 91 09 94). Coach excursions to Dordogne high spots are organized from this office during summer. Day trips (from 9.30am to 6pm), include visits to picturesque villages, ancient churches and natural beauty spots and there is a lunch-break at a small farmhouse auberge, noted for its regional cuisine. Also adjacent in Pace Marbot, there are regular exhibitions of paintings by local artists held at Easter, July, August and September.

There is a regular bus service to Brive, Tulle and Argentat, plus a connection bus service to the nearest railway station (Bretenoux-Biars), 6 kilometres to the south. A private taxi service operates, details from the S.I.

Accommodation: the 3-star Hôtel Turenne (Tel: 55 91 10 16) recommended restaurant, open form May to September. Also Les Charmilles, Relais hotel-restaurant, popular family pension by Dordogne (Tel: 55 91 11 54). The attractive fourteenth-century youth hostel is strategically (and scenically) located on a major rambling and cycling circuit of the Dordogne. It is open from April to September, accommodating a total of 45 persons (Tel: 55 91 13 82). An imposing and traditional Logis de France 2-star hotel is the Fournie, Place du Champ-de-Mars, with a restaurant specializing in regional dishes. Open from mid-March to mid-November (Tel: 55 91 01 34).

Leisure Amenities: Situated as it is on the banks of the Dordogne, there is much emphasis on water sports, especially canoeing. One of the leading canoe and kayak hire companies is Copeyre, with hire stations (locations), at Argentat and Souillac and several in between. At Beaulieu, the Hôtel de la Plage, Place Monturu, supplies hire craft, camping gear and safety equipment (see also Sports section in part VI of guide). Mountain bikes may also be hired form the same location (Tel: 55 91 06 21). Local horse-riding centres are located at the Ranch de Chadenac, Chauffour (14 kms north-west), Tel: 55 25 41 45 and at Ferme Equestre de Mialaret, Camps St Mathurin – 14 kms east (Tel: 55 28 50 09).

Collonges-la-Rouge Beaulieu and its immediate area has enough of interest for at least a day or two. A little further afield are some outstanding high spots. The exceptional roseate cluster of Collonges-la Rouge lies 20km to the north-west of Beaulieu, on the D940 and then the D38. Nothing like any rustic French village of the Middle Ages, this was a show-piece collection of country retreat houses and mansions, of doll's-house design and dimensions in places, representing an extraordinary architectural exercise. It is authentic, yet – especially in bright sunlight – it is almost *too* colourful.

Collonges is unique in France, the result of indulging the whims of over-wealthy medieval minorities, at a time when most of the populace was living at subsistence level. It basks sleepily now in a half-hidden valley, once a convenient 8km from Turenne, once power-house of Corrèze politics and impregnable stronghold of the powerful dynasty of the Dukes of

Collonges-la-Rouge – a fascinating medieval indulgence

Turenne. Built as a rest and recuperation centre from the pressures of seventeenth-century ruling-class life, the houses in Collonges are exclusively of glowing red sandstone. Almost every house is different, a riot of pepper-pot towers, galleries, fish-scale roofs, quaint dormer windows, and a host of elaborate ornamentation revealed between trained grape vines clinging to the rose-red walls.

The tiny main square is charming, as it should be in one of the 'prettiest villages in France', with an imposing (mainly) sixteenth-century church on one side and a Chapelle des Pénitents museum on the other. The square is on the site of a much earlier settlement that was centred on an eighth-century Bénédictine priory. For the Turenne overlords, Collonges was not only novel in concept, but literally a completely new town.

Collonges can be fully explored in a couple of hours' strolling. Don't miss the Manoir de Beauvirie, the Castel de Maussac, the Château Benge, or the fine church which, very usually, has two naves, one Catholic, one Protestant – the most powerful of all the Turenne *vicomtes* was a Protestant for much of his life. The original structure dates back to the eleventh century and, while the church was largely rebuilt in the sixteenth and seventeenth

118

centuries, a sculpted white-stone tympanum from the earlier period, depicting the Ascension, remains in the doorway.

There is a comfortable two-star hotel at Collonges, Le Relais de St Jacques (well named, since the village was a pilgrim stopover along the Compostela Trail centuries before its conversion to a red-stone showplace). There are also agreeable restaurants and cafés, as well as a well-run campsite (with swimming pool and tennis courts). Collonges is a source of craftsman-made souvenirs, notably in leather and ceramics, and a range of Dordogne gastronomic treats like *foie-gras* and *confit* (duck or goose preserved in its own rendered fat). This way of preserving food (now very expensive), has been handed down from earlier times.

Turenne is much more a typical Limousin hill town of medieval origin, although little remains to signify its immense importance throughout most of France's turbulent history. From the tenth century to the eighteenth, this was the capital of a vast domain stretching across the lower Limousin, the Quercy and Périgord, embracing hundreds of towns and villages. It was a feudal empire, with its own army, laws, taxes and coinage, which owed allegiance to none save the King of France. A succession of *vicomtes* governed from a position of indisputable strength. Today there are only remnants of their mighty hilltop castle; it was almost destroyed by revolutionaries in the eighteenth century. You can still see, however, a complex defensive system of castle, rampart walls and protective towers.

Of all the fiefdon chiefs who held sway across thirteen centuries, Henri de la Tour d'Auvergne was probably the greatest, and was certainly the most famous. Born in 1611, he was destined for a soldier's career and was eventually much favoured for his military prowess and courage in battle by the influential Cardinal Richelieu. After many brilliant campaigns, often won through audacious boldness, he was appointed Marshal of France by Louis XIV – despite being a staunch Protestant! He eventually converted to Catholicism later (hence the twin naves in Collonges church), and was killed in battle in 1675. He was lastingly mourned as a military genius and one of France's greatest generals, and his ashes were moved to Les Invalides in Paris on the orders of Napoleon.

119

Martel, named in honour of the legendary eighth-century hero 'The Hammer'. This photograph show the approach to the famous covered market

120

No rose tints decorate Turenne, but this imposing relic of bright limestone, now slumbering gently as a backwater settlement, is able to rely on tourism to fill its once fabulously-rich coffers.

Old Turenne is, so well preserved (at least in part), that it is not too difficult to visualize the medieval war-lord striding the village streets between the fifteenth and sixteenth century houses on his way up to the great castle. He would still recognize the thirteenth-century Tour de Caesar. From here there are some spectacular views across Corrèze countryside, and you can easily appreciate the wonderful defensive site this ancient village occupied.

Don't miss: The thirteenth-century ramparts; Church of St Maur; Maison Fabri; Hôtel de la Raymondi.

Martel South of Turenne on the D20 and then, from Les Quatres Routes hamlet, on the D96 is the township of Martel. For a long time under the protection of Turenne, the town dominates the Quercy plateau, the Causse Martel. The stony terrain and relatively sparse vegetation of the plateau enhance the powerful beauty of ancient Martel, as well as contributing to the atmosphere.

Martel was named after the eighth-century hero Charles Martel, 'The Hammer', King of the Franks, grandfather of Charlemagne and victor over the Moors who, after their defeat at the Battle of Poitiers in AD 732, were at last routed here on the high and stony plateau. Even today, the town can transport you back to medieval France, especially as you stand under the massive, wormy timbers of the magnificent covered market. Do this, if you can, at lunchtime, when the great and universal French quiet descends.

Martel possesses and enviable surfeit of architectural riches. The remains of the thirteenth-century ramparts are evidence of how stoutly this most important town of the Turenne empire was defended. The fortified Gothic church of St Maur – outwardly all battlements and buttresses – testifies to the constant threat faced by the township during the Middle Ages. Visit, too the magnificent Maison Fabri, where Henry 'Chartmantle', the son of Henry II of England, sought refuge after revolting against his father and sacking nearby Rocamadour to replenish his campaign funds. He contracted a fever and died here – of remorse, it is said, for his sacrilegious act – in 1183. Also of interest is the splendid

Hôtel de la Raymondi, built at the turn of the thirteenth century, where the viscounts of Turenne held their high court.

Martel was occupied by the English form 1360 to 1374, and only attached to the French crown by Louis XV in 1738.

There is a good choice of accommodation in and around the ancient town, including the comfortable and central Le Turenne and the Lion d'Or, as well as atmospheric cafés and bars, and a convenient shady municipal touring site for caravans and tents just of the N140 on the northern outskirts (Camping Callopie). The tourist office is in the centre of this 'Town of the Seven Towers'.

For riverside accommodation, there is a most attractive hostelry called the Auberge de l'Ile, at the quiet and secluded village of Creysse just to the south of Martel. Their restaurant is noted for its local delicacies. To get there, take the D23 south to the banks of the Dordogne, about 10km distant. Creysse is a backwater village, with a fine Romanesque church and some lovely old houses.

Bretenoux and Castelnau East from Martel on the D703 is Bretenoux where the D940 is rejoined. This lovely old village, on the banks of the river Cère, has covered arcades, venerable houses and fifteenth-century mansions around the picturesque Place des Consuls. It is a peaceful and friendly place, with two hotels and a camping ground plus a number of *gîtes ruraux* (self-catering cottages) in the area.

Château de Castlenau, near Bretenoux was one of the most powerful fortresses of medieval France

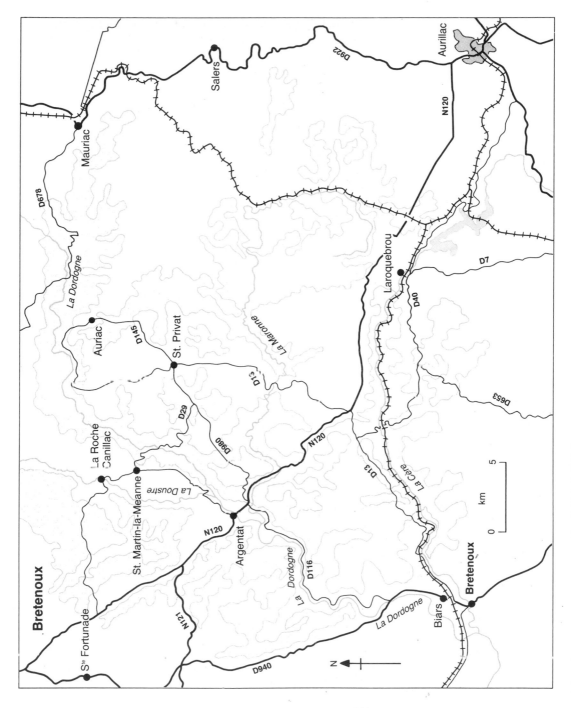

However, Bretenoux is not the main attraction. In the 'land of marvels', as this district of the Dordogne and Cère valley is called, the majestic Castelnau *château*/fortress commands a breathtaking and dominant position. On its lofty wooded bluff, this huge red-stone fort oversees the strategic heights and the communication routes of the Dordogne, Cère and Bave valleys; even today it is formidable, almost threatening, and very impressive.

Castelnau was the biggest military fortress in southern France, a fearsome stronghold since the eleventh century, when Hugh of Castelnau enclosed his feudal domain behind almost impregnable walls. It was the scene of savage skirmishes during the Hundred Years War, between the feudal barons and the forces of Henry II of England, and later again when the ramparts were breached and the castle taken by storm by Simon de Montfort. During the seventeenth century, in a more peaceful interlude, the battle-scarred building was converted to a princely residence, and huge bay windows were let into the old walls to improved the interior lighting. Around this time the fortress came under the protection of the Dukes of Turenne. Two hundred years later, another vast programme of restoration was undertaken (largely to repair the ravages of the French Revolution) by a wealthy opera singer and finally, in 1932, the magnificent building was handed over, in excellent order, to the French nation. The stout rampart walls, studded with defensive towers, enclose a main courtyard overshadowed by the thirteenth-century Saracen's Tower. The courtyard is a perfect setting for a music festival that is now held annually in the summer. The *château* is open to visitors daily throughout the year, except on Tuesdays.

The Souillac Circuit Lying on a major north to south route (the N20 between Brive and Cahors), Souillac has to tolerate a steady throughput of road traffic, particularly in high summer. Its location on the banks of the Dordogne, although it is officially within the *département* of Lot, means that it is a town well known to most Dordogne explorers. Apart from a magnificent twelfth-century abbey church, Souillac has little to offer, except a riverbank location and the fragmentary old town around the narrow river Borrèze, which meets the Dordogne here in the heart of a fertile valley.

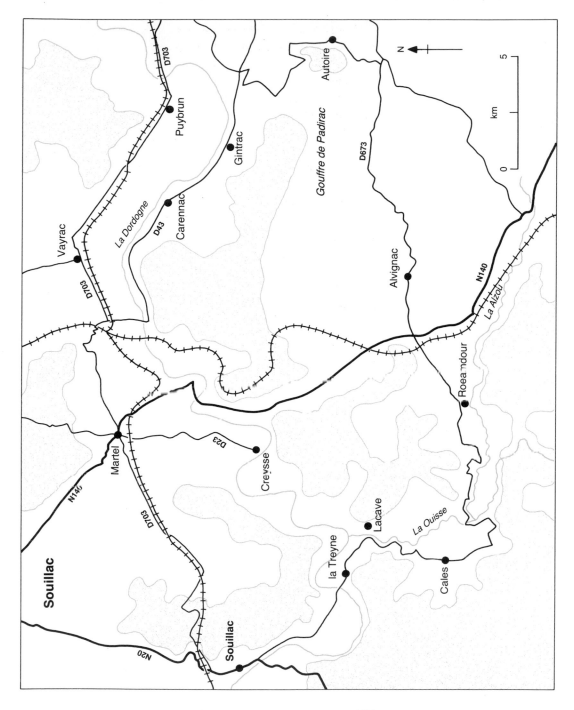

However, the town has been a strategic crossroads of the region for a long time, and it has an important history; traces of human habitation have been unearthed in the vicinity, and carbon-dated to a period around 40,000 years ago. On hillsides above the town the remains of numerous dolmen, menhirs and tumuli testify to the importance – and frequency – of both Bronze Age and Iron Age settlements, which were established in this obviously bountiful area. The Romans used Souillac as a strategic staging-post throughout their long occupation, while in AD909 the Count of Aurillac bequeathed funds for the foundation of a priory, around which developed first a village and then a town.

The priory became an abbey in the late fifteenth century, and an architectural masterpiece which suffered ravages, by English soldiery during the Hundred Years War and again in 1573, during the Wars of Religion, by Huguenot forces. However unremarkable the rest of Souillac may be, this magnificently restored abbey church glows in the sunlight, and is a structure of beautiful proportion. Byzantine more than Romanesque, the great domes, graced with mellow *lauze* roof tiles, blend with perfectly contoured walls. Some truly remarkable Romanesque carvings are housed within an interior of surprising light and spaciousness. There is a large car park adjacent, which also provides an excellent viewpoint of the building early in the day.

The rest of the interesting part of town can be seen in a short time. Visit the twelfth-century belfry tower in the Place St Martin, and a number of medieval buildings in the fragmentary old quarter of Souillac, including a pilgrims' hospice and a former tobacco warehouse that is now a mechanical-model museum with robotic figures from the nineteenth century to the present day. In the Place de l'Abbaye, the museum is open daily. The delights of old Souillac are frequently missed by many tourists, put off by the busy main N20 road, which effectively cuts the town centre in half.

Souillac is not so much a place to explore, more a good town to use as a touring base. The *Syndicat d'Initiative* immediately off the N20 in the town centre is helpful, and there is a good choice of hotel accommodation, as well as a smart shopping centre that caters especially to holiday visitors, with a wide

**Opposite
Souillac**

127

Souillac. The twelfth-century St. Mary's Abbey Church is one of the finest Romanesque buildings in the region

choice of local produce. The efficient local transport system gives access to major Dordogne attractions; some of the finest gems of both ancient Quercy province and Dordogne *département* within a 50-km radius.

Of the hotels in Souillac, the three-star Granges Vieilles (with restaurant), in the Route de Sarlat, is the best, closely followed by the three-star Hôtel du Puy d'Alon (no restaurant), in the Rue de Présignac. All the hotels in town, even the most modest, are of a standard appropriate to a recognized *Station Verte*. There are also a number of *chambres d'hotes* (bed and breakfast houses) and *gîtes*, and the best camping ground is the municipal Des Ondines, in the Avenue de Sarlat. Full lists of accommodation and amenities are available from the tourist office.

The tourist office also supplies information about local travel by train or excursion coaches, which operate throughout the summer season, as well as the addresses of car, cycle and canoe-hire centres. Remember to ask for a free map of pedestrian circuits around the town too. One or two tourist-office pamphlets are memorable for their valiant attempts at English. One accommodation brochure ends with a flourish, thus: 'By maximal and according as availability, I should respect you wishs. We request not a deposit, but I shall receive you in person. Thank you for your prettiness.' One can only warm to such sentiments!

In many places along and alongside the Dordogne, English *is* spoken and understood to a reasonable degree, perhaps not surprisingly, since this is such a popular area with the British. If you *must* speak in English you can do so in limited fashion at the Souillac tourist office and in some of the specialized shops; incidentally, the town *charcuteries* are famed for their delicacies.

Souillac, not an outstandingly beautiful town, attracts a steady stream of leisure visitors at almost all seasons of the year, partly because it is at an important road and rail junction, but mainly because, according to locals and hotel-keepers, it is an efficient comfort-station in a strategic location. It is a particularly good place to stay in order to take in two of the most visited and most coveted tourist targets in all France – Rocamadour (21 km away) and the Gouffre de Padirac (32 km away).

Souillac – Useful Information *Syndicat d'Initiative:* Boulevard L.J. Malvy, (Tel: 65 37 81 56). Open all the year round. Comprehensive information and address lists of furnished accommodation available for the holiday period from June to September. Details also available about SNCF excursions in the Dordogne region, which operate from mid June to mid September, departing and returning to Souillac. There are 18 hotels in town (six with no restaurants), plus a choice of 18 more within close proximity. There is also a selection of *chambres d'hotes* and *gîtes ruraux*, together with a *village vacance* at Calviac on the Dordogne, some 15 kilometres south-west. There are 8 caravan and camping parks in the vicinity.

Leisure Amenities: There are 6 canoe-kayak centres within easy distance of Souillac, with the Copeyre base adjacent to the camping ground by the river bridge, the nearest. Their main office telephone number is 65 37 33 51. Other centres will be found at Creyesse, Siorac and Vitrac. There are 4 horse-riding centres within reasonable distance of town (two near Pinsac just to the south) and 4 cycle hire locations including the railway station (Tel: 65 32 78 21). For indoor entertainment there is a cinema in Avenue Charles de Gaulle, and a discoteque Le Moulin à Blazy (Tel: 65 37 84 60).

There are 5 banks in Souillac, a comprehensive range of shops, 3 repair garages and car-hire form Garage Renault in the Avenue de Sarlat Tel: 65 32 73 03. There is a good choice of cafés, bars, pizzerias and restaurants and, of course, a taxi service and regular bus service to places like Sarlat and Brive.

The Road to Rocamadour From Souillac drive south on the N20 to the town fringe and the Dordogne river, then, staying on the north bank, take the signposted D43 for Rocamadour. This secondary road crosses the river just beyond the village of Pinsac via an iron bridge, and from here you will catch a view of the beautiful cliff-top *château* of La Treyne. This formidable medieval redoubt of impregnable strength coupled with elegant beauty, seem to hang precariously from its lofty limestone bluff high above the water. Today it positively welcomes invaders, although only those with deep pockets, for it is a luxury hotel. It is sometimes open (notably the gardens) to casual visitors during summer.

Equestrian trekkers crossing the Dordogne close by the Château La Treyne

This impressive seventeenth-century *château* almost pales into insignificance beside the next piece of history along the riverbank. Belcastel château, elevated and hovering above the Dordogne and Ouysse confluence waters, is considered by many to hold the most breathtaking position anywhere along the length of the Dordogne river, and from a distance it seems to be the epitome of the noble fortified French château. The towering limestone crag is complemented beautifully by the man-made cluster of towers and turrets in a site which mirrors medieval France perfectly.

Alas, your eyes can play tricks on you, and upon closer inspection much of this ancient redoubt, created originally in the turbulent fourteenth century, is revealed to be nineteenth-century restoration (and by no means an ideal example of the restorer's craft). Still the views from the vicinity of the *château* (which is open in July and August for guided tours) are superb.

While you are in the area, you might also consider a visit to the grotto of Lacavel. Like almost every grotto in the Dordogne it

Rocamadour is the second most-visited site in all France. This is the view from the narrow and winding road to Couzou

Belcastel chateau

is fully commercialized, with a miniature railway, and elevator access to some 2km of subterranean stalagmite displays, elaborately stage-lit for maximum effect. Children of all ages will love this place, which is open daily from Easter to mid-October.

To continue to Rocamadour, go south then east from the attractive village of Cales on the winding D673 road. You will ascend through increasingly rugged and sparsely populated country to traverse part of the northern rim of the Gramat *causse* before approaching L'Hospitalet and its neighbour, Rocamadour

Rocamadour is the second most-visited historic site in France (after Mont St Michel), and one of the most renowned pilgrim shrines along the Compostela Trail to north-west Spain. No medieval sanctuary could be more dramatically located, nor more impressively constructed. It hangs from a south-facing rock precipice, that seems too sheer to hold the huddle of ancient buildings, beneath a limestone overhang with a crowning *château*. The finest distant view is perhaps from L'Hospitalet, where there is a purpose-built *belvédère*, but the prospect form below the shrine, along the snaking D32 towards Couzou, is also memorable.

Don't miss: Rue de la Merceries; Hôtel de Ville; Chapelle Miraculeuse; View from L'Hospitalet.

The town is, of course, much visited and therefore beset by awful traffic congestion at times, but this does not detract from its visual impact upon first-time visitors. As the French assert, it is one of the most impressive religious havens of the Middle Ages. To see it comfortably, try to arrive early in the day to enjoy atmospheric terraced streets like the Rue de la Mercerie, the wealth of medieval dwellings, and other extraordinary buildings like the fifteenth-century Hôtel de Ville.

The real treasure of Rocamadour is reached via the famous 216 pilgrim steps which have been trodden by kings and commoners alike through many centuries. (A lift is available for those who cannot walk).

The goal is the magnificent Chapel of Notre Dame (Chapelle Miraculeuse), which contains the sacred Black Virgin and Child, a walnut carving known to be well over a thousand years old. The chapel also contains a mysterious bell, almost as ancient, said to toll of its own accord to herald miracles, and the alleged battle sword of Roland, the legendary eighth-century hero of Christian France (*see also* under Blaye in the *département* of Giroude).

The chapel is just one of seven churches, a defensive fortress and cliff-top *château* which make up this fascinating cluster of medieval architecture. Some remnants of genuine eleventh- and twelfth-century Rocamadour do remain, but much of it is nineteenth-century restoration carried out after centuries of wanton attacks. Rocamadour had rich pickings (donated by countless pilgrims) for those bent on pillage during the Hundred Years War, the Wars of Religion and the tumultuous anti-religious period of the French Revolution.

To appreciate this remarkable place to the full, the visitor should understand why it became such a hallowed patch of ground in the first place. Archive material records that in the mid-twelfth century a grave was discovered beneath the floor of an old cliff-top chapel, said to contain the remains of an original disciple of Christ who became known as St Amadour. This gave a name to the place of his discovery – Roque Amadour. After the saint was re-interred, a series of miracles were claimed and from then on Rocamadour became one of the great religious shrines of western civilization. Kings and paupers came in increasing numbers to pay homage, and the shrine, despite its desolate wild-country setting, became more famous, more rich and therefore more tempting to would-be ransackers like Henry Curtmantle.

The lowly medieval pilgrims fully aware of the dangers of which such an opulent must have been beset, must be admired for their courage and resilience. Many were already sick (this was an age when a holy happening was often the only hope), so it is extraordinary that so many devout souls made it to precipitous Rocamadour in its hostile terrain at all. L'Hospitalet, at the top end of the gorge, was the site of a medieval first-aid centre for exhausted and often desperately ill pilgrims. It was no leisurely stroll to reach Rocamadour from the twelfth to the fifteenth-century period, when the pilgrimage flow was at its highest; considering the distances, the primitive roads and the facilities *en route*, the journey must have been arduous in the extreme. Even today, a walk around the ravine location of Rocamadour is enough to show you what kind of physical stamina an early Christian traveller needed.

Keen walkers might consider the ancient pilgrim route (now

the GR6 long-distance walking trail) from the Rocamadour, along the course of the fast-flowing river Alzou, to the half-hidden fourteenth-century water mill of Cougnaguet, approximately 6km away. This stretch of country reveals, to either side of the narrow river, a harsh and splintered landscape that is starkly beautiful yet extremely hostile. Those travellers of old would have had to cross this for days on end, and surely only the most indomitable spirit and unshakeable faith could have sustained them. Today, for the car-owning visitor, the hazards are not quite so life-threatening – though finding a parking space can be exasperatingly traumatic!

To enjoy Rocamadour to the full, arrive early in the day, leave your car at L'Hospitalet's spacious car park and viewing *belvédère*, and walk down the hill to Rocamadour, as the pilgrims of an earlier age did. Better still, consider overnighting; there really is a great deal to see, and there is a good choice of hotels in Rocamadour, while L'Hospitalet provides a caravan and camping park with adjacent café and information pavilion. Rocamadour boasts a number of restaurants and cafés, and one or two deserve high marks. The tourist office in the Grande Rue is open daily from Easter to 30 September.

Gouffre de Padirac About 12km east of L'Hospitalet, via the narrow and winding D673, is Padirac village, now largely devoted to providing refreshment for the cohorts of tourists who emerge from France's mightiest natural chasm just to the north of the village – the Gouffre de Padirac.

This phenomenal subterranean rift is the greatest (among many) of those which characterize the limestone *causses* of the region. These arid, notably bare heights or harsh grandeur remain dry, since any rainwater quickly disappears into the clefts and abysses which craze the limestone crust. These *igues*, as they are called, are found primarily in the Causse de Gramat and Padirac is the most famous of them.

For long time the caves were a complex and secretive underground refuge for those fleeing persecution (especially during the Hundred Years War and the Wars of Religion), and it was only in the late nineteenth century that their breathtaking immensity was fully realized and subsequently exploited. Even today, there are unexplored sections of natural tunnels branching

136

Rocamadour's neighbouring attraction, Gouffre de Padirac

away from the 'Cathedral of Nature' which lies just below the surface of the Gramat plateau.

In the summer, it is often necessary to queue for the guided excursion, which lasts about 1½ hours. It begins with lift descents to a primeval setting, seen firstly from walkways and then from small boats. There is a rain lake (Lac de la Pluie), a staggering display of gigantic stalactites, vivid coloured pools and sparkling cascades, all enhanced with dramatic lighting. The *pièce de résistance*, however, is the enormous cavern, Le Grande Dome, almost 100 metres high, where surrealist rock outcrops dominate a wet and chilly underworld, almost hostile, but certainly exciting and irresistibly intriguing. Padirac is open every day from Easter to the second Sunday in October.

Padirac to Souillac From Padirac, drive east, then take the D38 to the village of Autoire, at the head of the Autoire gorges, as scenic in their way as the Alzou ravines near Rocamadour. Autoire is lovely, a wonderfully preserved enclave of old France and officially another one of the prettiest French villages. Still dominated by an ancient *château*, a country manor largely reconstructed during the seventeenth century when Autoire was a small but important outpost of the Turenne, the village retains a number of fine Renaissance buildings, while the church chancel is opulently sculptured. On a nearby plateau above the valley settlement, there is a ruined castle (said to be a Hundred Years War fortification), still called a *château des Anglais*, and a picturesque waterfall cascading down a cliff face.

Loubressac has an even more ancient history, occupying the site of a Gallo-Roman settlement. The village grew up behind the ramparts of the fourteenth-century *château*-fortress to become a stoutly defended *bastide*, first under the protection of the Turenne family and later – through a high-born marriage alliance – part of the Castelnau dynasty. From this cliff-top spur there are fine views of the Dordogne and distant Castelnau fortress.

Loubressac village is an interesting blend of medieval and renaissance architecture, and the church has a highly decorated sixteenth-century portal. There is a municipal swimming pool here, and *gîte* accommodation, while for those who enjoy walking, the village lies on the route of the GR480 which takes in Haut-Vivarais countryside.

To return to Souillac, from Loubressac take the road north-west, back to the banks of the Dordogne, via the half-timbered houses of Gintrac village clustered on its limestone outcrop above the river. Carry on to Carennac, renowned for its Romanesque church portal, and rich in fifteenth- and sixteenth-century buildings, with a fine *château* overlooking the river and a priory founded in the tenth century. Francois Fénelon was the prior (1651-1715), author of a romantic work entitles *Télémaque* and an esteemed figure of French literature. The tympanum of the twelfth-century church compares favourably with the spectacular example at Beaulieu. Carennac enjoys a delightful setting, facing the Dordogne island of Calypso (which so enchanted Fénelon), and today it is popular to canoe and kayak explorers who base themselves at the campsite.

From here the Dordogne south bank begins to level off into water-meadows just to he west, where it is possible to cross over to the north bank near Floirac. From here you can rejoin the D708 for Martel, and then continue back to Souillac.

Worth a visit: Autoire; Loubressac; Carennac.

The Cère Valley One extended excursion into the Cantal mountains which really deserves consideration by the visitor reveals the invigorating Cère, a sister-river of the Dordogne, which rises near the Plomb-du-Cantal and joins the main river just west of Bretenoux. The countryside alongside this watercourse is pleasant, becoming more dramatic to the southwest of the Plomb-du-Cantal. This is the second-highest mountain in the *Parc Naturel*, rising to 1,858 metres and dominating this southern extremity of Auvergne high country.

From Bretenoux, you can trace the route of the Cère reasonably faithfully via minor roads across sparsely populated countryside. You will touch the Cère gorges in places, and come eventually upon Laroquebrou, about 30km to the north-east. This picturesque little town, sited on the north bank of the river, has a ruined medieval *château* and an interesting fourteenth-century church. Just 5km upriver from here is the man-made lake of the Barrage de St Étienne Cantalès, which covers much of the valley floor between Laroquebrou and Aurillac, a distance of about 20km.

Aurillac, to the north of the Cère on the Jordanne river, is one of the largest towns in the Auvergne region with 34,000 inhabitants. This *préfecture* of Cantal is second only in size to Clermont-Ferrand, and is busy and very crowded at times. Still, it is nicely atmospheric and *almost* Mediterranean in atmosphere, with a wide choice of accommodation. There are a couple of three star hotels, and an agreeable three-star municipal camping and caravanning park on the banks of the Jordanne, 1km north of town on the D17. The tourist office is in the Place Square.

Although essentially modern, Aurillac has an old heart, and the interesting part is around the fifteenth-century church of St Géraud. This church occupies the site of a much earlier monastery, where Géraud himself, a local monk who later became the first-ever French Pope in AD999, once worshipped. He was an exceptionally holy man by all accounts, with an extraordinarily inventive mind.

There is more of old Aurillac alongside the river Jordanne, including a number of fifteenth- and sixteenth-century buildings, of which the best view is had from the Pont Rouge. Don't miss the Maison des Volcans either, housed within the Château

St Étienne, about $1/2$km north of the town centre. This is obligatory for those who seek detailed information about the peaks and craters of the national park, or indeed about volcanology worldwide. The *château* was built during the eleventh century, although little remains of the original. The Parc des Volcans is one of the most favoured areas in France for walkers, and the *château* also has an information office concerned with *randonnée* routes and guided rambles.

There are several other permanent exhibits of past Auvergene in Aurillac, including a display of medieval tapestry of Flemish origin in the imposing Palais de Justice, located in the town centre, and a Cantal folklore exhibition in the Musée Rames, south of the town centre off the Rue des Carmes near the railway station. Aurillac is also noted for the quality and variety of its restaurants specializing in regional dishes, and for its shopping facilities which are among the best in the Auvergne region.

For a much smaller enclave of old Auvergne, take the N122 north-eastwards, more or less parallel to the river Cère, until you reach Vic-sur-Cère. Vic is a most attractive little town, not much more than an overgrown village with some excellent hillwalking in the immediate vicinity.

There are particularly scenic routes: one goes through and above a charming part of the old town, while the other, longer route, leads via quiet back lanes towards the regal Plomb-du-Cantal, and the waterfall of the Pas de Cère. Vic is just within the Parc des Volcans boundary, and the splendid walks that are within easy reach are over terrain that is exhilarating and virtually undeveloped, away from the fast-flowing river, the road and the railway.

The town of Vic is close-knit and probably pretty much the same around the centre as it must have been centuries ago. Of a number of fine houses, the most famous is the town mansion of the ancient Princes of Monaco, constructed in the fifteenth century and sandwiched between buildings of equally imposing mellowness.

There is a good selection of hostels *auberges* and *gîtes* in and around town, plus an excellent large, level and well-equipped municipal touring site just a few minutes' stroll from the centre, with a convenient supermarket opposite the entrance.

A town house in the attractive Vic-sur-Cère, amid the beautiful Cantal countryside

Part Four: **Central Dordogne**

Domme

Central Dordogne The definitive 'Dordogne' for most of the holidaymakers who visit the region each summer, is the area embracing both the Dordogne *département* and the great river itself which flows between Souillac and Bergerac. This is a landscape blessed with scenery that is always impressive, frequently dramatic, occasionally breathtaking; and indeed its treasures of history and pre-history are world renowned.

The actual *département* – covering some 9,065 kilometres square – was named after the river following the French Revolution (with Solomon-like wisdom), by the literary giant Mirabeau. He also perceptively proclaimed that every man has two countries, 'his own and France'. Mirabeau successfully ended the grumbling of inhabitants, who complained that the huge new Republican *département* (the third largest in the country, being created from old Périgord in 1790), was impossibly divided by the wide watercourse. Suggesting the new name of 'Dordogne', placated all parties, even ardent traditionalists, who continued to call the whole area Périgord anyway; and do so even to this day!

The richest of the regions which denote the boundaries of the ancient province, is unquestionably Périgord Noir, the boundary of which is crossed just west of Souillac in the *département* of Lot. The mere names of Périgord towns, *bastides* and *châteaux*, like Sarlat, Domme and Montfort are enough to invoke visions of glory to those who already know the area well. For newcomers, however, since there is really so much to see and enjoy within a somewhat convoluted geographical compass, a strategic base is all-important.

Sarlat, or Sarlat-la-Canéda to give it its full title, is rightly much-favoured, not only for its own medieval riches, but for the

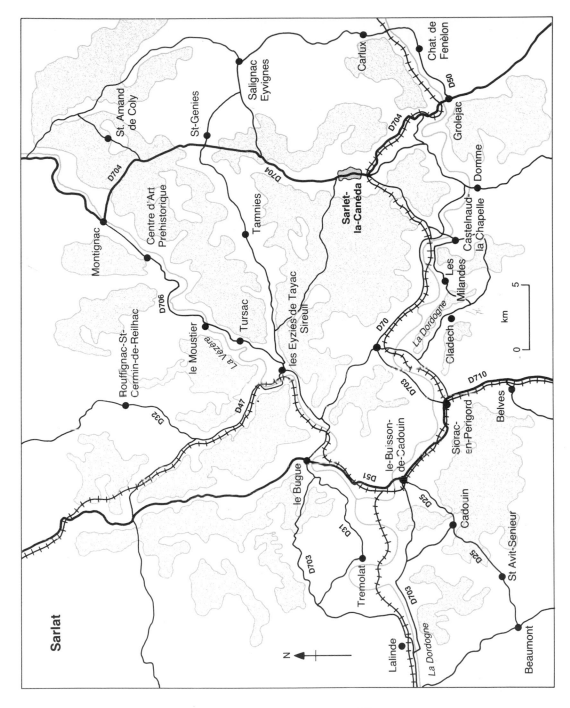

Sarlat

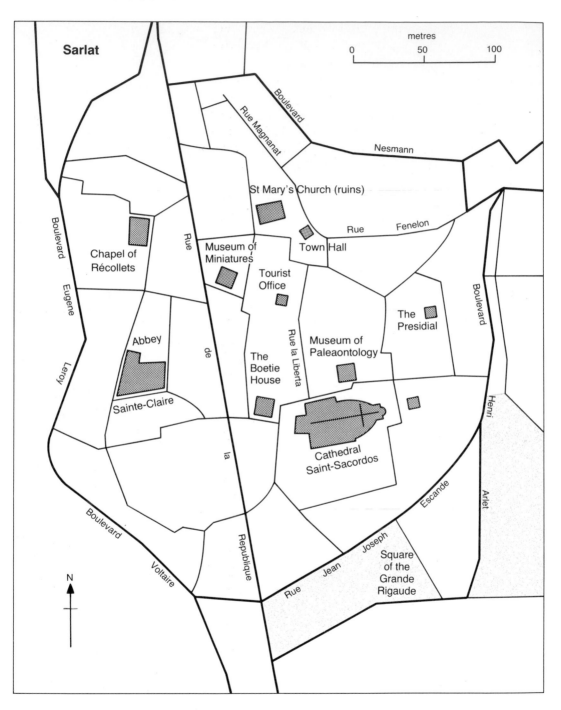

Sarlat

metres

0   50   100

Boulevard

Rue Magnanat

Nesmann

St Mary's Church (ruins)

Rue   Fenelon

Boulevard

Eugene

Chapel of
Récollets

Rue

Museum of
Miniatures

Town Hall

Tourist
Office

The
Presidial

Boulevard

de

Abbey

Rue la Liberta

Museum of
Paleaontology

Henri

Leroy

Sainte-Claire

The
Boetie
House

Cathedral
Saint-Sacordos

la

Boulevard

Republique

Escande

Arlet

N

Voltaire

Rue   Jean   Joseph

Square
of the
Grande
Rigaude

many natural and man-made treasures which can be found in virtually every direction. It is located within an expansive V formed by the Dordogne and Vézère rivers, and is dominated by massive limestone cliffs and outcrops, and steep-sided wooded valleys which are served by narrow lanes. It is here that the landscape provides a delightful visual surprise at almost every turn.

The region around Sarlat is a real fun-spot in high summer too, where swimming, canoeing and every conceivable outdoor pursuit is available to all age groups. Event the stuff of pre-history is made enjoyable and instructive for children, by pragmatic enterprises like the Pre-history Parc near Les Eyzies. Add an almost embarrassing richness of preserved medieval relics, including some of the finest *châteaux* (castles) in the world, and the unrivaled amenities available to visitors – be they gourmets or aesthetes – Périgord Noir provides the traveller with some of the very best of pastoral France.

The name, by the way, is often said to have been acquired because of the blackness of the mysterious truffle found in relative

The central Place de la Liberté in Sarlat

147

profusion here, while others maintain it is the rich dark and almost black appearance of the countless chestnut, walnut and oak trees which cloak the landscape. There may be more validity about the latter theory, since it was the Romans who originally introduced the valuable chestnut and walnut trees in Aquitaine (along with the even more valuable grapevine).

However, there is nothing black about the recognized heart and hub of Périgord Noir. For it is golden and glorious as it basks in a splendid valley setting, and is arguably the best preserved medieval city in the whole Republic. With an envied heritage, Sarlat, even though it is now just a modest sub-*préfecture*, has a history as colourful – and as long – as France herself.

Sarlat is built on the site of a Roman settlement where Clovis created a religious monastery and later Pepin the Short built an abbey in the eighth century, which his grandson, Emperor Charlemagne, had mightily extended. The city was a revered religious and prestigious regional centre during the Middle Ages, and was at the heart of a war-zone during the century-long conflict between the royal houses of France and England and again during the Wars of Religion. Indeed, the city was also one of the first places to flower during the Renaissance. Sarlat reached a pinnacle of elegant beauty during the late sixteenth and seventeenth centuries, remaining thus by a miracle, and preserving, almost in its entirety, a unique example of medieval France for the contemporary world to enjoy.

It is not *quite* perfect of course, for admittedly much of the restoration work is obviously detectable, while there are only vestigial remnants of the stout rampart walls which once embraced the town. There is also the wide, straight Rue de la République (colloquially called 'the traverse'), which is invariably traffic-choked and an intrusive concession to the car age that slashes old Sarlat in half.

Notwithstanding, there is medieval magic wherever you happen to turn on either side of *la traverse*, where ancient ghosts of a long-dead past may be sensed around almost any corner. I urge you to reserve a day or so to hunt for them, amid a venerable stone-pile that even Hollywood could not surpass for atmosphere and bygone realism.

Before exploring, a congenial base is of prime importance. Certainly in and around Sarlat the traveller could hardly be better served – as might be expected at a fount of French history which is visited by some 600,000 people every year. Opt for central city accommodation, though if arriving by car, it is advisable to ensure parking space is available, for the whole of the old town is subjected to pay-parking and there are traffic wardens ready to exact instant fines. Despite the priceless heritage value of the old town, there are relatively few concessions to pedestrians (save in high summer), and it is not only the Rue de la République which is traffic-thronged; cars dodge and weave along the narrowest of alleys and ancient passageways, often to the chagrin of strollers trying to absorb the ambience of another age.

From the old city perimeter park-and-pay areas, the tourist office is well signposted, though again it must be said the staff are hard-pressed to such an extent most days that the enquiring visitor – French or otherwise – is given but scant assistance. There are though, ample self-explanatory pamphlets on display (one of two of which are in English), so personal contact is hardly vital for your basic travel needs. If you've found your way to the tourist office anyway, you are at the virtual heart of the medieval city, for the Place de la Liberté is to Sarlat what St Mark's Square is to Venice. You could do worse than begin your sightseeing by taking a drink at one of the delightful people-watching pavement cafés and restaurants which line this expansive but crowded, square.

If this introduction appears a trifle derogatory, so be it, however, it also serves as a timely warning. The old town simply cannot be studied leisurely, or envisaged in its original slow-paced medieval majesty, during any high day or holiday. There are simply too many people who will be trying to enjoy it with you. The best advice on offer is to go out of season, or make your foray to the centre really early on a Sunday morning. If either alternative is impossible, then grit your teeth and go anyway, for it is truly an architectural resurrection of the European Middle Ages.

Sooner or later, wherever your feet wander, they will lead you to the most famous and elegant of medieval landmarks the Italianate town house and birthplace of Étienne la Boétie (1530-63), friend and contemporary of Montaigne: a magistrate and another gifted son of Périgord, who died so tragically young.

149

Briefly, la Boétie was an anti-royalist, an idealist – of course – whose major literary work was published after his death. Maison de la Boétie reflects a subtle blend of architecture that is at once flamboyant yet subdued, to perfection; this is an extremely difficult combination to achieve. Here in Sarlat, the house is proof-positive that medieval stonemasons knew the secret.

The architectural centre-piece of Sarlat is the largely sixteenth-century cathedral of Saint Sacerdos (originally built in the twelfth century). A visitor will expect imposing dominance on a grand scale, at the heart of a living medieval city; so gazing upwards from the Place du Peyrou you will be impressed, though not surprised. Not so at some of the other high spots which cluster within this tight golden circle. Aspects of the Presidial, capped with a pagoda roof, the inner courtyard of the Hôtel Selve de Plamon, the Chapel of the White Penitents which displays the finest of Romanesque architecture, are all stunningly sublime. And these buildings are just a few of the many principal monuments.

Don't miss: Maison de la Boétie; Cathedral of Saint Sacerdos: the Presidial; Chapel of the White Penitents; Place de la Liberté.

At the heart of this film-set city (which becomes precisely that at frequent intervals for mammoth productions like *Les Miserables*), is the Place de la Liberté, where corbelled towers, *lauze*-covered roof pitches, some incredibly steep, pepper-pot cappings and rich ochre walls surround the visitor in profusion. From this city hub, arched alleyways radiate, some of them uphill, to quaint venerable dwellings lining cobbled ways, which are punctuated by miniscule courtyards. Others lead past celebrated and enduring buildings that are heavy with ornate cornices, and above colourful art galleries interspersed with cafés and restaurants. The whole area is an exciting re-creation of Renaissance city life for those with a little imagination. For a fine elevated view, visit the cathedral cloister quadrangle.

For the rest of your sightseeing, be it deliberate or meandering, there are yet more rewards ahead, while if you wish to go shopping for anything from *haute-couture* clothes to souvenirs of gift wrapped *foie-gras* or marzipan frogs 'the traverse' await – either to your left or right – like a tarmac canal, lined with all the necessities (or whim-wants), of twentieth-century living.

Close by however, medieval France is still ruling supreme, epitomized by the fifteenth-century watch-tower *tour de guêt*; by

150

the former Poor House of Saint Claire's Abbey; by the Executioner's Tower which is to the west of 'la traverse' and by the strange, artillery-shell of stone, the Lantern of the Dead, in the old cemetery of St Benedict. On this site with its religious connections, it is recorded that St Bernard performed a miracle of healing in 1147.

The city's other most noteworthy residence is the Consul's House, one of several in the Rue des Consuls, dating from the fourteenth to the seventeenth centuries. While another near-authentic scene of medieval France is captured adjacent to the Place de la Liberté every Saturday, where the original market place is thronged with vendors and buyers of traditional Sarladais fare, including live ducks, geese and rabbits. Witness all this and perhaps one of the vivid seasonal costume plays, acted out most convincingly in the cathedral precinct, and you really do begin to feel a little like a medieval citizen for a brief interlude.

There is an annual drama festival which takes place each summer from mid July to mid August, as the city is after all, a

The Lantern of Death and cathedral spire in Sarlat

151

principal art and culture centre of Périgord. There is invariably some stimulating event on offer during the summers months, ranging from music concerts (classical and jazz), through art exhibitions of international repute, to theatre, dance and open-air performances. At these times, the streets are filled with local players re-creating *son et lumière* spectaculars. At the height of the season, numbers of streets in the old town are reserved for pedestrians only, which does make sightseeing much more pleasant – and safer!

There are five museums in town, including an aquarium specializing in fish species resident in the Dordogne basin; a motor museum, and another devoted to pre-history. For visitors arriving by train, the first view of Sarlat is not stimulating; it seldom is in the vicinity of mainline railway stations and it is approximately 1 kilometre of uninspiring urban build-up before one reaches the golden cluster which is old Sarlat. There is an efficient local bus or taxi service and the infrastructure of the city is well geared to tourists. There are numerous hotels ranging from the three-star La Madeleine, to a youth hostel and there is a four-star caravan/camping ground close to the centre, plus twelve or more others in the neighbourhood.

Sarlat – Useful Information

Sarlat is the capital of Périgord Noir and is a sub-*préfecture*. The tourist office is at the Place de la Liberté and is close to the town hall in the old town centre, Tel: 53 59 27 67. It is open daily (including Sundays in high season) from 9am to 6pm. but is closed between 12 noon and 2pm.

The train service is the SNCF, Route de Souillac, Tel: 53 59 00 21.

The distance by rail from; Bordeaux: 167 kms; Paris: 525 kms.

The police (*Gendarmerie*) are at the Place Salvador-Allende, Tel: 53 59 10 17.

The hospital is at Centre Jean Leclaire; Le Pouget (direction Périgueux), Tel: 53 59 00 72.

Taxi hire: Allo Sarlat Taxi Rue J. J. Rouseau Tel: 53 59 02 43, or 53 59 00 49, open day and night. There is also a small group transport service by mini-bus.

The emergency ambulance service, Brajot is La Trappe, Tel: 53 59 06 46

Cycle hire is available from the SNCF office (*see* above for address).

Scooter and cycle hire (including mountain bikes), is available from L'Aventure a Vélo, 16 Rue Fénelon, Tel: 53 31 24 18

There is a car hire service, Avis, Station Total, 10, Avenue Aristide Briand, Tel: 53 59 04 83. This is open every day (up to 11pm in summer) and is one of five car-hire firms in town.

There are a dozen car-repair garages catering to most popular makes and models, including British marques.

There are nine banks and the post office is in Place du 14 Juillet. Principal hotels, include:

La Madeleine (three-star), Hôtel/restaurant, 1, Place de la Petite Rigaudie, Tel: 53 59 10 41; Meysset (three-star), hotel/restaurant, Argentouleua. It is 3kms from the centre and is on route from Eyzies. Tel: 53 59 08 29; La Hoirie (three-star) hotel/restaurant is 2 kms from Sarlat, Tel: 53 59 05 62; St-Albert-Montaigne (two-star) hotel/restaurant, Place Pasteur, Tel: 53 59 01 92 and La Verperie (two-star) hotel/restaurant, Allée des Acacias, Tel: 53 59 00 20.

There are six hotels providing accommodation only, in and around the town centre.

There is a youth hostel (auberge de jeunesse), at 15, bis avenue de Selves (open all year round), Tel: 53 59 47 59 or 53 59 48 31.

Camping and Caravanning; Les Périères (four-star), Route de Sainte-Nathalène, Tel. 53 59 05 84. 1 km from the centre, it is open from April to September.

There are some thirty restaurants in and around old Sarlat, open all year round and twelve or more open during the summer season only. These of course range from Gourmet establishments like the restaurant Rossignol in the Boulevard Henri-Arlet et Rue Fénelon, (Tel: 53 59 03 20) specializing in regional dishes, to pizza parlours and even an English-type 'pub'.

There is a variety of leisure amenities including, Cinema 'Le Rex', Avenue Thiers Tel: 53 59 39 10 (it has four screens).

Discoteques: Le Griot, Route de Souillac, 2km from the centre, Tel: 53 59 20 13; Le Basroc, Avenue de la Dordogne (Route de Bergerac), 1 km from the centre, Tel: 53 59 16 17.

The swimming pool is open-air and heated, Stade Municipal de Madrazès, Route de Souillac. It is open from 1 July to 5 September, daily except Tuesdays. (it is 3km south-east of the centre).

Tennis: Jardin Public du Plantier (three open-air courts); there are also facilities at Madrazès which has three open-air and three covered courts.

Horse riding: Centre Hippique Fournier Sarlovèze, Bonnefond (5km south-west of city centre, off D57), Tel: 53 59 15 83.

Golf: The Country Club, Domaine de Rochebois, Vitrac. This is 6km south of Sarlat (on the D703 Route de Montfort) Tel: 53 28 18 01.

Open-air activities: Maison du Plein-Air et de la Rendonné, 16, Rue Fénelon, Tel: 53 31 24 18. This centre organizes weekend pursuits like riding, rambling, canoeing and cycling (road and cross-country), especially for children and young adults, and is part of the commercial l'Aventure a Vélo enterprise.

Economy accommodation units are available in abundance in the Sarlat area, including over 150 rural *gîtes* and self-catering hostels. Certain areas are highly favoured as bases amid pastoral settings yet are conveniently close to Sarlat particularly Tamnies for its choice of country hotels and leisure lake (approximately 12km to the north-west of Sarlat) and St Nathalène for its neighbourhood camping parks (approximately 6km east of Sarlat).

To orientate yourself to the Sarlat district easily and pleasantly, limited pedestrian exploration is available. This is provided by a useful short-walk brochure which is distributed by the tourist office free of charge. It features four pedestrian routes, from $2^1/2$ to $5^1/2$ km in length with estimated walking times from $1^1/2$ to 3 hours. Each walk leads to a nearby village or hamlet, and returns to Sarlat centre via a circuit route, individually signposted with distinctive symbols. The circuits and destinations have been selected for each of the cardinal compass points and each takes in attractive viewpoints and the prettiest stretches of wooded valley flanks where possible. For walking inside the historic city centre, the visitor can take advantage of the guided lecture tours which are organized weekly during the summer season, and depart from the tourist office. Just one of the historic facts which may be learned during any educational ramble, is that Sarlat was ceded to England in 1360. During brief ownership it is to our credit that this medieval jewel was allowed to remain intact!

Sarlat - north, south and east   Ideally, every foray should embrace a stimulating objective, and none could be more exciting than that which takes the traveller north from Sarlat along the D704 for the 26 kilometres or so to Montignac on the Vézère river. For this route takes in the most renowned prehistory site in Europe, the caves of Lascaux.

Lascaux II a technological masterpiece of cloning, which is located barely a couple of hundred metres from the unique original Lascaux I, is described elsewhere. Here it is the final approach to the site which must be praised for it is no easy task to sustain the illusion of time long passed, when countless thousands of contemporary visitors from the world over converge on the hallowed spot every summer.

Don't miss: The caves of Lascaux; Regardou; Montignac; Salignac; Roque-Gageac; Castlenaud; Domme.

Somehow the French have managed it, while armies of visitors have co-operated consciously or otherwise, in respecting and preserving the fresh nature of the almost isolated woodland setting. Car parking places have been sited with care, the pedestrian approach has been left cunningly casual, so that even today there is the feeling that this once-secret hillside glade has been stumbled upon almost accidentally.

Commendably (and unusually), commercial overtones have also been kept very low-key There is the inevitable souvenir outlet alongside the pay-kiosk, but it is appropriately modest, as is the small cabin drinks bar. No picnicking is permitted. Thus, you enter the subterranean treasure-house almost forgetting that it is a replica you are about to see. However, a fake it is not and the experience for some at least, can be quite profound.

Half a kilometre from Lascaux II, is another interesting centre, that of Regourdou on the site of a geological strata dating back to the Paleolithic era. A small museum displays prehistoric artefacts, including restored remains of early man, together with other exhibits revealing biological and sociological evidence about the life of Neanderthal. The huge mammal that once shared his caves – and was apparently revered to the point of worship – the brown bear, can be seen living happily here. Regardou is open all year, children up to the age of twelve are admitted free.

Montignac, is just 4km north of Sarlat. It is a riverside market town that is close-knit and has been lovingly restored, especially along the old river quay. For visitors Lascaux is the great magnet

The quay, church and ruined château in Montignac, a delightful base for northern Périgord Noir

but the town of Montignac is one of charm and character. One celebrity who chose to live here was the novelist Eugene le Roy, whose historic sagas have now been widely televised. His namesake museum in Montignac, houses accurate re-creations from the era of his most famous epic, *Jacquou le Croquant*. In due course you can visit the infamous *château*, that the fictional hero Jacky, and his peasant compatriots, supposedly razed to the ground. The real history of Château de l'Herm is far more sinister.

Since the creation of Lascaux II (opened to the public in 1983), Montignac has basked in reflected glory, thriving rightfully from the swelling volume of Lascaux visitors. There are now a number of attractive hotels and restaurants, plus a selection of *gîte* accommodation in the vicinity. The four-star Château Puy Robert, just outside town on the Sergeac road, is highly regarded by gourmets, while there is, of course, a Lascaux hotel/restaurant, a Logie de France, offering comfortable quarters and good value for money. There is also a small municipal camping ground, which is adequate though nothing special.

156

For those who enjoy the medieval remnants of France as much as pre-history evidence, Château de Losse is a superb example of fourteenth- to sixteenth-century military and civilian architecture, the *château* residence being in part a defended fortress, sternly towered and moated. It lies just 6km south of Montignac on the D706, and is a stone sentinel of massive beauty with *lauze* roof pitches, situated on a terrace setting above the Vézère. It is open to visitors from July to mid September.

From Montignac too, it is only a short distance to yet another mighty monument to the past. This is a twelfth-century fortified church towering above a tiny village, when its massive proportions really demand that it graces the centre of a great city like Paris. The church of St-Amand-de-Coly, is strangely misplaced, though it cannot fail to impress with its stark, utterly simple cruciform shape, as unadorned outwardly as it is inside the vast domed nave. As a defensive structure it still appears formidable; as indeed it would have needed to have been in former days, because of its vulnerable valley-floor setting. It is a memorable medieval building.

The Vézère river is no less popular with waterway explorers. This reach meanders below regal Château Losse, south of Montignac

Another quiet corner of Périgord prevails hereabouts, with pleasant accommodation amid rural surroundings being provided by the nearby village of Coly. There is also the Manoir d'Hautegente providing top-class comfort in grand country house style, which has a well-run if very secluded campground complete with swimming pool and self-catering cabins for hire.

Returning to Sarlat via the D704, travellers might care to make a short diversion to the Château de la Grand Filolie, one of several Perigordin Renaissance manor houses which characterize the mode of living of medieval families, where nobles and commoners frequently shared fortified farm complexes. Filolie is a particularly fine example of the fifteenth-century communal manor farm.

Périgord Noir is handsomely green and slumbers to the north-east of Sarlat, particularly where it flirts with neighbouring Corrèze (Limousin), just to the east of Salignac-Eyvignes. This landscape of rich pastures is reached once more via the D704 and then the D60, although the leisurely explorer will probably want to make the small detour *en route* to St Genies.

Just a small farming village, but largely unchanged by progress and possessing some fine examples of Perigordin *lauze* roofing, which caps a neat cluster of medieval buildings, especially the Romanesque church and the Chapelle du Cheylard. The latter of which contains some expressive fourteenth-century frescoes. An enjoyable, almost traffic-free drive to Salignac follows.

Salignac-Eyvignes is a small hill town of pleasing aspect and an ancient patina, lorded over still by the proud *château*. This was originally erected during the twelfth century and named after the illustrious Salignac family who ruled hereabouts for centuries. The most celebrated member was the illustrious Francois de Salignac de la Mothe-Fénelon (1651-1715), Archbishop of Cambrai, but famed lastingly as Fénelon the writer (*see* Carennac). The actual birthplace of the author of *Télémaque* is Château Fénelon at Ste Mondane, overlooking the Dordogne river.

Salignac is a place to visit on a summer morning, when the sun highlights the ancient fortress ramparts and towers to their best advantage. There are several dramatic viewpoints from the narrow encircling hill road. The whole town is compact and completely encircled by an area that was once walled. It graces the commanding high ground with strength, as it has done for centuries. It is surrounded still by a delightful and sparsely populated region. The community serves the traveller well and is a recommended lunch stop on any day outing from Sarlat.

The gradual descent from Salignanc is through deep and verdent combe country along the D61 and D47 to Carlux, a pretty little village with an old English connection of less-pleasant memory. Here, during the Hundred Years War, English troops almost burned down the castle that dominated this river flank – the stark ruin of the remnant keep still exists as a reminder to what was probably wanton destruction. It towers still standing with stubborn permanence at the southern end of the short and scenic main street.

Just below here, the Dordogne is bridged at a spot popular with picnickers, campers and swimmers in high summer. It is overlooked by the eyrie-perched Château de Rouffillac which shines, newly golden in its restored state, against a background of dense woodland. St-Julien-de-Lampon, on the southern bank, is another favoured gathering point, with a choice of cafés and

Salignac-Eyvignes – a beautiful backwater north-west of Sarlat

159

restaurants in an ambient setting, that is conjured from a one-time farming and fishing village, now highly geared to tourism.

From neighbouring Ste Mondane a brief uphill drive leads to a setting as deeply wooded as that of Rouffillac on the opposing north bank of the Dordogne, as well as to the birthplace of Fénelon. Château Fénelon, though much restored and extended, still retains a martial air with its massive double walls, formidable machicolated towers and lofty limestone ledge location. Modified and modernized it may be, but assuredly as much a feudal fortress as it was when first constructed by the mighty Salignac dynasty in the fifteenth century. Today it does not repel strangers with boiling oil, but welcomes them seasonally to admire the birthplace of a literary lion; and it also has a museum devoted to prestige early motor cars.

Just downstream from here is another rustic village, that of Veyrignac, which is pleasantly sited, if unremarkable. The principal building here, a once handsome sixteenth-century *château*, was also subjected to invasive violence, this one much more recently than nearby Carlux; it was put to the torch by a retreating German army in 1944. So back in Grolejac, the Dordogne river bridge once more and the D704 to Sarlat.

Jewels in the Dordogne Crown Now for the short circuit to the south of Sarlat which takes in four of the most glittering of Dordogne's historic gems – two on the north bank of the river and two on the south. Start by taking the D57 to Vezac, continuing due south on the minor road if you are a keen gardener. The Château de Marquayssac, built in the seventeenth century, is renowned for its formal gardens laid out high above the river, from where there are majestic views across that much-esteemed village La Roque-Gageac, and feudal Castelnaud la Chapelle together with its rival neighbour fortress Beynac. There is yet another pre-history site close by here, the Grotte du Roc.

Continue south-east along the D703 to La Roque-Gageac, drive on directly across the river bridge to Castelnaud-la-Chapelle. The first choice will reveal one of the Dordogne's most celebrated waterside villages which has been awarded the national accolade of beauty for its setting and the preservation of its medieval buildings. Built literally into a limestone cliff overhang, the narrow and precipitous streets are hewn from the towering cliff side and in places there are remnants of cave dwellings,

160

**La Roque-Gageac is a
fascinating waterside village**

**The medieval might of
Castelnaud fortress**

especially on the upper levels of the old settlement. Clinging precariously, the miniscule houses, now resplendent in their renovated and flower-bedecked state, line cobbled alleys and staircase passageways which wind upwards tortuously and very steeply in places, from the waterside. It is a very popular tourist target, and is heavily patronised throughout the summer. So, see it early in the day if you can, to appreciate its ancient charms – and to find space in the river bank car park. Hour-long river trips on the traditional *gabarre* (flat-bottom boats) depart from here, to view five famous waterside *châteaux*.

The second option is to cross the river immediately from Marquayssac to see at close quarters the majestic, still mighty, ruins of twelfth-century Castelnaud. The castle is the very epitomy of a medieval warlord's eyrie. Its purpose was purely military, to be a watch-tower of formidable strength overlooking nearby Beynac castle and the cliff-bordered valley of the Céou to the south. Castelnaud was much fought over during the Hundred Years War, the whole castle is consequently a mix of both French and English fortifications (the keep was erected by the latter), and it is now undergoing very extensive and prolonged restoration. Bend low as you climb the narrow tower staircases, admire the fortitude of those who manned its stark quarters and shudder for those imprisoned in its fearful dungeons, where wall-scratched graffiti has been recently uncovered.

Climbers, walkers and canoeists all converge on Castelnaud, not so much to admire the gaunt ruins of the castle, or the picturesque village nestling at its foot, but for the limestone cliffs, valley walks and both the Céou and Dordogne waters. There is a scenically sited and well-run camping park called Maisonneuve, 1km distant from the village which has a small supermarket and a popular riverside *auberge*.

Domme So the most famous and spectacular of all the Republic's Périgord towns, the *bastide* of Domme, built in 1280. This is scenic nugget, a true French *bastide* smothering the crest of a limestone promontory and overlooking one of the finest panoramas along the entire Dordogne river valley.

This town is raved about with justification, by poets and writers from Mirabeau to Henry Miller – even today when highly geared to tourism, it does not disappoint. The approach, by

163

An outsider's view of Domme's rampart towers where Knights Templar were once incarcerated

graded tarmac now (though once by a steeply ascending cart track), is impressively evocative of its thirteenth-century beginnings when it was founded by King Phillip the Bold.

The formidable ramparts and the three surviving ports, or gates, illustrate military architecture at its most powerful, and even today they are enough to inspire a certain awed respect from strangers. Despite massive fortifications and the eyrie location, Domme was taken by the English during the Hundred Years War and retained for a couple of decades. It was invaded again, alternatively by Catholic and Protestant forces during the later religious struggles. It was battled over consistently during the Middle Ages, but somehow most of the original architecture survives, even if it has been enthusiastically restored in parts.

There is much to see and appreciate here, from nobles' mansions like the old Hôtel des Gouverneurs, to commoners typical dwellings lining narrow and sometimes steep alleyways. The history of the town ranges from a fine feudal market place (complete with pre-history caves immediately below) to a belvédère unsurpassed in Périgord for its vistas of the great river

164

The belvédère overlooking the most famous viewpoint anywhere along the Dordogne river

and includes: an Augustine abbey and a house once occupied by the famous author, Eugene le Roy. The three surviving gateways are perhaps the most reminiscent of medieval times, especially the Port des Tours which were once used to incarcerate Knights Templar, some of whom recorded their enforced stay with graffiti. An even more gruesome location is the Place de la Rode, where wrongdoers were once drawn and quartered. Today, visitors trundle through the ancient streets aboard a miniature train, patronize the plethora of shops that seem to specialize in canned *confit*, or marvel at the stage-lit underworld of the grotto. For those fascinated by the France of the past, the town itself (together perhaps with the folklore museum), is reward enough. Domme is indeed a *bastide royale*. For those with deeply-lined pockets wishing to view the old town from the most spectacular angle, helicopter sightseeing trips are available from nearby Domme airport! For gentler study of the surrounding hill country, three colour-coded short walks from 3 to 5km (2 to 3$1/2$ miles in length), complement the long-distance GR64 which is routed through the *bastide* centre.

After the ochre-stone glow of Domme, visit the dazzling symmetry of white-knight Montfort which is every bit a fairy-tale castle in the classical mould. Alas, it is only to be admired from a distance because it is privately owned. However, and there are several magnificent middle-distance viewpoints in the vicinity, while in the hamlet itself, which basks in the very shadow of the great *château*, you can refresh yourself in the time-honoured French manner, with a drink or a meal.

While doing so, you may reflect on the turbulent history of this masterpiece in stone and the man after whom it is named. The original fortress which stood upon this bluff above the snaking Dordogne bend to *cingle* was razed by Simon de Montfort during the savage crusade against the Albigensians (1209-1229), his son, also called Simon, continued with merciless zeal.

Simon de Montfort was born in France in about 1200 and was a complex character who bestrode the stage of thirteenth-century France and England like a colossus. He was French by birth but an Englishman at heart, was seen to be a cruel adventurer to his enemies but a brave and wise warrior to his friends. He was made Earl of Leicester, became leader of the baron-lords and ruler of

Opposite
Domme

Dominating the Cingle-de-Montfort, the mighty *Château* is named after Simon who razed the original to the ground

England briefly after defeating Henry III at the Battle of Lewes. Simon de Montfort was determined to wrest absolute political power from the king's hands. He failed and was killed by the forces of his own godson, Edward I at the Battle of Evesham in 1265. While nothing of the original Montfort castle remains, the fifteenth-century replacement would assuredly have met with his approval.

A skein of minor road lead back to Sarlat from hereabouts with the prettiest area perhaps being the D46 which winds between a wooded scarp and the narrow thread of the Vitrac river. Vitrac is a sort of French equivalent to an Upper Thames enclave, complete with golf course and consequently very popular with some tourists. For others the appeal will be the concentration of canoeing and camping facilities.

Using the tarmac artery the D704 once again moves south from Sarlat, and here, there are several scenic high spots to be seen without much deviation from the main road, which eventually leads to Gourdon. This is an interesting drive, which takes the best part of a day if the travel is leisurely. The first delight along this 26km route is of course, the Dordogne river, which can be reached directly or via quieter country lanes that lead through the tiny settlement of La Caneda, the latter part of the Sarlat appellation.

Pause awhile here to admire the very unusual medieval church, around which is clustered a surprisingly atmospheric village which is marvellously pastoral in its setting, despite the proximity of Sarlat and the approach route which at one point skirts a small industrial estate. There is a well-appointed touring site at La Caneda called Les Acacias, which is quiet, shady and not over-publicised, with some nice woodland footpaths in the immediate vicinity.

Go down to the Dordogne banks and the distinctive Cingle-de-Montfort snake-bend. Take the D703 alongside the water for a short distance to Carsac-Aillac, where there is a gem of a twelfth-century Romanesque church in a near perfect state of preservation. It even enhances the green and tranquil setting. Beside it, on a jutting scarp, are the remnants of a once imposing *château* which the tiny church originally served. There is a second medieval church – weirdly, almost identical in both construction and surroundings – at neighbouring Aillac village about 3km upriver. After admiring either or both of these stone splendours, cross the river to Grolejac, where there is a well-stocked general store with expansive parking space. It displays a wide selection of fruit and vegetables in season and this is very popular with travellers because it is an area not overly endowed in this respect.

From the rich wooded flanks of the sometimes steep-sided Dordogne river valley, the countryside now becomes more open and less tree-clad as you approach to the elevated Quercy *causses*. The Grottes de Cougnac, on the northern outskirts of Gourdon, lie at an altitude of 264m and are the Lot *département* equivalent of Dordogne's Lascaux, as it is yet another remarkable cave system, graced with some beautiful wall paintings by primitive man some 50,000 years ago, depicting both mammals and human figures. The caves are open seasonally, and are about 4km north of the town, off the D704.

Gourdon's configuration is rather akin to that of a whipped-cream walnut, with its winding streets rising and converging

169

The *causse* country south-east of Domme, seen beyond the rooftops of Gourdon

above a massive fourteenth-century church that is ornately Gothic, and a once fortified town hall which retains its medieval character, almost in defiance of very extensive restoration. The whole of the old town has undergone an enthusiastic renewal programme, with newly cut golden stone glowing on all sides.

Above all, inside the perimeter of ancient residual ramparts, which are reached by wide and shallow steps once rising to a great *château*, is a *belvédère* rewarding the climber with panoramic views across the wide Quercy landscape. There are many charming alleys and passageways radiating upwards and outwards from the old town centre, itself a pleasant, tree-lined conglomeration of shops, hotels, restaurants and cafés. There is a nice three-star campground sited by the lake on the outskirts of town and a helpful tourist office. There are two supermarkets on the Route de Eumel and for walkers, two long-distance routes (GR6 and GR64), plus several short circuits in the vicinity. For those wishing to use Gourdon as a base, there is a choice of hotels and some two hundred bed and breakfast houses in the area. Gourdon

Left
A typical Périgord 'Borile'.
The region is dotted with
many such reminders of the
Neolithic age

Below
One of the most worthwhile
souvenirs of the region –
miniature replicas of the
prehistoric wall paintings

Biron – the mightiest redoubt of the Purple Périgord

is a colourful, friendly and lively town, proud of its past and its claim to be the Gateway to the *causses* of Périgord.

Sarlat West – The Short Circuit Tour The road to the south-west of Sarlat revels three more Périgord splendours which are comparable in every way to any that have gone before. The first, arguably the most regal of Dordogne riverside *châteaux*, is Beynac-et-Cazenac, a medieval fortress that actually appears to dwarf the towering limestone cliff upon which it squats. It is quite overpowering in its dominance of the river valley.

Certainly the *château* must have posed a menacing threat in its original thirteenth-century form, for Simon de Montfort ordered the destruction of the great stronghold. Earlier still, it was a bastion of Richard the Lionheart. It was rebuilt in time to suffer many assaults during the Hundred Years War and later. The structure surviving today is mainly fifteenth century in origin, though with some notable remnants of the two preceding centuries. Beynac, one of the four principal baronies of Périgord was given by Richard the Lionheart, along with Biron,

173

Bourdeilles and Mareuil to the bloodthirsty Mercadier. He conducted a ruthless campaign of brigandage from the impregnable eyrie, in the name of the king of England. (Mercadier was the man who had the crossbowman responsible for Richard's death at the seige of Chalus, flayed alive. He was himself murdered a year later, in AD1200.)

Two distinctive viewpoints present themselves to the visitor, the first, from the riverside road being perhaps the most impressive of both village and *château*; it must have been daunting in the extreme to any potential medieval aggressor. For contemporary intruders however, access to the heart of the ancient stone complex is easy via a 3-km (2-mile) approach road, but it is far more romantic to travel via the direct pedestrian route, even if it is a trifle on the steep side. Predictably, there are commercial overtones, with a restaurant, café, antique outlets and a pottery within the hilltop confines. But these are not too intrusive and the eagle-eye views over the Dordogne from the ramparts make the climb worthwhile.

Places to visit: Beynac-et-Cazenac; St Cyprien; Berbiguieres.

Along the river bank, traces of the old *gabares* (quays) survive, from where modern versions of the flat-bottomed boats depart regularly on a sightseeing trip. Beynac, as with most other important historic sites in the Dordogne, has had a lot of restoration work done during the past two decades, and yet the visitor cannot but help feel that the power and strength of this might stronghold is still totally medieval. It is hard to visualize but Richard the Lionheart actually stormed and captured Beynac castle in the twelfth century. Today, conscious of its illustrious reputation as one of the leading high spots of central Dordogne, Beynac-et-Cazenac now has a small archaeological park and an interesting museum of folk history. While some 3km to the north-west, little Cazenac village (rather like La Canéda near Sarlat), has a notable fifteenth-century Gothic church, plus some fine high-level vistas over the river valley.

Follow the D703 westwards now for a short distance, to where St Cyprien cascades down a steep hillside above the Dordogne. Glowing quite golden when the sun is bright, the great twelfth-century church is unmistakably the most important medieval building jutting proudly above the surrounding ochre stone houses. Drive along the main road and you will see little of this colourful old town, because it reveals its numerous terraced

**Opposite
Beynac-et-Cazenac**

174

charms only shyly to those prepared to explore on foot. St Cyprien is a working town, only moderately furnished for the benefit of tourists and none the worse for that. The upper town streets have character which is the stimulating patina of centuries.

There is good food shopping here, as the town has two supermarkets, plus a popular and well-run municipal touring site on the banks of the Dordogne which is much patronized by conoeists during summer. There is also a choice of comfortable hotels, like the three-star l'Abbaye, where traditional Périgord dishes are served. The vicinity of St Cyprien is not dramatically scenic, though there is pleasant riverside walking with distant views of wooded hills to either side. There is also the restored Château de Fages on its nearby hilltop perch, commanding a wide panorama over the wide river valley.

There is no shortage of scenic beauty, nor pastoral seclusion, on the next stretch of the circuit which begins almost at once for those opting for the narrow and winding D48 which bridges the Dordogne directly south of St Cyprien. This is a fine hill route, lushly wooded in parts, offering distant views sporadically and a road which carries only very light traffic. The route takes in the pretty hill hamlet of Berbiguieres, where there is a favoured restaurant and overnight accommodation below a privately owned seventeenth-century *château*.

Eastwards from here the ridge road D48 becomes the D50 and winds around the Welsh-sounding village of Cladech, before descending on the D53, towards the river again and the celebrated *château* of Les Milandes. This elegant fifteenth-century cluster was bought by Josephine Baker, the famous black cabaret star of the 1930s, who attempted to create a multi-cultural orphanage here after World War Two. The project failed, leaving the one-time sweetheart of Paris in dire debt. The gardens of this much restored mansion are now a principal attraction, while there is some nice hillwalking in the immediate vicinity of the secluded setting.

The descent continues from Les Milandes over a scenic winding road, leading to a second *château*, this one is more of a medieval castle with its magnificent outline, immediately beside the Dordogne river. Like Montfort, Château de Fayrac is privately owned and no access is possible. You many still admire the turreted contours however, from a particularly open aspect roadside viewpoint. It was built in the sixteenth century and much restored in the nineteenth, and is a splendid example of the double-walled medieval bastion-cum-country mansion. Just south of here, the massive military structure of Castelnaud is unmistakably and functionally warlike, in contrast to the more delicate elegance of both Milandes and Fayrac. Cross the Dordogne once more here at the foot of the mighty castle, and return to Sarlat via Vezac.

Further south-west from Sarlat Like the excursion from Sarlat to Gourdon in the east of the area, this is a western equivalent which also has many interesting places. It takes in yet three more justly lauded objectives in both Périgord Noir and Périgord Pourpre. Take the St Cyprien road once more to begin the foray this time continuing along the right bank of the Dordogne to cross the river at Siorac-en-Périgord.

Places to visit: Urval; Belves; Montpazier; Biron.

This waterside village is in parts, one of photogenic charm, as you might expect at a site which has been inhabited since the Gallic era. There are a number of ancient dolmens in the vicinity, and just to the west another authentic medieval village called Urval, has itself been occupied since the Romans conquered Gaul. Siorac reached its civic height of importance in the twelfth century, when it was the location of an important religious priory. The site is now occupied by a large if somewhat unimpressive *château*, housing municipal departments. There is an attractive touring site here, with riverside walks and a popular *auberge*.

It is Belves,though, some 5km southwards along the D710, which is the first of that illustrious trio of high spots. This town is a much favoured Périgord base with those using public transport, since it lies on the mainline railway to Paris. The approach road for drivers, will illustrate why Belves has been inhabited since the dawn of history, for it is a typical hill-crest settlement, with sweeping bird's-eye views across the Nauze valley. It even has a fortified eyrie dating from the beginning of the Christian era, which during the thirteenth century, was an English stronghold for a time, though never a true *bastide*.

Belves was once completely walled and moated, and the handsome if crumbling remnants of the original centre, epitomized by the fourteenth-century Tour des Fillols in the Place d'Armes, are still strongly evocative of a long-dead age.

The vaulted arcades of Monpazier

Belves is a place to stroll around at leisure, for there is much to see and appreciate of old France in the vicinity of the tourist office, including the fifteenth-century covered market, museums of history and folklore, glowing vestiges of the past like the Maison des Consuls, the thirteenth-century Benedictine church and the maze of narrow streets lined with medieval dwellings.

It is not all bygone France at Belves though, which actually provides good traveller facilities and leisure amenities, including a heated swimming pool, tennis courts, marked pedestrian circuits, plus golf and horse-riding opportunities in the near vicinity. On the first Sunday in July, there is a colourful antique fair which sees the old town thronged with visitors. Many visitors come to Belves during most of the summer when the terraced gardens flanking the rampart walls are ablaze with flowers and the distant views are at their most impressive.

If Belves is charming, Monpazier which is reached via a delightfully quiet green road route along the D53, is stunningly memorable. It is unquestionably the finest of all the genuine

178

bastide, and is a superb example of medieval architecture, that is a subtle blend of military necessity and civilian aestheticism. Created on the orders of Edward I of England in 1284 by Pierre de Gontaut and Edward's steward Jean de Grailly, the old town is very French in conception, though conforming to the standard British grid-pattern of street layout.

The main square which is gloriously spacious, shows a combination of delicacy and strength that is reflected in the perfectly proportioned vaulted arcade, Les Cornières, and the whole area is highlighted by a medieval covered market place. Even today you can sense the one-time strategic importance of Monpazier, as you enter the garrison town through portals into the cross-hatch of dead straight alleyways and narrow straights which are punctuated by symmetrical squares. Monpazier is still very compact and self-contained. It commands the pinnacle of a handsome green bluff which rises above the river Dropt, as it resolutely stands guard over the ancient route between Périgord and Agen to the south.

Pick a sunny day to see it if you can, and allow yourself time to explore it at leisure, because there are many delightful nooks and crannies here. The thirteenth-century Maison du Chapitre (the old tithe barn) and the fourteenth-century church with a particularly fine carved portal, are two of the most outstanding buildings among other interesting medieval dwellings, lookout towers and ramparts walls. (Needless to say, the town was frequently fought over, especially during the Wars of Religions). It is one of the most atmospheric of all the *bastides* and it really is possible to capture a whiff of the distant past here.

The third and final objective on this extended route from Sarlat, is the most dramatic of all – it is the *château* at Biron. Biron has one of the largest and most dominant *châteaux* in all France. Seen at its best under vivid blue skies, this massive stronghold of the turbulent Middle Ages is almost breathtaking in its powerful splendour. The *château* is magnetic yet intimidating, and the towering limestone outcrop it occupies oversees the region for 30km or more in every direction. It is a stern and regal landmark of formidable dimension and enduring strength.

When you approach Biron from the north the great castle looms compactly and ostensibly unified. However, the southern aspect reveals the clutter of disordered architecture which is testimony to the turbulence of its history. It has a past which is not least remarkable for the fact that one family held Biron for eight centuries, only relinquishing ownership just before World War Two. The all-powerful Gontaut dynasty were kings of this particular castle (the same family responsible for the creation of Monpazier), and in the early days of the bastion's existence, the Gontauts were sympathetic to the Albigensian cause. Thus Biron came under the baleful eye of Simon de Montfort, who besieged and fired the castle, and showed scant mercy to the unfortunate inhabitants. The Gontaut family lost, then regained their base, (even though the English held it for a while during the Hundred Years War), each succession of occupants repairing, modifying or enlarging the main structure and its ancillary buildings. For the whole of the seventeenth century, the Gontaut dynasty was out of favour (Henry IV having Charles de Gontaut executed for plotting), but early in the eighteenth the barony was again granted to Charles de Gontaut, who became Marshal of France. During the Renaissance period, the great complex was gradually converted, from one of bleak defensive sternness to that of a more gracious *château*.

Today, under the benevolent protection of the regional authority, Biron is a telling combination of historic architecture, spanning the centuries and reflecting the many periods of peace and war which the ancient stones have survived. It dates from the stout twelfth-century keep, to the seventeenth-century state rooms, which have now been lovingly restored. Inside the mighty rampart walls, which actually enfold Biron hamlet, there is ample evidence of baronial life on the grandest of scales, topped by some truly splendid panoramas from ancient sentry walks. Biron, like Monpazier, really should not be missed, for it is an almost awesome legacy of old France and is far and away the most monumental of all the *châteaux* of Purple Périgord.

A Base at Le Bugue Le Bugue, a small market town close to the confluence of the Dordogne and Vézère rivers, has escalated in popularity as a riverside resort of late, though it is still a relatively backwater base amid pastoral Périgord Noir. There are two recently created attractions, which have contributed to the increased visitor influx, a fossil museum and an aquarium. Neither may initially sound extremely exciting, but both are really quite exceptional examples of their respective field. The Musée de Paleontologie exhibits a fascinating collection of fossilized early-planet creatures, some of which have been carbon dated to an era some 150 million years ago. The museum has added interest because the majority of the collection is composed of fossils discovered in the Dordogne region.

The second unusual amenity is a new, custom-built aquarium. This low-rise complex has a very imaginative design, with the exterior incorporating a series of landscaped cascades. It is assuredly one of the largest, and most comprehensively stocked private enterprise aquariums in Europe, and it emphasizes the aquatic world of south-western France. It is a great favourite with children and naturalists of all ages and is an extremely popular wet-weather objective, only slightly less patronized when the sun shines brightly.

Don't miss: The Musée de Paleontologie; the Aquarium.

However, it is the marvellous evidence of the past – both prehistoric and medieval – which lies in profusion close to Le Bugue that is the major magnet for visitors. The fact that these high spots are located for the most part amid unspoiled country is also a bonus. The little township has for a long time been patronized for its strategic position, making its title, 'The Gateway to Périgord' quite apt.

It is a semi-rural base really, and is favoured by those seeking facilities and amenities akin to those of Sarlat, within a much quieter and more compact source. The services and amenities provided are comprehensive enough for most visitors, while the setting alongside the Vézère river is pretty enough in parts. There is a good choice of hotels and restaurants of all categories, there are two high-standard touring sites (one municipal and one private), two supermarkets and a variety of diverse shops in the lively town centre. Open markets are held every Tuesday and Saturday and there is an enthusiastic seasonal programme of rustic fairs, including a celebrated bric-à-brac event in August.

Like Belves to the south, Le Bugue lies on the main railway line to Paris and thus provides a good bicycle hire service for train travellers. There is also good canoeing potential on the Vézère, together with several local waymarked footpaths and sections of the long distance GR6. A particularly pleasant pedestrian route

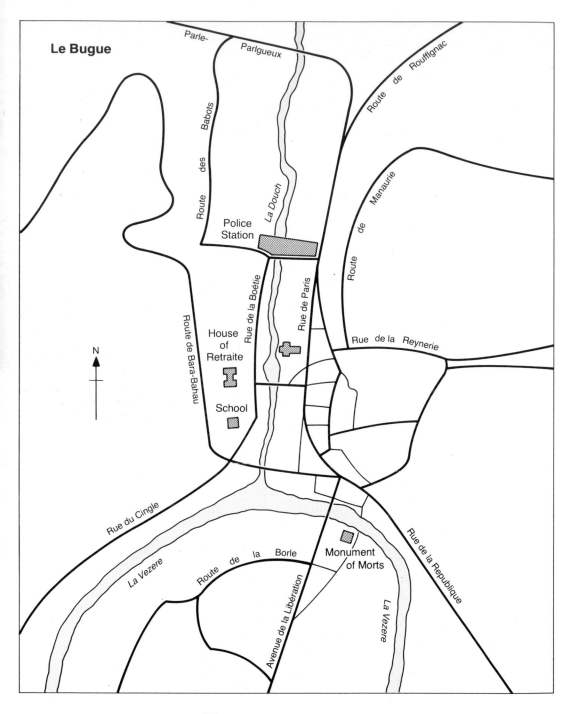

Le Bugue

leads from the municipal touring site and swimming pool complex to the town centre. This travels along beside a nicely renovated bank side promenade, passing the new aquarium on the way and avoiding the busy main street traffic. A steep flight of steps lead directly from the waterside to the market place and the helpful tourist office beside the town hall.

A particularly scenic stretch of the Dordogne river, much favoured by canoeists

There is little that is historically outstanding except in Bugue (although the town has a very long past), for a venerable water mill in the process of restoration. It is simply a workaday market town of unpretentious and relaxed charm and is none the worse for that. It possesses character, the local people are friendly and as a touring base it is definitely commendable. From the vicinity of the Bara-Bahau caves about half a kilometre outside the town (*see* Périgord's Pre-history Trail). there are revealing elevated views across the town. Regrettably, Le Bugue also lives up to its other nickname rather too literally as the Crossroads of Périgord because the traffic is almost insufferable at times, in the town centre. Inhabitants and visitors alike have

183

to endure a heavy and seemingly continuous north–south flow of commercial vehicles along the D710, as well as a cross-country stream of tourist traffic moving between Bergerac and Sarlat. Le Bugue somehow survives the noise, dust and danger, while incredibly, there *are* quieter periods when pedestrians can capture traces of a past-age tranquility in the streets which lead off the main riverside square.

Le Bugue – Useful Information

Le Bugue is the chief town of its canton, in the *arrondissement* of Sarlat, supporting nearly 3,000 inhabitants. It lies on the SNCF mains line between Agen and Paris. It is 30km distant from Sarlat and 40km from both Bergerac and Périgueux.

Syndicat d'Initiative office is the Place de l'Hôtel-de-Ville, Tel: 53 07 20 48.

The Gendarmerie is in the Rue de Paris.

The Medical Centre, Tel: 53 07 26 87.

The taxi/ambulance service (Claude Dupuy) is 24 hours, and is at the Rue de la Faure Haute, Tel: 53 07 22 97.

Accommodation includes: Royal Vézère hotel/restaurant Place de l'Hôtel de Ville. Three-star, fifty-three rooms, Tel: 53 07 20 01. There are five other one- and two-star category hotels, plus the Auberge du pre Saint-Louis in the Place de la Farge (ten rooms), Tel: 53 07 15 14 (it is open all year round). The Hôtel de Paris (it has no restaurant), No 14 Rue de Paris, is open all year (one-star, eighteen rooms), Tel: 53 07 28 16. There are camping and caravanning sites at Le Port camping municipal (this is open 15 June to 30 Sept), Tel: 53 07 24 60, 1 km (1/2 mile) town centre; there is an alternative three-star private site; plus Le Val de la Marquise at Campagne, 4 km east, (this is open same dates as Le Bugue), Tel: 53 07 23 65.

There are half a dozen restaurants and cafés in town, the Albuca in the Place de l'Hôtel de Ville, providing a variety of regional dishes. There is a popular pizzeria in the Avenue de la Liberation, La Pergola.

There is a variety of leisure amenities including: the town sports centre; three tennis courts (one covered); a mini-golf course; two swimming pools; and canoe or bicycle hire facilities with excursions in season. (*see Syndicat d'Initiative* office for details.)

The Musée de Paleontologie is located at 42 Rue de la

République and is open all year, Tel: 53 07 16 79. L'Aquarium du Périgord Noir, is situated alongside the Vézère, half a kilometre from the centre, Tel: 53 07 16 38.

For most visitors to Le Bugue, the first excursion objective is Les Eyzies only 10km upriver on the banks of the Vézère. It may be the capital of French pre-history, but it is in truth, just a small and somewhat straggling village lacking any obvious focal point and now coping valiantly with an ever-growing influx of summer visitors. There is much expansion and renovation in progress, though there is a limit to what can be done to a settlement originally nestling in a very narrow valley defile, with distinctly restricted terrace space. The authorities have done what they can, but car parking is always difficult during the summer, and at times it borders on the impossible within the village confines.

There is no shortage of accommodation however, with nine hotels and many bed and breakfast houses and camping grounds in the vicinity being ready to cater to the steady visitor flow. The main street shops in Les Eyzies seem primarily concerned to dispense the ubiquitous Périgord tinned *confit*, fancy goods, or souvenirs. Due to the shape of the village there is no central square, the village centre vaguely defined as the stretch of street below the famous national museum. This half-concealed building itself occupies a medieval castle site, beneath a massive limestone overhang which is landmarked by the controversial carved figure of early *Homo sapiens*. The tourist office opposite is constantly busy catering to the international clientele (except on Tuesday when it is closed).

Les Eyzies is now one of the Republic's great heritage centres that you either love or hate to visit. However, it must be said that the museum is one of Europe's most significant and impressive. The pre-history sites in the near vicinity are, of course unique.

Drive north from Les Eyzies along the D47 and then the secluded and largely traffic-free D32 which skirts the Grotte de Rouffignac. This road leads eventually to the small market town of Rouffignac-St-Cernin. The town is an attractive place, with the stonework of every building, from the town hall to the most modest private house, glowing in pristine condition, as though the whole town was built but yesterday. In effect it was, because

185

Les Eyzies. The prehistory museum and its primitive man 'guardian'

in 1944 the retreating German army burned Rouffignac to the ground, with only the imposing Renaissance church being rescued from the flames. The restoration of the entire old township has been faithfully followed however, to re-create the layout almost exactly as it was before the war. One must marvel at the industry and expertise which this architectural resurrection must have demanded.

From this tranquil settlement with its tree-shaded square and proudly preserved church, there is a signposted minor road which leads north again for a few kilometres to one of my great personal Dordogne delights. For Château de l'Herm assuredly evokes a genuine glimpse of rustic life in medieval France.

In a very secluded – indeed almost isolated back-country setting – the gaunt shell of a once majestic sixteenth-century mansion, is now just a stone skeleton of towers and tall walls clad with undergrowth in places but retaining their regal presence. The *château* is surrounded by a tiny cluster of wondrously medieval-looking dwellings, one or two of which are inhabited whilst others are picturesquely tumbledown. These once served the great estate. It is highly atmospheric but as yet totally uncommercialized, though there is a programme of restoration scheduled. I urge you to see this miniscule remnant of bygone France before it is placed too prominently on the tourist map.

The *château* was imaginatively used as a film-set for the recreation of *Jacquou le Croquant* (the famous novel by Eugene le Roy). However, there is a grisly infamy which is stranger than fiction about *Château* de l'Herm, as the mansion was occupied by a succession of black-hearted owners. The most notorious of all was the homicidal Anne d'Abzac, who participated in the murder of her own daughter. Gazing at the opulent stone tracery around the main portal of the old manor or upwards at the stark towers now with tree growth thrusting through in places, you can feel slightly chilling vibrations still. The humble dwellings of the hamlet seem very cosy and orthodox by comparison. This is a most revealing day trip north from Le Bugue then, taking in Les Eyzies, the caves of Carpe-Diem and Rouffignac, the town of Rouffignac-St-Cernin and *Château* l'Herm. A more direct return route to Le Bugue is available if required, via the D710, a few kilometres to the west of *Château* l'Herm.

The Treble-B Triangle The triangle formed by Bugue, Beaumont and Belves, almost a golden one in terms of scenery is, as it takes in some notable high spots that are both natural and man-made, within the final swathe of hills in Purple Périgord, eastwards of Bergerac and the predominantly plain country. The area south-westwards of Le Bugue, along the right banks of the Vézère on the D31, reveals the first feature of beauty, the Chapelle St Martin, a medieval gem on the outskirts of Limeuil village.

The chapel is situated by the confluence of two great rivers, and therefore is predictably a much-visited but interesting venue. the waters are doubly spanned where they meet by arched bridges, creating a much photographed scene, because you can clearly see the Dordogne/Vézère division from the large bankside car park and picnic area.

Don't miss: Chapelle St Martin; Limeuil; Cingle de Tremolat; Lalinde Cadouin; Montferrand-du-Périgord.

It is the village of Limeuil proper, high above the water line, that is the real beauty however, and anyone who has ever visited Clovelly in north Devon, will assuredly experience a pang of *déjà-vu*. The place comes as a surprise to most visitors, myself included, since its praises are sung but modestly in most guide books. Limeuil snuggles on its precipitous and lushly-wooded hill flank. It consists of a compact collection of low-roofed cottages covered with ivy and vines that flank the most delightful of steep and narrow cobbled alleyways and passages. There has been some restoration to this ancient and once fortified hill town, but much of the original ramparts and the venerable church with its open belfry, remain admirably original. On no account miss this cluster of old Périgord which is every bit as splendid as it renowned riverside counterpart La Roque-Gageac upriver.

After Limeuil, there is a bonus of natural splendour, the Cingle de Tremolat, the most famous snake-bend in the Dordogne river. This is a mighty loop of water dramatically revealed at the lofty viewing *belvédère* alongside the narrow D31, where there is a car park beneath the pine trees, a pay-and-peek telescope and a hotel called, what else, *Le Panoramic*. Tremolat village is pleasant and mellow if unremarkable. Nowadays its main claim to fame is as the location for Chabrol's celebrated spine-chiller *Le Boucher* (The Butcher), now something of a cult movie. A more venerable attraction is the fortified twelfth-century church, occupying the site of a shrine erected in the time of Charlemagne.

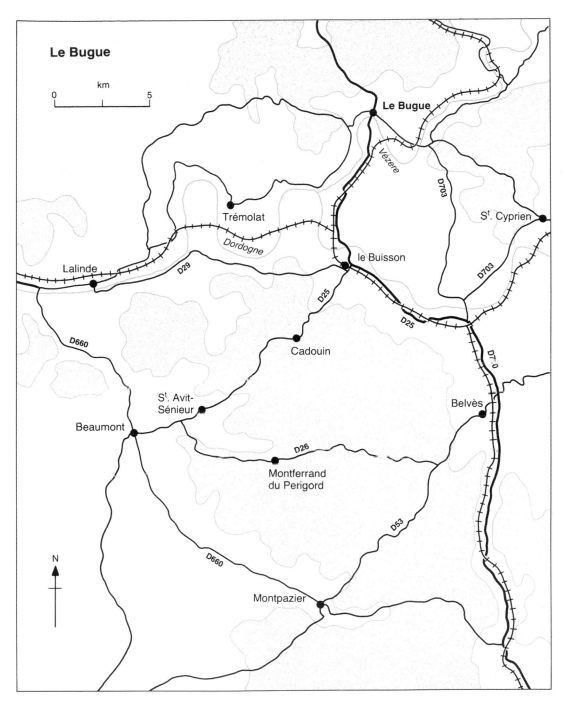

Le Bugue

km
0 — — — — 5

Le Bugue

Vézère

D703

St. Cyprien

Trémolat

Dordogne

le Buisson

D703

Lalinde

D29

D25

D25

D660

Cadouin

DT-0

St. Avit-Sénieur

Belvès

Beaumont

D26

Montferrand
du Perigord

D53

N

D660

Montpazier

The western bank of the mighty river bend is now a leisure base, almost a full-blown summer holiday resort, with every kind of water sport available and supported by a well-run and extensive caravan and camping park. A short distance west of here, you are again transported from a super-modern complex to more medieval delight in the shape of two very distinctive English *bastides*, once again illustrating the stimulating contrasts with which this part of south-western France abound.

The first of these, Lalinde is built on a spot where Roman legions once forded the Dordogne. It was raised in the late thirteenth century with most of the defensive rampart stones being pillaged from Roman remains. Like so many of the fortified enclaves in the Dordogne region, Lalinde retains even today a faint martial air. Strolling the ancient streets you can more readily understand how those medieval inhabitants developed a siege mentality, for there must have been a comfortable feeling of security behind those massive rampart walls, even though it frequently proved to be fatally false!

Beaumont, the second medieval *bastide*, lies across the river and 10km to the south along the D660. It was built at the same time as Lalinde, on the orders of Edward I of England. It was the chief *bastide* of the English occupying Aquitaine province, though today it seems very tiny to have been of such strategic importance. The main square has suffered much alteration since the Middle Ages and there are only partial remnants of the original vaulted arcades. One ancient rampart entry survives though, the evocative Porte de Luzier which was only relatively recently deprived of its great portcullis. The massive thirteenth-century church is still the pride of Beaumont. It was once fortified of course and is still standing proud and half soldierly, being unmistakably the work of a medieval military architect. It is an atmospheric hill town, although it lacks the stunning architectural flair that pervades Monpazier, and is a favoured lunch stop or overnight way-station for tourists on the Circuit des Bastides.

From Beaumont, the return to Le Bugue begins with the green road D25 which leads eastwards to Cadouin, some 12km away. The route takes in yet more of ancient France like the twelfth-century hilltop monastery ruins of St-Avit-Senieur,

which is surrounded by its once fortified medieval village. There is also a geology museum here.

Cadouin is famous for its great Cistercian abbey, which has stood here since the early twelfth century. The cloisters are considered to be masterpieces of medieval craftsmanship. It was believed for centuries that this fount of religion once housed fragments of the Holy Shroud. Alas, like those of Turin in Italy, they were proved fakes by twentieth-century experts. Today, the abbey, church and village, once a settlement of spiritual isolation, endures more than its fair share of visitors throughout the summer months. The old abbey is partially ruined and has not weathered the centuries well, though it must be said that the many signs of deterioration add to the atmosphere.

There are a number of ancient carp ponds amid forest clearings which are mute evidence of the monks past and present industry. The village itself is quite picturesque, since it was once partially fortified and the medieval Porte St Louis archway still stands solidly. From here, the direct return route to Le Bugue is via the D25 and the Dordogne river bridge at Le Buisson.

Beaumont is an early English bastide that Simon de Montfort might still recognize today. This is the only remaining rampart gateway

For those with the time available, the extended circuit, taking in the road from Beaumont to Belves is recommended, for it takes in yet another magnificent hilltop town, Montferrand-du-Périgord. The town is located in the very tranquil and pretty valley of the river Couze, and is wonderfully evocative of a past era, complete with ancient covered market place and a twelfth-century *château* ruin, which has a fine surviving donjon and defensive wall remnants.

On the backroads of the Le Bugue circuit the traveller will be wellserved – a comforting thought for any who may be a trifle apprehensive about leaving the mainstream tourist areas. Lalinde, Beaumont, Cadouin and Belves all provide hotel *gîte* or camping accommodation while more secluded backwaters like St Avit or Montferrand will often surprise you with the services or amenities available, especially during the high season. Monteferrand for example, has a very comfortable *Logi-de-France* hotel/restaurant; St Avit provides for conducted tours around the old town in July and August. While Cadouin organizes guided tours of the Gothic cloistered abbey, and has some 18km of marked footpaths in the neighbourhood, amid a delightfully tranquil countryside.

Périgord's Pre-history Trail This area is named with genuine justification, the Valley of Pre-history because the Vézère watercourse between Le Bugue (at the confluence of the Dordogne) and Montignac market town to the north-west, is regarded today as one of the prime birthplaces of *Homo sapiens*. The area around the little village of Les Eyzies is now acknowledged by eminent prehistorians as the area in Europe where man lived around a million years ago and left behind vital evidence of his existence.

Les Eyzies is now a monument to mankind and, of course, an obligatory pilgrimage centre where nearly every visitor to the Dordogne area feels compelled to pay homage. It is however, just one example among a liberal scattering of primitive settlements, not only along the banks of the Vézère and the Dordogne, but also along neighbouring river valleys of Périgord, like the Dronne, the Isle, the Beaune (both Grande and Petite), and the Gouze.

The Vézère certainly enjoys the giant's share of these world heritage sites, and it is also true that most lie within the compass of Périgord Noir, but almost anywhere you travel within the

Places to visit: Les Eyzies; Lascaux; Le Thot Research Centre and Museum Park; Grotte de Rouffignac; La Roque Saint-Christophe; La Madeleine; Grotte Font de Gaume; Bara-Bahau; Gouffre de Proumeyssac.

Prehisto Parc, Vézère. An exhibit of Neanderthal hunters with a ruminant antelope species, itself extinct for 40,000 years. The replicas are all as scientifically accurate as possible

Dordogne *département* (or even beyond its boundaries in places), there will be some evidence of our primitive ancestors. Here is a selection of some of the most interesting.

Lascaux I and Lascaux II. The first was discovered in 1940 by four schoolboy potholers. However, it is now inaccessible to visitors because it was closed in 1963 to prevent further bacterial damage to the astounding wall-paintings; these are some of the most significant and beautiful works of art created by the hand of primitive man.

With masterly modern day skill and ingenuity however, Lascaux II has been created close by – the location being just to the south of Montignac. In an appropriate woodland setting, this technological marvel has been fashioned largely with ferro-cement. It re-creates a world of 15,000 years BC, down to the smallest rock face detail and the most exact of polychromatic colours, by copying original methods to produce magnesium dioxide blacks and iron oxide yellows and reds. Lascaux II may be a carbon-copy, but is is forgivable and eminently excusable in the circumstances. It helps to know that the real thing lies close by, safely and permanently protected by layers of clay. The replica cave displays long-extinct auroch bulls, wild stallions, long-horned antelope and bison that are exactly like the originals. In

193

Lascaux II, France's most famous ancient site

places, the very contours of the chamber walls are used to emphasize the physical features of the astoundingly lifelike animals depicted. Many of these are captured in what we would now describe as action poses. They are images that remain long in the mind, with perhaps the most notable being those adorning the cave roof near the main entrance, which are dubbed with perception by the archaeology world as, 'the Sistine Chapel of pre-history'. Lascaux II is open daily, except Monday.

Le Thot Research Centre and Museum/Park is located between Montignac and Belcayre. It contains ancient rock shelters (*abris*), and many fascinating re-creations of the prehistoric era, including an animated mammoth and illustrative material giving an insight to the everyday life of Cro-Magnon man. Much of the material comes from the encampments and authentic impediments discovered here during archaeological digs. The centre, which is just off the D706, is open seasonally.

Some 15km west of here, via quiet minor roads, is arguably the most impressive of all the inhabited cave systems in Périgord, that

194

of the Grotte de Rouffignac. It is sometimes called 'the Cave of the Hundred Mammoths', because there are no less than 8km of underground galleries here! The cave system is so extensive in fact, that a miniature electric train is employed to ferry visitors through it. It is also the oldest known cavern in France.

The entrance to the vast Grotto de Rouffignac 'Cave of a Hundred Mammoths'

There are hundreds of primitive wall-paintings here, many of which are of mammoths (hence the name), together with other intriguing long-gone mammals, like the woolly rhinoceros and the ruminant auroch. The paintings were created some 11,000 years BC with the first of which adorning the walls almost a kilometre from the diminutive, half-hidden and low-roofed entrance. The Grotto de Rouffignac is signposted from the village and is open daily during the summer season.

If you travel back south-east again, to the banks of the Vézère, three more of the Republic's most precious pre-history sites follow in quick succession. Upstream of Les Eyzies village, Le Moustier is the original archaeological gem, with Cro-Magnon man being first unearthed near here during the nineteenth

195

century. Le Moustier now lends its name to the geological 'Mousterian Era'.

La Roque Saint-Christophe creates one of the largest natural rock terraces to be found anywhere on the European continent. It is situated just above the waters of the Vézère. The rock formation is unique. It is some 83m (250ft) high and covering a riverside stretch in excess of 1,000m (3,000ft). The limestone, sculpted by water erosion, lent itself admirably to defensive modification by the early settlers. The most notable section is the Grand Abri, a massive cavern, once a medieval fortress which is one of several on different cliff levels. The site is open to visitors seasonally.

The village of Tursac, just to the south of here, is rich in pre-history surroundings. The most celebrated is the troglodyte settlement of La Madeleine, yet another of Périgord's early-world gems. This is the place that gave its name to the archaeological Magdalanian period which lasted from 15,000 years BC to around 10,000BC. The excavation area is out of bounds to visitors, but the fortified cave complex and latter-age troglodyte shelters (occupied even at the beginning of the present century), generate a distinctive atmosphere of the ancient world, evoking our primitive ancestors.

Cave systems downstream of La Madeleine follow thick and fast now towards Les Eyzies. They are situated principally on the right bank, with the most magnificent (from the archaeologist's viewpoint), being Laugerie Haute and Laugerie Basse, where extensive multi-layers of rock (nearly fifty in some places), have facilitated scientific dating of the pre-history era. Gorge d'Enfer (Hell's Mouth), is one of the most dramatic of caverns hereabouts and it is surrounded by a number of smaller valley shelters.

About 1km from Les Eyzies itself, along the Sarlat road, is the Grotte Font de Gaume, discovered in 1901. It is a subterranean jewel adorned with vivid, beautifully executed animal paintings and engravings, which are comparable to the replicas on display at Lascaux II. Because these are original, the number of eager visitors is limited, as is the time allowed for each group within the cave. Spray-on protection of the walls, together with low-level lighting, inhibits the spread of micro-organisms which are the potential destroyers of a priceless national treasure. Font de Gaume is open every day except Tuesdays.

A little further along the Sarlat road from Les Eyzies is the Cave of Combarelles which was discovered at the same time as the Font de Gaume. This one contains not wall-paintings, but engravings, etched deeply into the relatively soft limestone strata. There are literally hundreds of representational animal figures in outline, including all those species of mammals known to have existed during the Magdalanian period. Among others, there are a number of sensational lion etchings, plus some of the human form. Combarelles is open to visitors seasonally.

Le Bugue's contribution to France's treasure trove of pre-history, are the caves of Bara-Bahau. Here, the erosion of a subterranean river has created huge caverns which are again scoured from exceptionally soft rock. And the wall surfaces of one cave in particular are deeply inscribed with engravings of stylized wild creatures. Some of these graphics are estimated to be 20,000 years old – this is relatively modern for the pre-history era. Access to the caves is possible for physically handicapped visitors with the guided tour taking about half an hour. Bara-Bahau is open every day, except during the annual closure period in December and January.

The *gouffres*, or chasms are distinct from the cave systems inhabited by primitive man because they are spectacular for their subterranean *natural* beauty. Of these, Padirac and La Cave in the neighbouring *département* of Lot are typical examples (*see* under Rocamadour). Périgord has comparable underground show-pieces, not least the Gouffre de Proumeyssac close to Le Bugue, and the Grotte de Domme, actually beneath the town's market place.

The first, Proumeyssac, dubbed descriptively a 'cathedral of crystal', is formed by massed stalactites and stalagmites. The petrified rock is displayed to breathtaking effect by stage lighting, creating a memorable and dazzling spectacular.

The Domme display is a little less grand in scale (though equally compelling), and is again shown to full advantage by special lighting effects. Both caves are open to visitors daily during the summer season. Like Bara-Bahau, Proumeyssac is accessible to wheelchair visitors.

Finally, for closer or more specialized study of the fascinating prehistoric era, three Périgord museums cater to the casually curious and the serious student alike. That of Les Eyzies is perhaps understandably the best known, the only museum in France devoted entirely to the subject of pre-history.

Accorded national status, this treasure-house of the past was opened at the end of World War One, occupying – appropriately perhaps – the site of an ancient fortress. The curators estimate that there are over a million artifacts in the total collection, many of which are displayed here, creating an impressive effect. Standing guard at the museum entrance, prominently above Les Eyzies narrow main street, is the controversial figure of primitive man, sculpted by Dardé in 1930. The museum is open daily except Tuesdays.

The Musée *Homo sapiens* at Sarlat, displays relics spanning a million years of man's existence, including the skulls, teeth and bones of many extinct animals. The museum is located in the Rue Montaigne, close to the cathedral, and is open daily during the summer season.

There is also the prestigious Musée du Périgord, at Périgueux. Here too, most of the exhibits are devoted to the pre-history era, with many priceless artifacts (like those found at nearby Chancelade which includes the skeletal remains of Neanderthal man), creating an accurate composite of our distant past. The more modern period is covered by fascinating evidence unearthed from the Gallo-Roman excavations at Vesone, almost literally a stone's throw away from the museum. It is a first-rate source of early European history, really not to be missed. The Périgord Museum is open daily except Tuesdays.

A further selection of pre-history sites in the vicinity worthy of exploration, if time permits, includes:

Prehistoric Caves

The *abri* (shelter), of Cap Blanc which exhibits primitive sculptures. It is 6km from Les Eyzies on the Tamnies road.

The *abris* of Castel-Merle at Sergeac which contain sculptures, and archaeological dig site and museum. They are 14km from Les Eyzies.

The potholes of Le Ruth (marmites), near Tursac.

The Bernifal caves with paintings and engraving which are 4km from Les Eyzies on the Sarlat road.

La Mouthe which has wall paintings is situated 2km on the Le Bugue road.

A primitive trogladyte cliff dwelling, extended by comparatively modern building. This one is at Gluges

Stalactite Caves

Le Grand Roc which is 1¹/2km from Les Eyzies on the Périgueux road.

The Carp Diem at Manaurie hamlet which is 4km from Les Eyzies.

Périgord Blanc The central belt of the Dordogne *département*, with the *préfecture* of Périgueux at its heart, is called 'white', after the limestone outcrops which abound alongside the principal river Isle which flows from the east to west. In contrast to the lush green of Périgord Vert, the countryside is subtly more open, marginally drier (being more southerly of aspect), with wider valleys, more urban development and consequently a larger population which is notably in the vicinity of the capital.

Nonetheless, Périgord Blanc is still essentially pastoral beyond the immediate environs of Périgueux and is just as agreeable to

The rustic charm of St Pardoux-la-Rivière at the heart of Périgord Vert

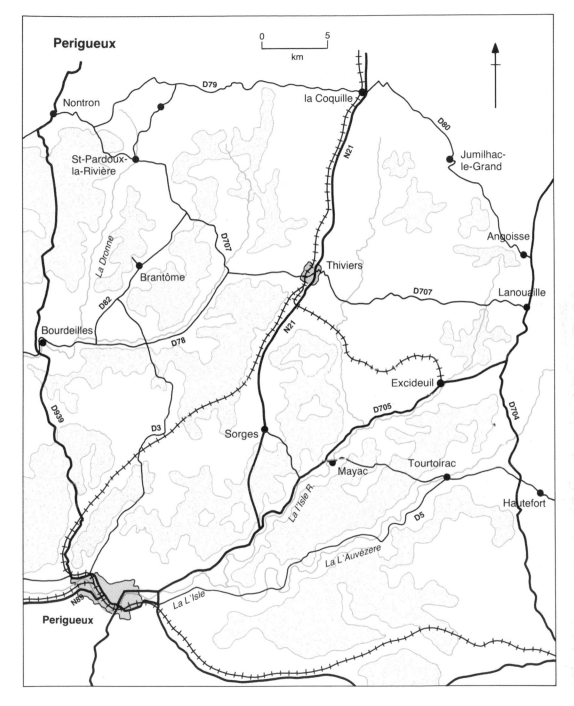

Perigueux

0 — 5
km

Nontron

St-Pardoux-
la-Rivière

La Dronne

Brantôme

D79

la Coquille

N21

D80

Jumilhac-
le-Grand

Angoisse

D707

Thiviers

D707

Lanouaille

N21

D82

Bourdeilles

D78

Excideuil

D705

D704

D939

D3

Sorges

Mayac

Tourtoirac

Hautefort

La l'Isle R.

D5

La L'Auvézere

La L'Isle

N89

Perigueux

explore as its northern neighbour. In some respects it is even more delightful to explore, not least for the number of historic attractions it has, but also for the diversity of appeal within the *préfecture*.

For those reliant on public transport the capital is an ideal base, since it is served by mainline rail connections to Bordeaux (convenient for those arriving by air), or via Limoges and Paris. Once comfortably installed – the range of tourist accommodation could hardly be wider – there are not only the charms of the old city awaiting, but also the best aspects of the Périgord Blanc, because the capital is very handily located, virtually in the centre of the region.

Don't miss: Tour de Vesone; Puy St Front cathedral; la Cité.

The city is situated in the ambient Isle valley, which is indeed the heart of ancient Périgord province. It is blessed with a benignly mild climate and a prevalently dry atmosphere. This famous redoubt of old Aquitaine is marvelously preserved – due in no small part to the arid atmosphere – however, it must be said that there are some areas which are a bit forlorn or even tatty on the outskirts of the city and in the vicinity of the rail terminus.

The programme of central city restoration, which was started in earnest in 1979, goes ahead at an impressive pace. There are, in any case, bound to be one or two frayed edges around a settlement that has survived some twenty centuries of existence. Anyway for some visitors such pockets of hard wear and neglect, simply add colour.

There are no signs of poverty in the now-vibrant centre. On the contrary, around the Place de la Libération, the vast Place Francheville and the Palais des Fêtes, there is more than a touch of affluence, even Parisian chic, which diplomatically extends to the area of the tourist information office in the Avenue Aquitaine. Périgueux is presently polishing its image, and doing so with patent success. There is an efficient information service here, dispensing all you need to know about the range of accommodation on offer, together with the local and more distant places of interest.

The long list of attractions – quite apart from the acknowledged world-wide reputation for Périgourdine gastronomy – is made readily available to enquirers and it includes details on such diverse matters as archaeology, coach-tours, evening and late-night entertainments, folklore and sport (especially tennis, angling, swimming and golf), plus the various market centres and where to find those specialized local dishes. For a city of only 35,000 people, the dedication to tourism is wholehearted.

Within the capital confines there are two three-star hotels; the Bristol, which is air-conditioned and with sound-softened rooms but no restaurant, and the Hôtel Domino which does have a restaurant serving regional speciality dishes. There are numerous

The Vesone Tower was once the centre-point of a great Roman temple and the heart of pre-Christian Périgueux

203

alternative hotel and hotel/restaurant choices to suit every pocket, some thirty in all within the city environs, together with a number of *Logis de France*, bed and breakfast houses and two touring sites for caravanners and campers, within easy reach of the centre of town. There are several alternative touring sites within a 20-km radius.

While initial confusion may afflict the first-time visitor, especially one trying to locate car-parking space at peak hours, the city soon captures the imagination, indeed affection, for it really does reward the diligent explorer who has the time to meander. There are any number of surprising delights, and not just the obvious if magnificent relics like the famous cathedral or the massive Tour de Vesone – though these are uniquely splendid in their timeless majesty. In short, Périgueux is an exciting city, more often than not bathed in warm sunlight and just south enough in latitude to engender an easy-going Mediterranean outlook on life, which can become infectious.

Successfully navigating around the old quarter of the city is made simple by the tourist office who dispense an easy-to-read numbered brochure with a map called 'the Circuit Vielle Ville'. Armed with this, you can plot a pedestrian route around the antiquarian centre taking in all the important and interesting sites, including many and varied refreshment places *en route*, such as the cosmopolitan eating houses. There are restaurants specializing in Vietnamese, Chinese, Greek and Spanish cuisine, and there is a popular Lebanese establishment called 'The Cedar', tucked away in a charming corner of the pedestrian precinct.

There are major architectural treasures which lay just to the south-west of the centre, and the are within a reasonable strolling distance of about 15 minutes. The first is the Tour de Vesone, which is well signposted and is located, appropriately, within a quiet green garden, in a less-busy residential quarter of the city. This tall, distinctive and now isolated monument, pin-points the exact centre of the colonized city of Vesuna, built by the Romans in the first century.

Vesuna was the original Gallic fortified capital of the Petrocorii tribe who were fiercely anti-Roman under Gaul chieftain (and now national hero), Vercingetorix. The existence of this Gallic city was only a short-lived thorn in the Roman side, which after

Roman arena, Périgueux – an entry tunnel which is still almost intact

the inevitable annexation, became the site of a great temple erected to the Gods. It marked the beginning of a long Gallo-Roman period of peace and prosperity, elevating the position of the new city to one of principal importance in all Aquitaine province.

Along with the Roman temple, of which the Vesuna Tower is the merest surviving fragment, a huge amphitheatre was constructed nearby, large enough to contain some 20,000 spectators. This followed the time-honoured and proven political strategy adopted in all annexed Roman provinces, that of bread

One of Périgueux's popular meeting places is the riverside quay below St Front Cathedral

and circuses. Ironically, the Vesuna Tower alone survives of the religious temple, while the outline shape, even a number of stair-wells, seating terraces and vaulted entry passages of the sporting arena are still very much in evidence.

The central arena is now a tranquil municipal garden, attractively landscaped and graced by playing fountains. However it must have been an area that was once a place of fearful apprehension for countless humans and animals alike. You can still imagine that there is a faint echo of a bloodthirsty crowd baying and gazing at the subterranean portals. None of the turbulent past seems to be conveyed to the locals, who bask languidly and happily amid the flowers oblivious, and perhaps rightly so, to the pagan past.

It is more difficult to imagine the great Vesuna temple, which must have majestically complimented the now lonely Vesuna Tower (once richly decorated with inlaid marble work, as evidenced by the stout iron fittings which are still visible). You can also see the distinctive narrow Roman bricks layering the half tower that survives, the 27-m pinnacle which was originally reached via a gracious spiral of stone steps. Like so many other glorious structures, especially those with religious connotations, half the tower was destroyed during the Barbarian era, when the massive free-stones of the lower storey were cannibalized to build defensive barricades.

Indeed, at the end of the Roman occupation and the start of the barbarous Dark Ages, Vesuna changed rapidly and radically. It changed from a centre of stable prosperity and even opulence to one of near-consistent turmoil which was to last for centuries. Dangers beset the city not only from afar but quite literally from neighbouring inhabitants. It is similar to Clermont-Ferrand in the fact that two distinct bastions arose in the early Middle Ages; one clustered around the cathedral known as Puy St Front, the other, la Cité, around the original Vesuna centre.

There was ferocious and sustained enmity between the two factions; one was largely monastic (on cathedral hill), and the other was more of an enclave of militant nobility. During the long Wars of Religion, la Cité sided with the English, the Puy St Front inhabitants with the French. It was not until the thirteenth century that reconciliation was possible, and the city was finally renamed Périgueux. Périgueux, having been almost razed in the third century, pillaged by the Saracens in the eighth century, and again by the Normans in the ninth century, does not seem to have had a happy past after the fall of the Roman Empire. It was even taken by the English during the Hundred Years War and was ceded briefly to England by the Treaty of Bretigny in 1356.

The somewhat stark if distinctive Romanesque church of St Étienne de la Cité is between the Tour de Veson and the ancient amphitheatre. This too once enjoyed cathedral status and though it has a stern outline with almost Spartan façades, it is capped by striking bee-hive cupolas — this is testimony to a past once as important as the hilltop St Front. And it too, like its more illustrious neighbour, was severely damaged during the medieval Wars of Religion. It was constructed during the twelfth century, on the site of a pagan temple, however, there has been much restoration over the centuries, including large areas of the interior during the seventeenth century.

The grandiose Cathedral St Front, with its highly distinctive multi-cupolas capping the Greek cross design was even more severely vandalized during the sixteenth-century turmoil. It is considered to be Périgueux's architectural gemstone. In truth, the whole structure is really something of a hybrid, for there were originally two churches side by side that are now linked by the lofty belfry which was constructed in the eleventh century. The great cathedral occupies a site where St Front preached Christianity in the fourth century. When he died, a monastery was raised above his tomb and the hallowed plot became Le Puy St Front.

In the nineteenth century, the building was in a desperately dilapidated state and was drastically – if interpretively – restored by Paul Abadie, a brilliant if controversial architect. He favoured a dramatic blend of Romanesque and Byzantine styling which was masterfully displayed by him, not only at Périgueux, but also at Montmatre in Paris, where the Sacré Coeur is perhaps the best-known example of the genre.

It is effectively striking if faintly misplaced, which always guarantees equal praise and criticism, though with St Front few observers fail to be impressed in one way or another. At any event, the Byzantine outline has a certain validity, since similar examples must have been a source of wonderment to medieval Europeans venturing eastwards as crusaders. Considering the depredations (caused primarily by the Huguenots in the sixteenth century and the Frondist rebels almost a century later), Abadie did create lasting beauty from almost total ruin.

The surrounding area of old Périgueux suffered equally of course. In the ancient la Cité district, the ruins of the twelfth-century *Château* Barriere still bears testimony to the protracted troubles, while the fourteenth-century Tour Mataguerre is the last remaining survivor of some thirty defensive structures which once ringed the St Front enclave.

208

The Musée du Périgord is one of France's leading museums specializing in pre-history and the Gallo-Roman age. The history museum lies just to the north of St Front cathedral and there is an equally absorbing military museum, depicting war from the Middle Ages to World War Two, just to the south.

The truly delightful old quarter is situated to the north-west and is now extensively and lovingly renovated. This vibrant and colourful part of Périgueux is just a step across the road from the cathedral portals, and is a haven of car-free, mellow stone buildings, enchanting tiny squares and an old town (superbly restored), appearing much as it must have done several centuries ago.

On a Sunday morning, when the celebrated food market is in full swing, it is a city centre that even the most country-loving devotee must assuredly enjoy. Saunter along the Rue de la Misericorde, the Rue Limogeanne or almost any of the narrow adjoining streets, to be rewarded by glimpses of the best of the half-hidden courtyards between tall house walls, which are cool and shady when the sun burns bright, and the riches of medieval

Sunday morning market in the old part of Périgueux

The king-sized strawberries for which Périgord is famous

architectural details like elegant balconies, quaint dormer windows and illustrative statuettes adorning upper-storey cornices. For a wide panorama of Périgueux, athletic explorers can gain access to the cathedral roof; there is a walkway between the Byzantine domes, affording fine views across the river and the wider city.

From this high vantage point, you can understand why Périgueux's past was so turbulent. Its ill-fated destiny is due largely to its situation because it occupies a strategic height and is an important crossroads of south-western France, being above the Isle river. Alternately Gallic, Roman Catholic and Protestant (both French and English), it was the administrative hub of the ancient Counts of Périgueux and the royal domain of the House of Bourbon. It has been dominated by religion since the early Christian era, consequently, there is not such a revealing concentration of religious architecture anywhere in the Dordogne region. It is befitting perhaps that it was at one time a major staging post along the Compostela pilgrim trail. Today, Périgueux is an absorbing blend of ancient and modern, and is rich enough in the splendours of one and the complex amenities of the other to call itself not only the capital of old Périgord and *préfecture* of the contemporary Dordogne *département*, but also to be proudly recognized as a Ville d'Art.

Périgord – Useful Information

The information office (including youth information centre) is at No 1, Avenue Aquitaine, 24000 Périgueux, Dordogne, Tel: 53 53 10 63, (youth centre enquires Tel: 53 53 52 81). There is also a small tourist office at No 16, Rue President Wilson, both dispense comprehensive accommodation lists covering city centre and outlying districts.

Travel information: the coach station, autobus Gonthier Nouhaud, Place Francheville, Tel: 53 08 76 00. There are local and distant road services.

Train services: Gare SNCF, Rue Denis Papin, Tel: 53 09 50 50.

The aerodrome is at (Bassillac 5km east of the city centre, Tel: 53 54 41 08.

The police (*Gendarmerie*) are off Boulevard Bertran de Born, Tel: 53 08 17 67.

The hospital emergency centre is at Avenue Georges Pompidou, Tel: 53 07 70 00.

Taxi hire: (Taxi Périgueux), Place Bugeaud, Tel: 53 09 09 09.

Cycle hire: Cycles Cumenal, No 41, Bis Cours Saint-Georges, Tel: 53 53 31 56.

There are camping facilities at Barnabé Plage, Tel: 53 53 41 45. It is 2km east of the town centre on Route de Brive-la-Gaillarde, and it is open all year. Camping le Grand Dague, Tel: 53 04 21 01. It is 3km north-east of the centre via the Route de St-Laurent-sur-Manoire et Chemin. It is open from Easter to late October.

Leisure amenities include:

Horse riding at Etrier Perigourdin Boret Petit, Champcevinel, Tel: 53 04 62 54; Haras de Bagnac, Route de Pommier Atur, Tel: 53 53 28 73; at Cravache de Trelissac, Poney Club, Tel: 53 08 14 58.

There is an eighteen-hole golf course at Domaine de Saltgourde, Route d'Angoulême, Tel: 53 53 02 35.

The swimming pool or Piscine Municipale is at Boulevard Lakanal, Tel: 53 53 30 36.

You can play tennis at Club du Breuih which is open all seasons,

Route de Saint-Alvère, Tel: 53 53 02 28; there is a tennis club for winter at Route d'Angoulême, Tel: 53 08 02 32.

The cinema, Le Montaigne, (seven screens), Tel: 53 53 20 24.

The theatre, Palais des Fêtes is at Avenue Aquitaine, Tel: 53 53 18 71.

There are several discoteques, La Regence, 16 Rue Chancelier-de-l'Hôpital, Tel: 53 53 10 55l; and L'Uba, No 3 Rue des Jacovins, Tel: 53 09 29 02.

The Musée du Périgord is at Cours Tourny, Tel: 53 53 16 42 and the Musée Militaire is at Rue des Farges, Tel: 53 53 47 36.

The bowling centre is at Rue President Wilson, (eight lanes) and brasserie and bar amenities. It is open every day.

There is a source of souvenirs with some quality antique articles displayed at specialist shop in old quarter.

Eatable treats include: Limousin beef with sauce Périgueux; Chocolate truffettes; Chabichou cheese (goat); and king-sized Périgord Strawberries.

Périgord Blanc is arguably the least-scenic of the colour-coded regions of the *département*, but it has nonetheless an agreeable swathe of countryside, is largely influenced by the wide valley of the river Isle. Low hills prevail to either side of the watercourse, which are lightly wooded for the main part, though with one or two richer forested areas, like the *Double*, to the west of Périgueux.

It is not quite so extensively watered as its neighbours to north and south, and with a high sun average (largely the reward of a landscape sparsely blessed with cloud-drawing hills), it is no surprise that the summer face of Périgord Blanc takes on a distinctive Tuscan tan. This goes naturally – and nicely – with the inhabitants attitude towards life, which is markedly Mediterranean in outlook.

While the country to either side of Périgueux is pleasant rather than dramatic, it is in no way bland or boring. There is much pastoral charm to both the east and west, once the environs of the capital are left behind. To the east, there is firstly, 'Au Pays des Pierres', one of the recommended tourist circuit routes. The prime objective here is the famous *Château* Hautefort, some 42km away. It is well signposted from the vicinity of Bassilac (Périgueux

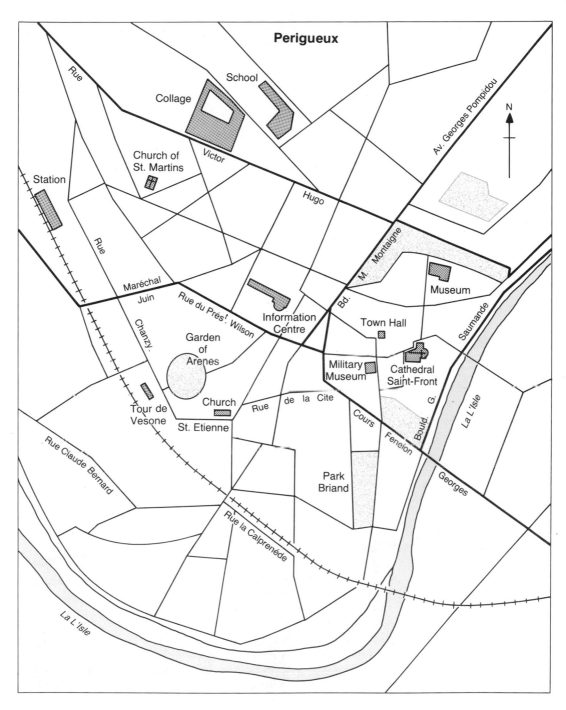

Perigueux

School

Collage

Rue

Victor

Church of
St. Martins

Hugo

Station

Rue

Av. Georges Pompidou

N

Bd. M. Montaigne

Museum

Maréchal
Juin

Rue du Prés.ᵗ Wilson

Information
Centre

Town Hall

Saumande

Charzy.

Garden
of
Arenes

Military
Museum

Cathedral
Saint-Front

La L'Isle

Tour de
Vesone

Church
St. Etienne

Rue   de   la   Cite

Cours   Fenelon

Bould. G.

Rue Claude Bernard

Park
Briand

Georges

Rue la Calprenéde

La L'Isle

airport) and from here, the D5 minor road threads its way through the centre of a fertile agricultural valley between distant wooded flanks. It largely follows the course of the Auvezere river through occasional villages like Le Change which boasts two *châteaux* and an imposing twelfth-century church. A little further along, Tourtoirac is a small and exceptionally charming market town, with a number of monastic remains and medieval fortifications. This is a recommended lunch stop and you will find a hotel/restaurant of some repute. For caravanners and campers there is a quiet and pleasant riverside base here.

Places to Visit: Château Hautefort; Sorges, St Astier; Mussidan; Montpon-Mesterol.

The prime magnet of this excursion though is Hautefort one of the mightiest of the Dordogne *châteaux*. It is the birthplace of the twelfth-century troubador knight, Bertran de Born. It was in the hands of one all-powerful family for almost seven centuries and the vast, intimidating castle is a real symbol of medieval power, even though the original hard lines have been softened by alterations and additions. There is still only one narrow entrance to the castle proper. Despite a disastrous fire in 1968, the great building has been meticulously restored to its full grandeur. The tiny village of Hautefort is almost as evocative as the *château* and is best seen early in the day, or out of season, when it is not thronged with too many sightseers.

There are a number of alternative routes which can be taken on the return to Périgueux, although by taking a northern loop from Hautefort through historic Exideuil (*see* Périgord Vert), along the D705, it is possible to visit another Périgord attraction – the village of Sorges, a diminutive agricultural hamlet astride the N21. It is firmly on the map nowadays as the home of the famous Truffle Museum, this is no gem of the past except for the building which houses the exhibits), because the Ecomusée de la Truffe, was only conceived, created and opened in 1982.

It is an original idea and is well executed as the steady flow of visitors every afternoon (except Tuesday), indicates. The regional authority assumed that visitors to Périgord *must* be interested in the mysterious *truffes*, and such has proved the case. Inside, among a host of exhibits, photographs and imposing charts, there is a monster replica truffle reposing under a perspex case, which is veined and blackened like something from outer space. The genuine articles, embedded in solid perspex cubes, are diminutive

A tableau of a truffle hunter with his trained pig in Sorges museum.

by comparison. An average truffle is about the size of a blackberry, while a king-sized version is no larger than a walnut. Indeed, in their natural state, these weird subterranean mushrooms, rooted form beneath oak trees by *truffieres* with their trained dogs or sows, do look a little like blackened walnuts. What they do for an omelette though is enough to make gourmets eyes glaze. It is hardly surprising they are extremely expensive!

The nearby Sentier des Truffieres (Truffle Hunter's Trail) is a logical development of the original Maison de la Truffe. This is a marked footpath, about 3km long, with a car-parking area off the N21 and close the the hamlet of Puycousin. At numbered points along the route, there are truffle interest points, including an ancient beehive shaped shelter; this is a typical Périgord *borile*, which was originally a Neolithic truffle hunter's lodge.

There is a contrasting tourist route of differing if equal interest, called the Vallee de l'Isle Circuit to the west of Périgueux, along the Isle river course. You begin the journey by taking the D710 just to the north-west of the city centre, to the village of Chancelade. One of Périgord's most imposing and ancient of monastic abbeys, with an adjacent church built in the twelfth century is situated here. It has a simple even somewhat severe

215

outline, yet is somehow elegant and a complement to its deep woodland surroundings. It was near this spot that the valuable prehistoric remains of 'Chancelade Man' were discovered; these are now in Périgueux museum. Chancelade has its own museum devoted to religion, and there are the picturesque ruins of an early mill.

Rejoin the N89 now for St Astier, another ancient and interesting little town, the old quarter hugely dominated by a mighty twelfth-century church which is built like a fortress high above the river. There is a most pleasant waterside municipal camping ground here (open all year round), within easy walking distance of the town centre. The town centre has a surprising number of modern service and leisure facilities which are half-hidden behind an old-world façade. There are also two supermarkets and a fine sports centre. It is a congenial base for exploring the Périgueux area, especially since the *préfecture* is just 17km away.

If you continue along the N89 you will find the two towns, Massidan and Montpon-Menesterol, which are both agreeable.

The modern covered swimming pool at St Astier

The first, which calls itself the 'Porte du Périgord', straddles a generously wide reach of the Isle and generates a friendly, unhurried atmosphere. The small town centre is attractive and spacious, with comprehensive service facilities. Mussidan too, has a fine swimming pool as part of a modern sports complex, an imaginative folklore museum, and a riverside campground from which you can stroll along towpaths.

Montpon–Menesterol is graced by an even larger and surprisingly swish main square, with a number of fashionable shops and a choice of hotels and restaurants which is somehow a

Picturesque old St Astier clustered around the massive medieval church

217

little unusual in such an ostensibly rural area. It is one of the factors that continue to make France such a land of surprise in places. There is, of course, yet another touring site here and more scenic riverside walking.

Now, turn north, along the D708 and in about 16km you will use the hamlet of Echougnac in the heart of the Foret de la Double. Just to the west of here, along the D38 minor road, the Abbey or Echourgnac, or to give it full title, Trappe Notre Dame de Bonne Esperance is situated in a secluded setting. The sisters here, when not at their devotions, provide the world with eagerly-sought gastronomic fare. They have done this since 1868 when they tentatively sold off some of their surplus home-made cheese. Today, during certain hours devoted to commerce, you can sample and buy their fare, which ranges from country pâté, *foie gras*, or pork in jelly, to home-made jams and crystalline fruits. The Abbey itself is in a very harmonious setting. The return journey is about 42km and is very largely along the D41 Double forest road as far as St Astier which is a delightful drive along a road you will have mainly to yourself.

Périgord Vert 'Green Périgord' forms a wide crescent of terrain covering the extreme north of Dordogne *departément*, and was so-named by the imaginative and observant science-fiction writer, Jules Verne. It is the least-visited part of the *departément* and in some respects I feel that it is the most pastoral of the whole of this region of south-west France.

It is aptly-named by Verne because rolling forests and meadow country unfold before the traveller, revealing kilometres of mixed woodland and verdant hill flanks grazed by cattle herds. It is wondrously green, due largely to the bountiful natural irrigation created by countless streams and lakelets stemming from major rivers like the Dronne and the Isle. Even today, it is a land dotted only by isolated farmsteads and occasional villages of old-world permanence and is inter-connected by a network of scarcely used country roads for the main part. Here, the telling statistic of French population is vividly revealed. You just *know* that in Périgord Vert, the national average people-density of ninety-five per square kilometre is true − compared with the crush of two hundred and twenty eight this can be for the same are in the UK.

Certainly only a very few people inhabit Périgord Vert which for the traveller seeking pastoral peace must be a delight.

The approach to Périgord Vert can also be one of rural tranquility for those travelling by road from the north. It is an intriguing backroad route really for those not too pressed for time. It begins at Chauvigny, not far to the east of Poitiers (in the Poitou-Charentes region). Chauvigny is a most extraodinary cluster of semi-detached castles on a half-kilometre-long bluff, high above the river Vienne. There are five towering structures in all, in various states of ruin or dedicated restoration and they form a memorable scene immediately above a well-run municipal touring site which is open all year round.

Places to Visit: Chauvigny; Confolens; Le Verdoyer; St Pardouz-la-Riviere; Saint-Jean-de-Cole; Jumhilac-le-Grand; Villars; Nontron; Brantome; Javerlhac.

From here, continue south, following the river course through the picturesque l'Isle Jourdain, on to Confolens (another medieval town famous for its annual folklore festival), then through Rochechouart and on, along the D901, to Chalus. Here, Richard the Lionheart was mortally wounded while laying seige to the castle. The tiny township is rightly proud of its vestigial *château* tower remains and you can follow a Route de Richard Coeur de Lion trail to evoke an imaginative glimpse of that 1199 tragedy. Just south of here you cross the Limousin boundary and the *département* of Dordogne stretches through wooded and wide scenery to a rolling and seemingly limitless infinity.

The small market town of St Saud Lacoussiere lies just to the west of the main N21 north-south road in a particularly pretty stretch of countryside, and about 4km or so west of here, you will find it well signposted on all approach routes. It is Château le Verdoyer which is a first-class, fully integrated accommodation base, which is most strategically centred for exploring northern Dordogne.

The imposing seventeenth-century *château* (built upon the site of a fifteenth-century castle) which was bought by two enterprising Dutch families in 1987, has been fully restored and the 9-hectare surrounding estate of woodland, lakes and lawns has been landscaped to incorporate a number of leisure amenities. The industrious resident owners can offer high-class, atmospheric accommodation to guests within the *château* itself, including bedrooms with four-poster beds which are furnished in genuine period style but are complemented by super-modern *ensuite* bathrooms and/or shower units. Full *pension* or bed and breakfast services are available and the restaurant, with its lakeside terrace and metre-thick castle walls, is one of warm character.

In the *château* grounds there are a row of self-catering chalets which overlook one of the property lakes. They are all furnished to attractively high standards, and for tenters and touring caravanners, there are pitches within woodland or on open lawn grass within hedged bays. Le Verdoyer has created a most pleasant atmosphere which is very efficient yet at once friendly and easygoing. English, as you might expect with Dutch owners, is the lingua franca.

Le Verdoyer has sport and leisure amenities which include, a 3-hectare swimming and canoeing lake, a separate fishing lake, a bar and snack-bar with take-away meals, an all-weather tennis court, two heated swimming pools, a large barn for social gatherings, special facilities for children including a nursery cabin and facilities for the disabled. All touring pitches are supplied with mains electricity, there is a multi-purpose shop and first-class toilets and laundry. Finally, there are field-session holidays available in subjects including French language, painting and drawing. The centre is open from Easter to the end of October, with booking for the July/August period being obligatory. Write to Château Le Verdoyer, 24470 Champs Romain, Dordogne, or Tel: 53 56 94 64/53 56 94 66 to speak to Richard or Ineke Ausems, or Jan or Lilian Janssen.

The area of extreme northern Dordogne which surrounds Le Verdoyer is literally Périgord Vert, because there is a cloak of near permanent green upon the landscape which is promoted by a particularly impermeable soil and a humid climate that encourages vigorous growth even during the driest of summers. Add to these favourable factors the widespread and generous watering of the land through countless streams and small lakes which spill from the great Dronne and Isle rivers, and you begin to understand which such lushness should prevail.

Not surprisingly, water is one of the great natural attractions of the region, whether it be in the form of the massive leisure park based on a 40-hectare lake at Rouffiac, to the west of Thiviers, or the celebrated waterfalls of the Saut du Chalard, close to the village of Champs Romain and just up the road from Château

Verdoyer. There is a spacious car-parking on the fringe of the village, from where you may take a green-coded pedestrian trail for a fairly lengthy walk into a considerably steep and densely wooded valley. Allow an hour and a half for the out-and-back excursion which includes the waters of the Dronne cascading noisily and impressively over a rugged valley floor.

If you want a target with a strong appeal for children, consider the Centre de Loisirs at Rouffiac, near the village of Lanouaille. There is everything here to amuse children of all ages, including a fine sandy beach, supervised swimming, a water chute, canoeing, archery, horse-riding, even a climbing wall and potholing. The park covers over 100 hectares in all and there is a three-star camping ground adjacent, open from mid June to mid September.

For somewhere a little less energetic, St Pardoux-la-Riviere is a charming and mellow old village with a history going back to pre-Roman times. There are a number of marked riverside strolls gracing the banks of the fast-flowing Dronne, which you can enjoy in the vicinity. In the village itself, there are several

The tranquil playground of Rouffiac leisure park, south-east of Jumilhac

thirteenth-century houses and the remains of an ancient Dominican convent. It is a very popular trout-fishing district (notably at Miallet), and the restaurants of St Pardoux specialize in game fish dishes.

Saint-Jean-de-Cole, a genuine medieval village to the south-east, is kept alive and well because it is gratefully exploited by film-makers who use the place frequently to create celluloid history. Certainly it is a photogenic cluster, with the centre-pieces including the twelfth-century abbey church of massive Gothic strength and the adjacent Château de la Marthonie, featuring some mighty fifteenth-century towers. The narrow streets around the attractive central Place l'Eglise, are graced by typical ancient Périgord houses, while the old bridge and mill add man-made charm to the natural sparkle of the Cole river. Les Templiers, the restaurant in the main square, has a reputation for fine cuisine and distinctive ambience, which is as you might expect from a community dubbed one of the *plus beaux villages de France.*

One of the most striking village settings in the region however, must be that of Jumilhac-le-Grand which is situated in the extreme north-eastern corner of the Dordogne *département*, almost on the Limousin boundary. It is a really prestigious site with the massive feudal castle topping a steep-sided gorge formed by the river Isle. The original fourteenth-century stronghold was erected by the Knights Templar, although much has been added to and modified over the centuries, however, it still bristles with turrets and towers majestically, complemented by an equally imposing adjacent Romanesque bell tower. The fiercesome stone-pile towers above the old village which is huddled subserviently below forbidding walls to create a scene that would be comfortably familiar to any medieval pilgrim nearing Jumilhac from the contemporary hillside road.

To the south of Jumilhac lies the attractive little market town of Excideuil. This is another settlement steeped in Périgord history and dominated still by a huge squat and aggressive eleventh-century keep. As with so many other fortified strongholds in the region, the builder made full use of the limestone outcrop which formed a naturally convenient base for the original defensive structure. Adjacent to the keep is the later *château* which is much more elegant and appealing to the eye, it is

the erstwhile home of the Viscount of Limoges. This is a pleasant base from which to explore the eastern sector of Périgord Vert, including a homely hotel/restaurant in the Place du Château. The surrounding countryside of the l'Isle river valley is green and undulating and there is a good variety of leisure pursuits available in the area. You can get information about all these things from the *Syndicat d'Initiative* office, also in the Place du Château.

Thiviers is a small if unremarkable town to the north-west, and while it does possess a long history there is little visual evidence of it. There is however, a popular visitor attraction in the *Foie-Gras* museum which is adjacent to a handsome and imposing church that dates from the sixteenth century. The town also boasts an attractive municipal park where an active programme of events is pursued throughout the year, from tennis tournaments to tranditional *concours de boules*. There is also a good shopping centre, with a large supermarket for self-catering, travellers.

It you continue west, the village of Villars has a two–fold attraction; it has an outstanding sixteenth–century *château*, the

Exideuil and the celebrated castle. In the background is the distinctive bell-tower of the old town church

Château de Puyguilhem which is much admired for its delicacy of structure and outline, and the nearby Grotte du Cluzeau which contains some remarkable ancient cave paintings, including some vividly alive hunting scenes, almost equal to those discovered at Lascaux. Both delights are open to visitors, while the village itself is colourfully picturesque and mellow, basking in the reflected glory of its local treasures, it proffers traditional fare in agreeable surroundings to its steady flow of summer visitors.

All the above-mentioned places are comfortably accessible – via scenic minor roads from the Verdoyer base for example – across richly-wooded hill country where traffic flow varies only

224

between light and non-existent for most months of the year. In truth, in the whole of Périgord Vert there are only a handful of sizeable towns and even these, like Thiviers and Nontron, are scarcely more than overgrown villages. However, this does for pleasurable exploration for visiting drivers.

Nontron, one of the major Périgord centres, is pleasant, congenial and mainly modern, though again it is a place with a long history and a vestigial old quarter, indicating ancient beginnings. It is no surprise, considering the strategic lofty location, to learn that there was a settlement here in the Celtic era and a fortified outpost during the Roman occupation. There is

225

also an eighteenth-century *château* which is built on ninth-century foundations and has a remnant tower and rampart wall dating from the twelfth century. The town's setting, which is quite dramatic, occupies the end of a promontory overlooking the gorges of the Bandiat river and must have seemed a formidable objective to any potential medieval aggressors.

Today it is just a charming and rather sleepy market town where no one seems in too much of a hurry. Its big cultural claim to fame is an historic puppet museum with collections of dolls and artefacts from the Napoleonic era. There is a large supermarket (dispensing less-expensive petrol), and a number of specialist restaurants, as befits a town dubbed locally as 'Gastronomic City'. Its specialities include the ubiquitous goose *confit*, trout dishes and truffle omelette. The *confits d'oie*, (goose quarters), served with parsley and potatoes are true gourmet fare. There are also one or two patisseries in the town, proffering such sweet-meat delicacies as chocolate truffles which is as much as Périgord treat as the Madeleine cakes from nearby Limousin. The tree-shaded town centre is a favoured strolling area and there are three hotels and half a dozen restaurants ready to receive those tempted to stay awhile. There is also a caravan and campingground beside the river Bandiat, about kilometre from the centre which is open from June to September.

The modern sports complex however is a bigger attraction for most, with its swimming pool, tennis courts and children's games area. The *Syndicat d'Initiative* in the Rue de Verdun dispenses free guide pamplets with maps, of scenic driving circuits ranging from 50 to 75km, together with marked local walks for those preferring to explore on foot.

Of all the townships in Périgord Vert, Brantôme is perhaps the best known and most lauded, as it represents such an historic architectural jewel in the valley of the river Dronne. It is known as the Venice of Périgord, and this tiny town, although supporting less than 2,000 inhabitants, is really an obligatory target for any visitor interested in ancient France.

Virtually an island cluster embraced by arms of the Dronne. This settlement of red-roofed old houses and maze of narrow streets, is massively dominated by the great abbey which has stood here in one form or another since the time of Charlemagne in the eighth century, and was probably on a strategic defensive island site many centuries before this. The ancient church is slightly less grand than the abbey, and has been extensively restored by architect Paul Abadie (the same architect who virtually rebuilt Périgueux Cathedral). The bell tower is original though, and remains one of the oldest in all France, parts of which stem from the time of the Norman Conquest. It tops a natural rock base, below which is a honeycomb of caves which are so prevalent in the district. In one cave, there are carvings on a vast scale representing a Judgment Day scene, dating from the fifteenth century.

While the abbey may be the crown-jewel of Brantôme, there are many lesser delights too, including a bijou Renaissance pavilion which now houses the tourist office, many fascinating alleyways which are still essentially medieval in aspect and numerous quaint waterside dwellings. There is also a great number of renowned eating houses (Brantôme is now firmly on the gourmet map), plus specialized *charcuteries* dispensing much-sought after locally cured whole hams.

On a summer evening, Brantôme really is a romatic place where you can stroll alongside sparkling waters within what were once monks gardens, amid a wealth of flowers, shrubs and tree-lined lawns, which surround the old-world houses opposite the great abbey.

Arrive early in the day if you can, for car parking is sometimes difficult and allow plenty of time to see the old town and its treasures properly. The Benedictine abbey is open every day (except Tuesday), as the Desmoulin museum of pre-history (between April and September). There are a number of high standard hotels, plus a selection of bed and breakfast houses, a full list of which is available from the tourist office, together with farmhouse and *gite* accommodation in the vicinity. The town now enjoys a very healthy visitor patronage from early spring through to late autumn.

The most famous son of this famous place was the medieval chronicler 'Brantôme', (1540–1614). This was the pen-name of Pierre de Bourdeille, who was Abbé of Brantôme, a soldier of fortune, a courtier and a staunch champion of Mary Queen of Scots. He wrote lustily, if not poetically, with uninhibited gusto, revealing vivid glimpses of the proletarian life of the period which

Brantôme. This view show part of the abbey and the Renaissance pavilion beside the old bridge

proved extremely popular – as must for the scurrilous content of his work as – with successive generations of readers, thus immortalized the adventurous soldier/churchman.

The Bourdeilles family seat can be seen about 10km to the south-west along the Dronne valley. The *château* is one of the original four baronies of the Périgord. It is a thirteenth- to sixteenth-century masterpiece of the stonemason's art, housing a significant collection of period furniture which was largely gathered by Pierre's sister-in-law. The ancient village huddled below the great *château* boasts several architectural gems, including a fine Gothic bridge and an ancient mill in the shape of a boat.

It is the *château* itself, however, that is the greatest attraction. It is a splendid edifice reflecting all the incredible skills and artistry of those medieval builders. Park at the bottom end of the village street and ascend the gentle hill across the Gothic bridge to gain one of the best views from the church gardens. There are two gems for the price of one here, for the mighty

Pierre de Bourdeille, better known as Brantôme

stone-pile is part thirteenth-century fortress, and partly a Renaissance palace never fully completed. The battlemented octagonal keep is the dominant structure amid a wealth of towers and ramparts. The palace interior is sumptuously furnished with many fine art treasures and period furniture. Bourdeilles Château is open to visitors every day in summer (closed Tuesday outside the high season).

The Dronne, which is the principal river valley of Périgord Vert, changes from a lively and invigorating torrent between St Saud and St Pardoux to a wider, more peaceful water between

229

Brantôme and Riberac. The drive, particularly alongside the river between Brantôme and Bourdeilles, is delightfully scenic and is marked by a series of huge limestone outcrops which become more frequent as landmarks, towards the south. Some of these massive slabs have been scoured by millions of years of water erosion, forming deep fissures and caves, many good examples of which may be seem on the outskirts of Brantôme. Such cave systems, culminating with those in Périgord Noir around Les Eyzies, are responsible for the claim of the region that here is *au pays de l'homme* (the land of man). These natural limestone havens played a crucial role in the settlement of wandering prehistoric tribes. It is claimed that the unique location – almost exactly halfway between the North Pole and the Equator – produced the most temperate climate in the world during that era, little has changed even today. Thus Périgord lays claim to be the veritable cradle of European *Homo sapiens*. It is certain that Renaissance man has left his mark along the Dordogne watercourses, and has done so nowhere more effectively than on the Dronne at Brantôme and Bourdeilles.

For modern mankind, the Dronne – together with its neighbouring waters – is not only a route of history but a natural playground where outdoor pursuit centres abound for enthusiasts of canoeing, horse-riding or rambling along marked trails. Canoes or kayaks may be paddled between Verneuil and Bourdeilles (about 19km), with Argos Adventure 2000 between mid June and mid September, either as day-ventures or overnighting at strategic camp grounds. This is similar to the Dordogne river enterprises. For details write to Argos, Boulevard Coligny, 24310, Brantôme, Dordogne, or Tel: 53 05 86 29.

There are several centres for horse-riding or *tourisme equestre*, in Périgord Vert, notably near Thiviers, Jumilhac-le-Grand, Lanouaille and in the vicinity of Riberac. Details are available from local *Syndicat d'Initiatives*, or write direct to the Association Departementale de Tourisme Equestre, Chambre d'Agriculture de la Dordogne, 4-6, Place Francheville, 24000 Périgueux, or Telephone 53 09 26 26.

For ramblers and backpackers there is a wide – and growing – choice of colour-coded paths and long-distance trails to explore throughout the region. The popular GR36 and GR4336 routes converge on Brantôme for example, where there is a municipal campground (as there is also at Bourdeille). In addition there are local leisure centres along the Dronne offering heated swimming pools, all-weather tennis courts and bicycle hire facilities for local exploration.

Finally, in the north-western corner of the area, there are three other high spots worthy of the explorer's attention. The first is the village of Varaignes near Javerlhac, and la Chapelle-St-Robert. This village is situated off the D75 north-west of Nontron. And you travel via another pretty approach road, alongside the river Bandiat to an intriguing old-world village graced by a central fifteenth-century *château*. Inside, within a particularly imposing courtyard of medieval character, an interesting folk museum is housed. Varaignes may be a little off the beaten track, but it is a lively village, putting on exhibitions of hand weaving and spinning periodically during the summer season.

At Javerlhac, about 4km away the twelfth-century Chapelle-St-Robert is an unusual architectural treasure. It is a Benedictine chapel in almost uniquely original condition, and although virtually untouched by restorers, it is in a remarkable state of preservation. Nearby here is a water-mill, still exploited occasionally, for extracting the renowned Périgord nut-oil from copious supplies of walnuts. Adjacent to this old mill is yet another relic of the distant past, a handsome pigeonnier, that was once an indispensible part of any prosperous pastoral community.

Take the very quiet country lane route south-west, from here, about 15km or so you'll come upon Mareuil which is the crossroads of the D939 and D708. There is another splendidly preserved early *château* here, complete with a formidable moat, great rampart walls and bulbous rounded corner towers all of which reflect fifteenth-century military architecture at its best. Mareuil was once a very important and strategic canton forming a triangle of protected countryside with Brantôme and Nontron, and was once one of the four baronies of Périgord. Now it is just the gateway to very green and pleasant terrain especially to the north of the Belle river upon which it stands. It is a popular area with both walkers and cyclists, there is camping and a small lake at nearby Vieux Mareuil and the GR36 long-distance walking trail bisects both places.

231

Part Five: **Lower Dordogne**

Monbazillac

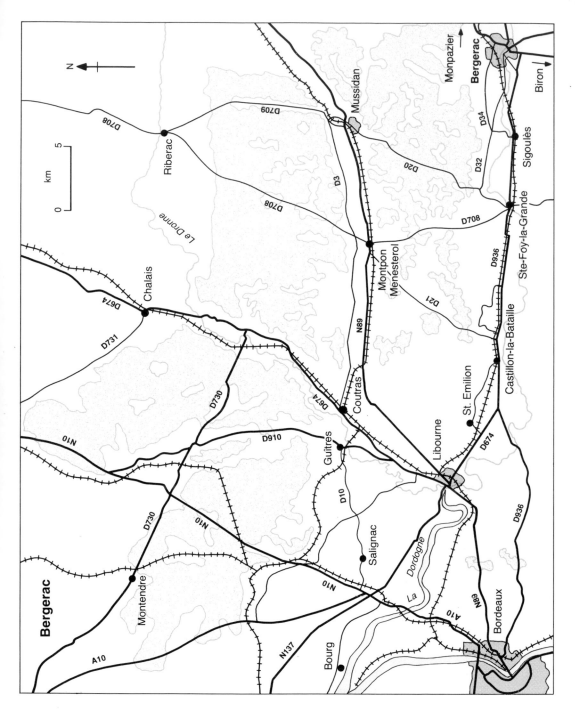

Bergerac to Bourg-sur-Gironde The wide reaches of the lower Dordogne join the waters of the Garonne to create the longest and, at times, fastest-flowing tidal estuary in France – the Gironde. Geographically and historically different in many ways from the upper and central regions the lower stretch of the Dordogne has an atmosphere of long-settled agricultural and commercial success, political stability and social affluence. This is the reward of living in a wide and fertile valley, served by an exceptionally broad and easily navigable river.

An added bonus in this area is the annual sunshine average, which becomes progressively higher on approach to the Atlantic seaboard, providing a near-perfect climate for exotic and consistently-demanded crops like grapes and tobacco. Although there has been something of a fall-off lately in trade of the latter, few would dispute the profit inherent in any well-run vineyard, especially those established on the much-envied hill slopes around Bordeaux.

Friendly, gentle countryside prevails around here and, although the river may run strongly, even fiercely, around its confluence with the Garonne, the landscape is marked by nothing threatening, of man-made or of natural origin. In the central and upper reaches of the Dordogne, on the other hand, further fortification of natural defensive high points like Domme by earlier warring generations was more or less unavoidable, while hostile gorge country slashed by unpredictable white water further upriver held limited appeal for settlers. Even today, the area is comparatively sparsely populated between Argentat and Bort-les-Orgues.

Within the Dordogne region today, the potential threats have been reduced to a uniform insignificance because of the taming

Bergerac seen from the left bank of the Dordogne

carried out by sophisticated civilization, but the scenery is still dramatic. One result of this difference in topography is perhaps the idea that the lower Dordogne is not very scenic and only marginally interesting, but there are many delights of bygone France alongside the river. This stretch of northern Aquitaine is richly endowed with treasures amid pleasing (if not spectacular) countryside, and offers the pastoral good life away from the hectic summer coastline. Cuisine and wine play a prominent part of daily life, and the sun remains hot from spring through to autumn.

Bergerac If you have just left the alluring country around the Vézère confluence for the busy D660 and the approaches to Bergerac, you may be disappointed. The traffic flow is heavy at certain hours here, and you will sense urgent urban vibrations. Grit your teeth, however, and carry on, for there is much of interest here, in the largest town on the banks of the Dordogne.

Of course, you might automatically link the name of this town with Cyrano de Bergerac, but, as far as is known, the real Cyrano never set foot in Dordogne. He was born, far to the north in 1619, Savien Cyrano, later calling himself 'de Bergerac' after the title of an estate near Paris. An adventurous and brave soldier, he possessed a brilliant and inventive mind and wrote plays and

Place de la Myrpe in Bergerac, where the old wattle and daub dwellings look down upon fictional Cyrano

science-fiction romances. He was also imprudent, dogged by ill fortune and he died at the early age of thirty-six. Cyrano was resurrected over two centuries later as the fictional swashbuckling adventurer with the enormous nose by playwright Edmond Rostand in 1897 – Cyrano de Bergerac.

The city fathers of Bergerac in the *département* of Dordogne do not readily own up to the fact that there is no connection. Some of their tourist revenue is undoubtedly gleaned from the myth that Cyrano was a son of this ancient and colourful town. There are statues of him in two prominent places (neither are very good), while restaurants, cafés and other commercial enterprises boldly infer that Cyrano was a true citizen of Bergerac by using his name.

One truth we do know about Bergerac is that is was almost certainly so named because it was a place where flocks of sheep were gathered and marketed, although this ancient connotation is today of little significance. We know, too, that Bergerac, during its long and frequently violent history, was once the principal centre of ancient Périgord. It was much more important than Périgueux, because of its strategic riverside location which, in early medieval France, led to commercial power and therefore influential administrative and political strength. It declined, languished and eventually became almost a backwater, largely because it was for a long time a staunch Protestant stronghold in a predominantly Catholic land.

Today, Bergerac is a place of growing prosperity, partially reliant on tourism, but primarily concerned with the wine industry and agriculture. At first glance there seem to be few visible signs of an earlier age, but the one or two clues that *are* there are more easily read by those who know a little about the town's history.

Modern Bergerac spreads busily though quite compactly to either side of the river, but the original and most interesting part covers the gentle hillside on the northern, right bank. Standing at the southern end of the gracefully arched bridge which links the suburb of La Madeleine to contemporary Bergerac's centre, you can see clearly the reasons for the town's importance. The contours of the natural terrain make it a perfect site for a settlement, south-facing, partly protected by the low hill line from prevailing westerly winds, and, above all, on the first really easily-navigable reach of river to be found south-west of the Dordogne source. The gentle bend of the river allowed good river-craft manoeuvrability and easy ferry crossings. Defensively, to medieval eyes, the site was perhaps not perfect, but there was sufficient elevation of a natural kind to give reasonable observation across the wide valley approaches. And the industrious stonemasons of old could soon throw up defensive ramparts, even in time a nearly impregnable citadel, to protect the town's inhabitants.

This important Périgord crossroads was established therefore, as a centre for transporting boat-loads of produce from the surrounding vineyards and tobacco-growing plantations to the other great ports of the day – Libourne and Bordeaux. From Gascony and Guenne in the fourteenth century, something like 100,000 tuns of wine were exported, and about a quarter found their way into England via the port of Bristol, while large quantities also went to the Dutch. For a long time the wine trade flourished supplemented later by the tobacco trade, and meanwhile stone quarries were established in the town's environs, along with tanneries, flour mills and iron foundries. Crops from the fertile soil were copious and also yielded its bounty including seasonal salmon. Bergerac grew more and more prosperous, populous and Protestant as the Middle Ages wore on. It also became more Anglicized. It was largely because of its Protestantism and its Anglicization that Bergerac deteriorated and then declined drastically in importance.

In the twelfth century, during the reign of Henry II of England, the royal domains stretched virtually from the Scottish borders to the Pyrénées, and half of France was the king's inheritance. Few citizens of either country felt themselves to be indisputably French or English at this time, and allegiance was essentially local. During the period from the Norman Conquest until the seventeenth-century reign of Louis XIV (despite the Hundred Years War between France and England), loyalty was to the neighbourhood baron-lord, who was himself often at odds with any crowned head, whether English or French.

Around the time of Edward Prince of Wales (1330–1376), Bergerac was definitely an English stronghold. The Black Prince set forth from Bergerac in 1336 with his army for the crucial battle of Poitiers, the most significant battle of the Hundred Years War. It culminated in the capture of King John of France, and Edward was proclaimed Prince of Aquitaine, with a vast and illustrious court at Bordeaux. For a while there was peace, until Charles V of France and his powerful baron allies declare all English possessions forfeit, by 1369 all south-west France was in revolt. Bergerac was stormed, besieged and fought over, being alternately occupied by both French and English forces, and finally being taken for the last time by the French in 1450.

Although there was again a peaceful interlude this was not the end of Bergerac's troubles. The town suffered cruelly during the debilitating Religious Wars of the mid-sixteenth century, which lasted (with a lengthy intermission between the Edict and Revocation of Nantes, 1598 and 1685 respectively), for another century and a half. Massacres were commonplace, and on St Bartholomew's Day in 1572 thousands of Protestants were butchered in Paris.

During the reign of Louis XIII (1601–1643), the government, more or less run by Cardinal Richelieu, became suspicious of Bergerac's religious loyalty and ordered the demolition of the ancient citadel and the riverbank fortifications. As you look upon the lowish line of contemporary ochre-coloured roofs, and the oddly spacious aprons of concrete that spread along the north-

239

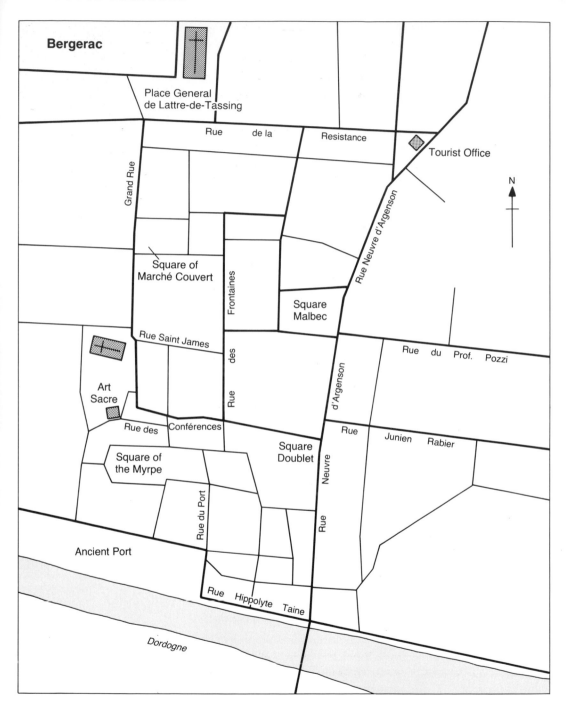

Bergerac

Place General
de Lattre-de-Tassing

Rue   de la   Resistance

Tourist Office

Grand Rue

N

Rue Neuvre d'Argenson

Square of
Marché Couvert

Frontaines

Square
Malbec

Rue Saint James

des

Art
Sacre

Rue

Rue du Prof. Pozzi

d'Argenson

Rue des   Conférences

Square
Doublet

Rue   Junien   Rabier

Square of
the Myrpe

Neuvre

Rue du Port

Rue

Ancient Port

Rue Hippolyte   Taine

Dordogne

bank waterside, consider how this town *would* have appeared before it was partly demolished in 1621. There was a fine medieval *bastide* and fortified bastion. The thought may help you to appreciate more fully the diminutive but delightful remnants of ancient Bergerac among modern buildings on the opposite side of the river.

The old town of Bergerac is a compact quadrangle to the west of the Rue Neuve d'Argenson (where the tourist office is situated), and north of the river. It is perhaps best explored by starting at the hilltop and working down gradually from the Palais de Justice, via quaint alleyways like Passage Bobinski, to the covered market. At the north-west corner of this square there is an interesting old building (now a shop), graved with a corner turret and gable-end, the remains of a medieval dwelling where Charles IX of France stayed in 1565. At the time the building was adjacent, not to the covered market of today, but to a Protestant church. This was destroyed 117 years later, just three years before the Revocation of the Nantes edict which had forbidden freedom of unorthodox worship.

Bergerac

Because of its geographical location, Bergerac was also on the pilgrim trail to Compostela. Evidence of this is in the St Jacques church, once a pilgrim hostel, and, in the Rue St James and the Rue des Fontaines, good examples of a preserved fourteenth-century hostelry, the Vieille Auberge, and some fifteenth-century houses.

The Rue de la Myrpe and the Place de la Myrpe have some really ancient wattle-and-daub dwellings enclosing a tree-shaded formal garden, where there is an unimposing statue of Rostand's Cyrano. Inevitably perhaps, someone has vandalized his nose. You should also see the monastery, now the headquarters of the regional wine council (its original chapel has been converted to a Protestant church by popular local request), the ancient cottages of the Rue de Conférences, and the Place Pélissière with its attractive fountain. On the site of the original wharves stood the medieval castle which was once flanked by two quays, constantly bustling with timber unloading from upriver Auvergne and with wine shipments being readied from export.

Don't miss: Area west of Rue Neuve d'Argenson; Rue and Place de la Myrpe; Rue de Conférences; Maison Peyrarède.

Another major crop of the region, tobacco, is commemorated by a museum (unique in France), housed in the distinctive Maison Peyrarède, a handsome turreted and arched fifteenth-century building, once the Hôtel de Ville. There are many fascinating exhibits devoted to the weed, including some magnificent carved pipes, as well as several paintings by old masters. It is open each day, save Mondays. This house faces the Rue d l'Ancien Pont – the original bridge (of which remnants can still be seen), destroyed in 1783. The oldest identifiable buildings of Bergerac are in Rue d'Albret, where, among some truly venerable traces, there are some massive thirteenth-century window arches.

You really need at least two or three days to see the old town properly. Away from the almost constantly busy Rue Neuve Argenson, it is delightfully tranquil, interestingly busy, small enough to enjoy as a pedestrian sightseer, and stimulatingly colourful. There are many cafés and good restaurants, including some serving regional dishes, and you will definitely find something, whether you want a snack or a *cordon bleu* feast.

For a leisurely evening stroll take the riverside route west from the heart of the old town and port. This is virtually traffic-free after half a kilometre or so, and has some nice views across the wide and gently-flowing Dordogne. After dark, evening entertainment during long summer season is provided by 'pubs', American bars, speciality restaurants offering a range of delicacies from *fruits de mer* to Moroccan *couscous*, *brasseries* and traditional wine bars and two discos.

Bergerac is one of the prime long-stay tourist towns in Périgord, with a good choice of accommodation. There are five three-star hotels (three with restaurants), three two-star hotels (including, of course, a Hôtel le Cyrano), plus half a dozen economy hotels and an agreeable municipal campsite in a pleasant riverside setting. Called La Pelouse, it is tree-shaded, close to the centre, and open all year round. The tourist office is at the top of the gentle hill in the modern centre. First-timers to the region might make a point of asking for a copy of the *Dordogne Telegraph*, a free guide printed primarily for the growing enclave of British residents. The tourist office is open all year round.

Around Bergerac The ancient region of Périgord was divided into two principal regions – Périgord Blanc, centred on Périgueux, and Périgord Noir, around Sarlat. Later divisional additions were Périgord Vert, to the north-east of Périgueux, and finally Périgord Pourpre which has Bergerac as its hub. These locations are rather vague and romantic today, within the boundaries of the official Dordogne *département*, which is much smaller than the old Périgord, the 'land of 1,001 *châteaux*'.

'Purple' Périgord includes some interesting places within easy reach of Bergerac, most of them adjacent to the Dordogne river and primarily to the west. (For that part of Périgord Pourpre east of Bergerac, *see* pages 143 – 231.)

Monbazillac The first delightful mini-excursion from Bergerac is to nearby Monbazillac, an imposing hilltop *château* of gleaming white rounded towers. This raised stone island sits in a sea of vineyards which radiate in all directions across undulating green slopes. The *château*, about 6km south of Bergerac, has been a massive landmark since the mid-sixteenth century, and the region around it has been producing some of France's finest sweet white wine for longer even than that, in a perfect wine-growing climate and terrain.

The great *château* is now the property of the local wine co-operative, and a museum open to visitors all year round. It is only partly devoted to viticulture nowadays, also dealing with the

Hunters among the vineyards below majestic Château Monbazillac

243

Protestant religious history that is so important in this part of Dordogne. There is a *dégustation* centre, as well as a retail outlet for the renowned *appellation*, and an atmospheric restaurant within the magnificent interior. The most famous of Dordogne wine, Monbazillac mellows with age, becoming more and more amber-tinted, and smoother and richer with the passage of years.

To reach Monbazillac from Bergerac, take the renowned Bordelais Wine Route, which begins along the D13. At first it goes through a flat and uninspiring landscape close to the local aerodrome, then it gradually ascends via minor roads to the great *châteaux*. There are fine views across the wide Dordogne valley from this hill ridge, with the tall spire of Bergerac church dominant.

Bridoire A short distance south-west of Monbazillac is Bridoire Château, which is worth seeing. Built originally as a Protestant castle in the mid-sixteenth century, it was badly damaged during the Wars of Religion, and then splendidly restored during the last and present centuries. Like a mini-Monbazillac, this castle with its white machicolations stands upon a knoll amid a particularly lush enclave of Bergeracois country. Visitors are not permitted, but a cat can look at a king and, despite the massive defensive walls, it is possible to see from one or two vantage points just off the minor road.

Eymet Between the vineyards, serried rows of immaculately tended vines on the small roads to the south-west are half-hidden old manor houses of old, isolated fortified farmhouses, atmospheric villages and marvellous *bastides* like Eymet.

Eymet's history goes back to the Iron Age. It was a settlement in the eighth century, a Bénédictine priory in the eleventh century, and a fortified *bastide* created by Alphonse de Poitiers in the thirteenth century. The main square, with some imposing fourteenth- and fifteenth-century architecture, is the Place Gambetta; see also the ancient castle keep, the *château* museum and the thirteenth-century bridge spanning the river Dropt.

Turn north from here for Sigoules and Pomport, where there is a lakeside leisure centre and camping park in countryside rich with ancient vineyards. This is a good area for *gîtes ruraux*, and *chambre d'hote* overnight accommodation.

Forêt du Landais North-west along the D15 from Sigoules, the Dordogne river is crossed at the village of Gardonne, and then you can return to Bergerac via La Force. La Force is pretty with a finely restored central square, an excellent *Logis de France* hotel and the remains of a great *château*, prominent during the Wars of Religion. A grand arched coaching entrance survives, dedicated to the first Duc de la Force (1558–1652).

Immediately north of here lies the extensive and beautiful Forêt du Landais, which covers a wide part of Périgord Pourpre above the Dordogne river. This is a vast haven of mixed woodland, networked by many minor roads, most of which carry only the lightest of traffic even in high summer.

Extensive though the Landais woods are, they are just part of a much larger forested area which covers almost all of Dordogne *département* to the north-west of Bergerac. And this huge wooded area is actually expanding, largely as a result of the massive tree-planting programme instigated after *phylloxera* (vine pest) decimated the Périgord vineyards towards the end of the nineteenth century.

Timber production in south-west France has steadily increased, but the Republic has not been heavily reliant on conifer varieties, which only account for about one-third of the total around here. The rest of the trees are broad-leaved, with many oak, and four or five species that are indigenous to this part of the world. Walnut and chestnut thrive in the soil and climate, and are richly

The richly arable slopes south of Bergerac

245

bountiful as well, and ash, poplar and lime are also encouraged and widespread. The Forêr du Landais is divided from the equally expansive Forêt de la Double by the narrow valley of the river Isle. Together they form a gloriously wide swathe of forest, river and lakes north-west of Mussidan.

Wine and Food For the wine buff, the countryside between Bergerac and Bordeaux is an Aladdin's cave, since the whole area is largely devoted to the grape. There are some 40,000 hectares of vine-covered slopes around Bergerac alone. The choice of local riches is almost bewildering: Bergerac dry, mellow Côtes de Bergerac, fruity rosé or Montravel, Saussignac, Monbazillac sweet white, and the superb, full-blooded red Pécharmant, cultivated in a very small area to the north-east of Bergerac.

Other superior appellations will be found *en route* between Bergerac and Eymet. Selections from a wide range of vintages will be served wherever you go, as the perfect accompaniment to renowned regional culinary treats like trout, pike, *foie gras, confits, cèpes* and the world-famous 'black diamonds' – truffles. The people of Périgord not only enjoy some of the best wines that France produces, but they also make mouth-watering meals, mainly quite simple, often very slowly cooked. In a quite recent peasant past, any Périgord housewife could produce a meal from basic ingredients. Game, fish, poultry, duck, and pork – staple of every old-time smallholder – were enhanced with mushrooms, chestnuts, walnuts, garlic and herbs both cultivated and wild, and eaten with potatoes and cheese. These ingredients came from the fertile local terrain, and were blended and cooked over wood-burning stove for hours. Although methods may not be so leisurely today the culinary reputation of the area is upheld in many family-owned inns and restaurants. One high-class restaurant in an atmospheric setting is the four-star La Closerie St Jacques (Tel: 53 58 37 77) at Le Bourg village near Monbazillac, where two couples have built themselves a name for gastronomic treats of the Périgourdine variety.

Bergerac – Useful Information

Tourist office: 97 Rue Neuve d'Argenson (opposite Place de la République) – Tel: 53 57 03 11 open all year, staff speak English. There are 14 hotels (8 with restaurants), in town, and a dozen restaurants, pizzerias and brasseries. Within the Bergerac environs there are a further 30 hotels with restaurants, plus half a dozen restaurants specializing in regional cuisine. As one would expect in a very popular tourist area there are also numerous furnished accommodations, urban and rural, full lists of which are obtainable on request from the S.I. The riverside municipal touring site is called La Pelouse, (Tel: 53 57 06 67) – well signposted on all approach roads.

Leisure Amenities: While most independent travellers probably prefer to explore Bergerac individually, guided tours of the old town are arranged by the *Syndicat d'Initiative* during summer, for groups of ten or more. Apart from the celebrated Musée du Tabac, there is the House of Wine, the museum of wine and traditional craft and the art museum of wine and traditional craft and the art museum, all of which are open daily during summer (save Mondays). There is ample evening entertainment in town, plus three discos in the vicinity.

All services are available in Bergerac, as might be expected from a town of this size including car repair garages, car hire, taxis, bicycle hire (SNCF). There is a pleasant leisure park (Base de Loisirs), a few kilometres south-west, providing good bathing, tennis and fishing together with camping and caravanning facilities (Tel: 53 58 81 94).

The Gateway to Périgord Sarlat and Rocamadour are synonymous with Dordogne valley splendour, but there are other, less well-known settlements near the river which are just as intriguing in their way. About 22km west of Bergerac, on the D936, is Sainte-Foy-la-Grande, a tiny centre that is a fine example of the preserved past, close to the Dordogne *département* boundary, in the neighbouring *département* of Gironde. Its history goes back to the thirteenth century.

Over a hundred years after the original alliance between Henry Plantaganet and Eleanor of Aquitaine, Edward I of England arrived in France (in 1254) to take up his inheritance of the duchy of Gascony. He kept a partial if tenuous hold on Aquitaine, partly through a second marriage to a French princess, but he was always opposed by powerful medieval barons. He had to make constant concessions to these dangerous warlords, since they could not be defeated by force of arms.

Aquitaine suffered a troubled era as a result, with towns and villages suddenly finding themselves subject to new and different

247

The gracious medieval arcades of Ste-Foy-la-Grande

powers that were not always benign. Predominantly English enclaves, particularly, were at risk. Consequently between the middle of the thirteenth and the middle of the fourteenth centuries, nearly one hundred and fifty *bastides*, both French and English were created throughout south-western France. These ingeniously fortified towns of geometrical grid layout, were stoutly defended and peopled by inhabitants who were granted special charters in return for their loyalty.

Ste-Foy-la-Grande (like the *bastide* of Eymet) was founded by Alphonse de Poitiers (1220–1271). He was a crusading son of Louis VIII, a pious if stern administrator, who helped significantly to restore political and social order after the height of the Albigensian Wars. The Albigensians, named after the town of Albi where they settled (although the majority were centred on Toulouse), were a heretic sect which infiltrated south-western France around the start of the thirteenth century. Also known as Cathars, their essential belief was that there were two gods, one good, one evil. They claimed to be true Christians, but were

248

damned by orthodoxy. The purest of the Albigensians, known as 'Perfects', practised total abstention from sexual contact with women, and from meat-eating.

Obviously (if only because of the risk of vital population increase!) this movement could not be allowed to escalate from its Languedoc stronghold, as it threatened to do at the start of the thirteenth century. Encouraged by papal decree, forces were dispatched from the north on a ruthless crusade which waxed and waned for decades, and in 1245 the Inquisition condemned and burned 200 heretics in a single day. The movement had been persecuted for over a century before this final Catholic assault, not only in France but also in Italy, Germany and England. Despite ruthless and widespread extermination, the Albigensians did survive in odd pockets within the mountainous regions of Ariège until the early part of the fourteenth century.

In this uncertain and dangerous era Alphonse de Poitiers had to establish a degree of stability. The existence of numerous, unstable fiefdoms held by rapacious barons across Gascony, Guienne and neighbouring Poitou, guaranteed attack at some time for any prosperous town or village. Especially vulnerable were those in strategic locations, with stretches of navigable river where trading barges and bankside storehouses might be plundered.

The oldest French *bastide*, Mont-de-Marsan in the Landes *département* of Aquitaine, was founded in 1141. A century later the building technique had reached a high level of cunning sophistication. The essence of defensive success lay in simplicity and uniformity. The streets ran, at right angles or parallel to each other, from a large central square often dominated by a fortified church or keep (donjon). The whole was surrounded by ramparts, with just one or two easily defended town entrances or *ports*. *Bastides* (from the old Provençal *bastida*, or 'building') were not formidable fortresses but simply new towns which could defend themselves against attack.

Ste-Foy-la-Grande was an important half-way river port between Bergerac and Libourne in medieval times so it was a prime candidate for conversion. Even today it is not too difficult to visualize the medieval original, which eventually became a staunch Protestant stronghold. Although only a kernel of ancient Ste-Foy remains, the grid pattern streets and vestigial ramparts are

249

Ste-Foy-la-Grande was once a very hectic barge port. Now only strollers use the massive quay

there to add atmosphere to this contemporary riverside town. It is fascinating to stroll around, conjecturing how the place might have appeared in 1337, when Edward III made his claim as King of France, thus causing the hostilities which lasted until 1453.

By the mid-fourteenth century, Ste-Foy was probably quite a good place to live, since it was commercially successful, and well defended. Its citizens are likely to have lived better that the average peasant, whose existence was often one of grinding poverty, overwhelmingly governed by religious devotion. Domination by the Church over such rural inhabitants was absolute, with eternal sweet after-life promised to the pious, and eternal damnation in hell to the wicked. Poorer families often slept in a communal bed, sharing room space with domestic

250

animals, vermin and a host of parasites. Privacy of a personal kind was virtually unknown to the majority of medieval Europeans.

For a very small minority, however, there was a degree of comparatively good living, and this minority included the more prominent citizens lucky enough to live in a *bastide* like Ste-Foy-la-Grande.

Almost no evidence of very early Ste-Foy remains, but there are traces of riverside ramparts, including a truncated round tower on the Quai de la Brèche, the fine turreted Maison de la Tour du Temple (now the tourist office), and the municipal library with its elegant arch supports, all mid-fourteenth-century structures in and around the delightfully arcaded central square. The square would have been a market place in medieval days, but it is now

251

occupied by a handsome town hall. Where the tall-spired Gothic church now stands, opposite the old town centre square, was once a thirteenth-century Knights Templar temple, but this was destroyed when the Knights were proscribed for becoming too powerful.

Today Ste-Foy is a lively, atmospheric town although there are reminders of hard times. Several plaques and flower-filled shrines around the town commemorate fallen Resistance fighters from World War II, while a plaque on a one-time mayor's house tells passers-by that it was deliberately blown up by the Nazis.

Don't miss: Traces of ramparts; Maison de la Tour du Temple; Municipal library.

Ste-Foy has many interesting nooks and corners on both sides of the Dordogne, and is a good base from which to explore either the Wine Trail or the Bastide Circuit in this part of Aquitaine. It is an officially-designated *Station de Longue Durée*, and there is a reasonable choice of hotels and restaurants, furnished self-catering accommodation, *chambres d'hôte,* and *gîtes ruraux* in the surrounding countryside. There is also a pleasant, well-run three-star camping site, the municipal La Tuilerie, with 250 pitches beside the river, within five minutes' stroll of the town. Tennis courts, a canoe-kayak centre, and coarse fishing are available in the vicinity of the river. There are five hotels in town; try the three-star Grand in the Rue de la République, or the modest L'Europe pension in Place Gambetta for value for money. This little town is a good starting point of any west-to-east exploration of the great river valley; hence the tag of Gateway to the Périgord. Equally, it can be your Gateway to the Gironde.

A Brief Excursion One pleasant drive-and-walk excursion from Ste-Foy begins at the hamlet of Le Fleix, some 5km east, upriver. Park here in front of the *mairie*, in the centre of a quaint village which was once a Roman settlement on a particularly pretty reach of the Dordogne. From here take the ascending lane, the D32 signposted to Fougueyrolles.

You have returned momentarily to the *département* of Dordogne and, though a degree of road walking is involved, the surroundings are rural and the traffic is very light. In about 1½ km you will pass a Resistance monument on your right among the trees, one of several in this region which commemorate August 1944.

There is a nice viewpoint over the river valley from this quiet road, and in 2½ km from Le Fleix, still ascending, you can take a

signposted track on the right, towards Capdefert. This is a section
of a *randonnée* (the GR6D) which circles through the isolated
hamlet of Ponchapt, just to the north. An agreeable, part-wooded
trail leads past a red and white radio tower, above a farm and on
along the ridge of the highest contour in the area. Even wider
views over the valley are now revealed; the return walk, all
downhill, takes much less time than the outward trip.

Travelling west from Ste-Foy-la-Grande, avoid the busy D936
by taking back-country roads, initially along the banks of the
wide Dordogne. Take the D672 from the western perimeter of
Ste-Foy, to Pont de la Beauze and the village of St-André-les-
Appelles, then join the D130 from Eynesse. This is a picturesque
Gallo-Roman site (Celtic name Ena), where there are remnants
of medieval fortifications reputed to have been a stronghold of
Knights Templar.

On the road between Eynesse and Pessac, look out for an
extensive commercial garden nursery, specializing in roses but also
having a wide variety of other species, and shrubs and trees. It is a
marvellous display, and illustrates how fertile this lower part of the
river valley is.

There are secluded camping grounds at Eynesse and at Pessac.
Pessac is an unspoiled village alongside the Dordogne, amid a
patchwork of well-rended fruit orchards and arable farm fields,
broken by a wealth of woods and coppices. Eynesse has a
distinctive medieval church and a *château*. This must have been an
exclusive, and secluded, reach of the Dordogne. From tiny Pessac
you cross the Dordogne (thus returning to the Dordogne
département) and then continue northwards to cross the D936 for
Montcaret.

There is evidence of a colourful and exciting kind here that this
area was much favoured by the Romans. Just up the hill from the
bustle of the main east–west transit road lies the slumbering village
of Montcaret, peaceful and slow-paced and coyly exposing just a
fragment of its ancient treasure to casual visitors who may be passing
the churchyard. Montcaret possesses a priceless heritage treasure
which dates back to a century or so before the birth of Christ.

Montcaret's treasure is a remarkable and brightly coloured
mosaic depicting fish and mythical beasts, as immaculately-laid
Roman flooring that makes the Middle Ages seem like yesterday.

There must have been a magnificent villa here, and the fact that remnants of it have survived is thanks to a Christian church being built on the site around the time of the Norman Conquest of Britain. Painstaking work by archaeologists later has preserved the remnants. To see the mosaic at close quarters you must acquire a ticket and a personal guide; enquire at the adjacent guardian's house. It is worth persuing – there are remains of thermal baths as well as those of a villa. The Pierre Tauziac National Museum is open all year round, but not from 12noon to 2 pm.

Montcaret lies just inside 'Purple Périgord'. A little to the north-west, adjacent to the village of St Michel de Montaigne, is the home of one of France's greatest literary figures of the sixteenth century – the Château de Montaigne.

Michel de Montaigne was born in 1533, doubly blessed by a towering literary talent, and a wealthy merchant father who could not have been more concerned for his son's future. He insisted that his son should be awakened by music each morning, and be spoken to exclusively in Latin until he reached the age of six. In an age of blind bigotry (the Wars of Religion continued virtually throughout Montaigne's life), Montaigne senior permitted two of his five children to become Protestant, although he himself was a devout Catholic. He insisted, too, that Michel should have local villagers as godparents, so that he should know ordinary folk as well as the high-born.

Michel de Montaigne became Mayor of Bordeaux, friend and advisor of kings, and above all a writer of uncanny perception about the human condition. His writings, staggeringly outspoken for the time – especially about sexual matters – placed him firmly and permanently among the giants of French literature. He advocated total equality between the sexes, and like most great thinkers, was centuries ahead of his time. His *Essays* contain lessons on decent human behaviour which remain highly relevant today. This gifted seeker of the truth outlived his great friend and fellow-writer La Boétie, and died in 1592.

The original family manor house was burned to the ground late in the nineteenth century and, while the restoration is impressive enough, with towers and machicolations, it contains nothing of medieval craftsmanship. The crucial structure of the ancient estate survives – the tower where he wrote his best work between 1572 and 1588. After his death, his heart, as was the practice, was buried separately in the village church Montaigne's tower and a section of the *château* are open to visitors.

Gironde and the Bordelais Over the Dordogne *département* boundary and westwards into Gironde, the Dordogne river continues its course across Aquitaine to the sea. Here again the character of the countryside changes subtly. The largest concentration of quality vineyards in the world spreads across the north-western corner of Gironde the largest *département* in France – 105km from north to south and 130km from east to west. Radiating from Bordeaux, the Bordelais vineyards cover a staggering 100,000 hectares, producing, on average, 500 million bottles of wine every year.

Wine is not the only attraction in the Gironde area (locally, the 'Pays de Castillon-Pujols'). The views are distant and the sky is almost invariably blue as you approach the wedge of wine-growing country between the Dordogne and the Garonne rivers, known as the Entre-Deux-Mers. The name was given because both rivers have tidal swells at their western extremities.)

The Romans built a military road in France, linking Poitiers (to the north) with the Pyrénées passes, and it crossed the Dordogne at a fording place near here called the Rauzen Pass. The ruins of a fourteenth-century feudal castle and a twelfth-century church can be seen at the little township of Rauzan, just off the D671 Sauveterre road. There are many other legacies of medieval France in this region, with fine architecture efficiently preserved by the favourable climate. Don't miss the splendid Romanesque church of Pujols, or the *château* and castle ruins of Lamothe-Montravel, surrounded by water-meadows and vine-covered slopes, and in a countryside that is invariably bathed in a bright warm light from spring to autumn. The landscape, networked by almost traffic-free minor roads, is delightful to explore, especially since at almost every village or hamlet, you can taste wine and perhaps enjoy some of the best local cuisine. Countless viticulture estates have at their hub an elegant *château* which makes the perfect setting.

These evocative *châteaux* from a more gracious age dot the skyline all across this Bordelais landscape. Some are just 'modest' country houses, or simply imposing farmhouses, while others are conversions or restorations of the most spectacular medieval fortress mansions, with towers, spires and protective walls. Many welcome visitors (though not all), to taste their vintage selection, follow a conducted tour and, of course, buy a bottle or two.

The Wines From sweet Sauterne to dry white Graves, from delicate Bordeaux Rosé, to the rich red of Saint Emilion and Médoc, all the famous names are local here. And a high percentage of names you haven't heard of will be on the labels of fine wines, probably bottled on the premises. Wine-tasting, choosing and buying has become almost an art form in this region for French visitors.

There is no question that the subject of wine – the minutiae concerned with its production and ultimate enjoyment – is the principal reason for visiting this part of Aquitaine. During high summer, clusters of eager *aficionados* file devoutly into *dégustation* annexes or *château* cellars, displaying a real enthusiasm. And it is very unlikely that they will find a bad wine, or even an indifferent one, in a Bordelais *château* cellar; I've been searching for years and it has not happened to me yet! For those aspiring to the exalted name of 'wine buff', the major Bordelais vineyards are as follows.

The Médoc is one of the most envied wine-growing areas in France. The superb reds are produced from a stretch of pebble and sand soil which stretches for some 85km along the left bank of the Gironde estuary, to the north of Bordeaux. The vines are rooted deep into a soil that is so thin, no other crop would thrive in it. The region is sub-divided into Médoc and Haut-Médoc.

South and east of Bordeaux, is Graves and Sauterne country, primarily located along the left bank of the river Garonne. Forty-three *communes* make up this region, covering about 50km and producing superior red and dry whites, together with sweet and semi-sweet varieties.

The Entre-Deux-Mers region is the home of the largest quantity of the Bordeaux *appellation* wines, including reds, rosés, and dry and semi-sweet whites. Across the vast plateaux, sandwiched between these two major rivercourses with their succession of valleys, streams and gentle hill flanks, is the most extensive concentration of vineyards in the Gironde *département*. They cover a huge triangle, from Ste-Foy-la-Grande in the east and Bordeaux in the west, to Langon, on the fringe of the vast Landes area, to the south.

Bordelais Wine regions:
Médoc; Graves; Sauterne; Entre-Deux-Mers; Côtes de Bourg; Saint Emilion; Libourne.

256

On the right bank of the Dordogne, and just to the north of its confluence with the Garonne, are the Côtes de Bourg. Here some of the best red wines are produced along the riverbanks, and some premier whites in the immediate hinterland hill slopes around Blaye on the Gironde estuary.

The final wine region, which the dedicated Dordogne explorer may quarter extensively, is Saint Emilion and Libourne. There are more envied *appellations* here, including some of the very best reds from nine *communes* which comprise the vineyards around Saint Emilion and across the extended hill flanks above Libourne and Fronsac, west of the river Isle.

In this one *département*, where nearly half of all France's fine wines are produced, you will also find the most famous of wine vintages, including Château Haut-Brion and Château-Lafite Rothschild (located in central Médoc). The *appellation d'origine contrôlée* (AOC) is a guarantee of fine wine authenticity. To be entitled to it, the wines must be made from grapes harvested in the precise areas named. Wines labelled 'Bordeaux' and 'Bordeaux Superior' *must* come from the acknowledged wine-growing enclave within the *département* of Gironde. All the 'superior' wines are subject to strict and arbitrary examination, performed regularly at a special centre not far from Libourne.

Certain wines, selected from several vineyard locations within the region, are blended and brand-named to provide consistent quality from one bottle to the next, and even from one year to the next. Others come exclusively from a particular *château*, and have their own personality developed by the grower, the cellar master, the oak-barrel cooper, the cork-maker and, of course, the merchant, who is constantly concerned for the quality of a product which will carry his signature.

For each wine-growing area there will be a *Maison du Vin*, where you can get local information, especially about those *châteaux* open to visitors. There are centres at Ste-Foy-la-Grande, Castillon-la-Bataille, Saint Emilion, Fronsac, Bourg-sur-Gironde and as far south as Langon. The main *Maison du Vin* is, of course, at Bordeaux. In addition, for those wishing to trace the origins of their favoured vintages, there are seven colour-coded road circuits around the Bordelais vineyards. Maps are freely available at *Maisons du Vin* and *Syndicat d'Initiative* offices in the locality.

257

Castillon-la-Bataille The first important township inside the *département* of eastern Gironde for those following the course of the Dordogne is Castillon-la-Bataille. If you are interested in Anglo-French history, this is one of the most significant locations in the country; the French won a decisive victory here in 1453. That battle, on 17 July, brought an end to the Hundred Years War, and dispossessed the English of the hold on a large part of French soil which they had maintained from almost 400 years.

At that turbulent period in the mid-fifteenth century, when Aquitaine owed allegiance to the English King (and, through its great capital and port of Bordeaux, gave him a lucrative living), the idea of liberation by the French held little appeal. For Castillon, as for other towns in the Gascony province England was the ally. However, the French ruling class were persistent with their claim to the territory, and heavy taxes were imposed where possible by the French King, Charles VII. Reputed to be the son of a madman Charles was unpopular already (he did nothing to save Joan of Arc), and the new taxes were the last straw. A deputation was sent to London, and Henry VI King of England and France, was asked to intervene against the French in Aquitaine.

Henry VI (1421–1471) was not a resolute king. He was deviously manipulated by his ministers, and his reign suffered many political disasters, including the loss of Normandy and part of the Aquitaine duchy (Guienne province), including Bordeaux. Simple, pious, trusting and humane, Henry was a gentle man, possessing virtues that did not serve a medieval king well. After a prolonged dynastic struggle, he was dethroned, and (almost certainly) murdered in May 1471.

During the 1450s Henry had rebellion troubles in England and his response to the French was to dispatch an aged general named Talbot. When the fiery old general landed at Bordeaux he quickly restored faith in English rule, and then, advancing inland along the right bank of the Dordogne, he overwhelmed a French garrison at Fronsac. The climax of the uneasy truce between the two royal houses approached. France was in turmoil, with famine and constant warring between various factions, but Charles's heavy taxes were enabling him to retain a large and well-equipped army. The English army had been drastically weakened by the Wars of the Roses at home, and the

powerful Burgundian princes had turned from allies into enemies in Europe.

The showdown came on the low hills above the Dordogne between Lamothe-Montravel and Castillon. Talbot led the English and Gascon troops, a stubborn, harsh warlord, brave but headstrong, with a very successful, if ruthless, military record. Presuming to overwhelm the Castillon encampment with the same ease and speed with which he had taken Fronsac, he ordered a cavalry charge without waiting for artillery support. The French had their own cannon *in situ* and the English forces were cut to pieces in one of the first concerted artillery barrages of history. Talbot, probably in his late sixties, was killed.

About 4,000 men lay dead at the end of the day, and eye-witnesses claimed that the waters of the Dordogne around the Pas de Rauzen ran red with French and English blood. Talbot himself spilled drops of each as he died, since his family were direct descendents of the Norman conquerors of England. His son was also killed in the battle. The French eventually erected a monument on the site, and called it the Talbot Memorial. This a pencil-slim landmark stands just to the east of Castillon.

The battlefield memorial column of Castillon-de-Mataille. It was here that the Hundred Years War finally ended

259

Charles VII was happy enough about finally annexing Aquitaine to the French crown, but he was angry with the Gascons for having elicited English help and he punished the region severely. Almost a decade of ruin and misery followed the battle, and not even the precious vineyards were cultivated. A pardon for the province was only forthcoming when the son of Charles, Louis XI, paid a state visit in 1462, to liberate essential commerce and instil social stability once more.

Contemporary Castillon is bustling and lively, with a mellow and picturesque waterfront, graced by individual old houses on either side of the river bridge. The town centre is tree-shaded and typical of southern French in its aspect and the layout of its streets, with narrow alleyways running off the main roads. There is a colourful general market held here every Monday and a flower market on Sunday mornings.

The inhabitants of Castillon love summer fêtes too, and they have a beer festival in August, and truly spectacular re-enactments of the battle in July and August. These are superbly arranged with a local cast of almost 1,000 in fifteenth-century costume, on strings of horses.

There are two hotels with restaurants in town, a municipal camping and caravanning site, a choice of *chambres d'hôte*, and a sports complex which includes a swimming pool and tennis courts. The *Syndicat d'Initiative* is at 5 Allée de la République (Tel: 57 40 27 58). The will give information about dates of the battle reconstruction, and availability of tickets.

Saint Emilion Situated about half-way between Castillon and Libourne, in tranquil green countryside, is an old settlement of true beauty. Saint Emilion must take the prize as the most important historic treasure of the lower Dordogne. Some 12km north-west of Castillon and about $3^{1/2}$ km from the Dordogne river, it perches in medieval splendour on a natural knoll, the highest point in the landscape for a considerable distance. This elevated position is an indication of the town's monastic beginnings – a wandering eighth-century Bénédictine monk, Emilien or Emilion, originally from Brittany, discovered a habitable grotto on what had been a Gallo-Roman site, and created the foundation of a hermitage there. He was joined by other monks in his new-found sanctuary, and gave his name to

the monastic centre, which grew slowly through a particularly gruelling type of expansion.

Saint Émilion. The rampart view

During the next century the industrious monks undertook to dig a monumental church to Emilion out of the solid rock. A massive extension of the natural cave complex which honeycombed the hill top, it took the religious order three centuries to complete. It survives today in the lower town, unique in Europe for its dimensions – it is about 38 metres in length – and enduring rarity and monument to an early faith that could, at times, almost literally move mountains.

This area is certainly richly endowed with archaeological and historic evidence of the past, going back to far antiquity. There are many castles, *châteaux*, monasteries and imposing ruins

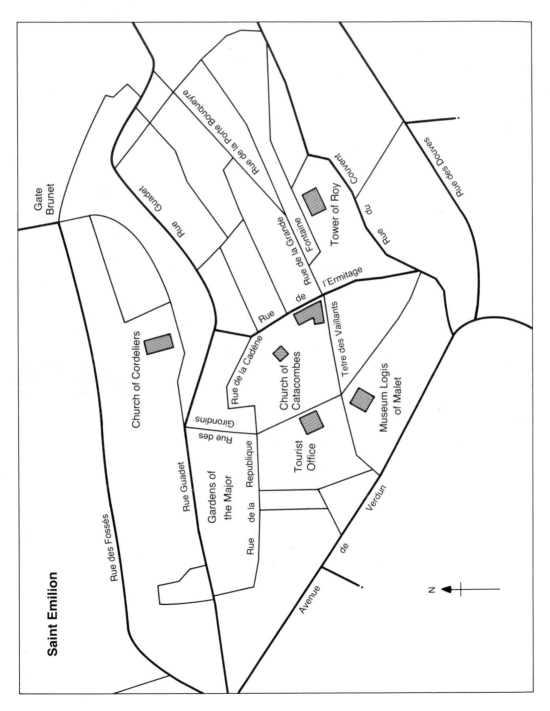

Saint Emilion

Gate Brunet

Rue des Douves

Rue de la Porte Bouqueyre

Rue Guadet

Rue de la Grande Fontaine

Couvent

Tower of Roy

Rue du Couvent

l'Ermitage

Rue de l'Ermitage

Church of Cordeliers

Rue de la Cadéne

Church of Catacombes

Tetre des Vaillants

Museum Logis of Malet

Rue des Girondins

Tourist Office

Rue Guadet

Gardens of the Major

Rue de la Republique

Avenue de Verdun

Rue des Fossés

N

scattered throughout the length of this fertile river valley, but none can really compete with Saint Emilion for a past of continuous habitation. This place was lived in not only in Roman times, but in the Neolithic Age, as proven by the discovery of polished stones, flint arrowheads and implements unearthed and retained by those beavering monks of the ninth to twelfth centuries. Such finds are commonplace in central Dordogne, but very rare along the tidal river.

Certainly the exceptional geographical location of the site, the climate, the abundance of natural shelter in the rock faces, the lushness of the vegetation (where Romans were cultivating vines in the first and second centuries), and the sweet spring water all combined to make this plateau setting safe and very appealing to early man. The disadvantage was that Saint Emilion was an envied prize and potential source of rich booty during the early Christian period, especially to periodic waves of Moorish invaders and later to even less scrupulous bands of marauders. Like most other settlements in this area, it suffered badly at times, but it did survive.

Little imagination is needed to envisage France as she was in the Middle Ages

Saint Émilion

In the twelfth century the town was at last made a military stronghold, with defensive ramparts and a massive citadel-keep, the Tour de Roy, being built as a direct result of the union between Henry II and Eleanor of Aquitaine. Their youngest son (King John, of Magna Carta fame, 1167–1216) was cruel and degenerate, but the charter was signed. Among other benefits, it bestowed commune status upon Saint Emilion, an early convert to the English dominion.

Saint Emilion changed hands several times during the Hundred Years War, but suffered much more damage in the sixteenth-century religious wars, when there was devastating looting and almost total ruin of the ancient monastic town and its precious monuments. Yet, despite repeated pillage across the centuries when almost all the principal fortified ramparts were destroyed, together with the medieval buildings, fragments of the former and a scattering of the latter did survive around the almost indestructible twelfth-century keep, as well as the monastic complexes, the monolithic and the collegial church.

In the fourteenth century certain parts and settlements along the lower reaches of the Dordogne and the neighbouring waters of the Garonne and Gironde were more important than others. These strategically sited strongholds, which came under the protection of Bordeaux, capital of English-dominated Aquitaine during the fourteenth century, included Castillon, Libourne, Cadillac, Bourg-sur-Gironde, Blaye, and Saint Emilion. Because of the significance of their location they were stoutly fortified and reconstructed when necessary. As a result much of historic interest is concentrated on this low hillside, where Saint Emilion sits above a sea of vines.

Don't miss: Twelfth-century monastic walls; Bouqueyre Gate; Rue de Clocher; Place du Marche; Tour du Roy; guided tour of vineyards.

Saint Emilion will present car owners with problems. It is too small and too concentrated, and the streets are too narrow to accommodate visitor traffic. You can park in designated areas outside the original ramparts, but you should arrive early in the day in high summer otherwise they will be full. Alternatively, consider spending the night at one of the five hotels in town (four of which have parking facilities for limited numbers), or use the scenic and well-maintained three-star municipal touring site for campers and caravanners, La Barbane. This is situated beside a small lake, about 3km north of the town – a short taxi-ride or a pleasant walk along vineyard access lanes to Saint Emilion.

Another idea is to make a base at Libourne and hire bicycles from the railway station. This is ideal countryside for cycling if you keep to the network of back roads which are more or less free of hills, with few cars. There are other interesting villages to see in the area too, but do leave the best part of a day to visit Saint Emilion.

A short distance from the old north gateway, the Porte Bourgeoise on the Libourne road, there is the sole surviving remnant of the twelfth-century monastic walls. Massive in construction and dimension, with huge Gothic window arches, this is the only evidence of a long-gone Dominican priory of colossal conception, which, because it was situated outside the town walls, was once destroyed by French army troops, in 1337. Even in this tiny town there were – and still are – six city gateways. (This probably contributed to the town's undoing in medieval times.) They range from an unusual doubly-arched entry, known as the Breach Gate, to the old southern approach, the most venerable of medieval portals, the Bouqueyre Gate, where a small look-out tower (the Counterfort) still survives.

There are some splendid views, across the town itself and the surrounding countryside, from the pedestrian perimeter circuit. This circuit is well worth completing before you enter the centre to enjoy the delights of the Rue de Clocher, or the atmospheric Place du Marché. There are guided visits to the Hermitage, Trinity Chapel, Catacombs and the Monolithic Church, conducted daily during the summer season from the tourist office (housed in a finely restored medieval building, La Doyenne). Alternatively, you can simply wander around the evocative fourteenth-century cloisters of the Collegial Church, ascend the steps to the top of the ancient Tour du Roy, or amble the steep sloping alleyways around the bell-tower of the Monolithic Church. Let your feet take you in ever-decreasing circles, from the ramparts to the church spire heart of town.

There are a dozen delightful places to eat in Saint Emilion, three three-star hotels within the town confines, and one four-star hotel-restaurant, the Hostellerie de Plaisance, in the Place du Clocher.

Wine One of the best things to do when you are in Saint Emilion is visit the vineyards, either on your own or on one of the guided tours that are available from June to the end of September. Wine culture began on the sun-blessed hillsides of

Quite apart from the famous wines, St. Émilion has an enviable reputation for its cuisine

Saint Emilion a very long time ago. When the Romans reigned supreme, Decimus Magnus Ausonius, a regional consul (and a poet), had a villa built here, and one hundred acres of vines placed under cultivation, according to the records. Then apparently, vines were not cultivated from the second to the twelfth century; only then was the vine planted and nurtured again, on comparatively safe ground by growers who, in exchange for allegiance to England, enjoyed the stability and social advantages forthcoming (for a while at least) to towns within the Bordeaux environs. In 1228, Edward I of England decreed the boundaries of the town's jurisdiction (among others in the region), which correspond exactly to the limits of today's vineyards.

In the following years there was a considerable increase in the wine trade, with much export to England and to the royal households. In 1312, Edward II restored to the town (among other privileges) the right to elect its own mayor, in return for a gift of fifty barrels of clear, pure wine, 'to be delivered to London by Easter'. Easter was the start of the medieval new year, so the king obviously intended 1313 to begin with a bang!

For a while, despite the ruination and depopulation caused by war and the epidemics which afflicted that era, Saint Emilion enjoyed cycles of prosperity. By the eighteenth century, all Saint Emilion wines were certificated and, to protect the high reputation of the ancient vintage, could only be despatched from the little port of Pierrefitte (on the Dordogne a short distance upstream from Libourne). Boats were to discharge their cargo only at the designated destination, and were forbidden to make drop-offs on the way.

In the mid-nineteenth century, there was another near-disaster, when the mysterious vine pest, *phylloxera*, ravaged the vines. The eventual vineyard renaissance began with pest-free vines imported from America, and the vines blossomed steadily throughout the twentieth century, annually fruitful except in very bad years like 1956.

Today, the Saint Emilion Premier Grands Crus are famous for their fine colour and high alcohol content, especially those which come from the higher slopes, where there is a predominance of limestone subsoil. These vintages benefit particularly from a long period of maturing. If an annual crop suffers serious damage because of adverse winter weather conditions, the growers' ruling body does not hesitate to declassify the entire year's production. No wine of inferior vintage is marketed under the Saint Emilion label.

If you are thinking of buying, apparently the younger and more powerful vintages have the greatest affinity with strong-tasting foods like cheese, cooked meats or game, while the older, more mellow wines go best with roast meat or fowl, or as an accompaniment to oysters. The vintage is also favoured for marinating fruits like pears or peaches.

Each year, there are colourful guild ceremonies (resurrected from the Middle Ages), including the Judging of the New Wine in June and the Proclamation of the Wine Harvest in September. Celebrated by the wine-growers, town burghers and crowds of visitors, such fête days capture for a brief spell the distant past.

Around Saint Emilion Saint Emilion is a jewel of the past, but there are a number of other delightful backwater villages and hamlets in the area for those who love quiet France. Just to the east of Saint Emilion, dotting the narrow ridge of low hills which rise above the Dordogne, are three which are certainly worth a visit.

St-Christophe-des-Bardes boasts a fortified *château*, largely rebuilt during the reign of Louis XIV. It also has remnants of much older architecture, including a medieval tower, making it the most ancient of outlying fortified settlements in this district.

St-Etienne-de-Lisse is a charming village with fewer than 500 inhabitants, situated on the minor road D130 just south-east of St-Christophe, with fragments of fourteenth-century castle ruins. It is a strong possibility that it was within this stronghold that the French army accepted the English surrender after the decisive battle of Castillon. Following this procedure of military protocol, the bloodstained combatants of both sides might well have made their way to the fortified village church, erected in the twelfth-century and still remarkably well preserved.

Three to visit: St-Christophe-des-Bardes; St-Etienne-de-lisse; St-Laurent-des-Combes.

St-Laurent-des-Combes is just to the south-east of Saint Emilion, and even more venerable in its beginnings, with parish records going back to the beginning of the thirteenth century, and architectural evidence proving it was the site of yet another, even earlier settlement. The ruins of a Gallo-Roman grand villa can still be seen, not far from a particularly fine Romanesque church in a superb state of preservation.

Finally, by taking the little road west of Saint Emilion, you will come upon Pierrefitte on the banks of the Dordogne, just off the D19. Here, at this tiny old port, there is a prehistoric standing stone, a sturdy, weather-eroded menhir that is a relic of Neolithic times.

Libourne Along the central reach of three enormous loops which the Dordogne describes before widening to estuary width, the Libourne location was near-perfect for a medieval river port. The water is tidal, yet partially subdued by wide bends and narrow enough to bridge, with a ready-made barge siding in the form of the river Isle tributary. In addition there are uninterrupted distant views both upriver and down, valuable for defence.

This first-rate site first attracted the Romans, who established a fortified settlement where the town now stands around the first or second century AD. However, they unwisely chose the Dordogne bankside (where Condat now stands, some 2km to the south), and Roman *Condate* was totally destroyed, probably by Visigoths, during the Dark Ages.

270

In the eighth century a new port was built, on the orders of Charlemagne, who made it much more of a redoubt than the Romans had. This settlement, too, deteriorated, languishing until 1269, when it once again became coveted as a splendid potential commercial and strategic centre by English occupiers. Under King Edward I of England, the governor of Guienne, Sir Roger de Leybourne, ordered the creation of a purpose-built new town and port, and named it after himself. The Keeper of Edward's Purse (before he was crowned king), Sir Roger was also a close and loyal friend. He was a warlord of some reputation, born at the ancient family seat of Leybourne, not far from Maidstone in Kent, of Norman descendancy. He is thought to have perished during a crusade to the Holy Land, but his heart, according to the practice of the time, was taken home to Kent and buried within the wall of Leybourne village church. His lasting legacy, however, lies in the town which bears his name in Gallic form.

Libourne

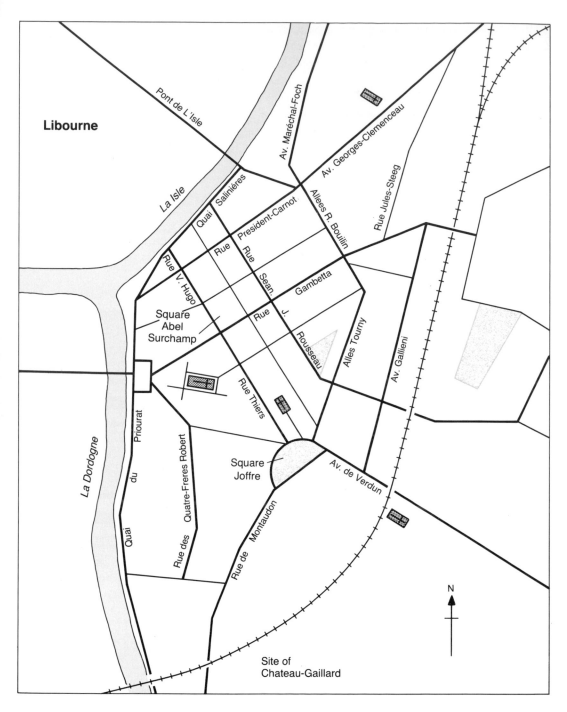

Libourne

Pont de L'Isle

La Isle

Av. Maréchal-Foch

Av. Georges-Clemenceau

Rue Jules-Steeg

Quai Salinières

Allees R. Bouilin

Rue President-Carnot

Rue V. Hugo

Rue Sean.

Gambetta

Rue J.

Rousseau

Alles Tourny

Square Abel Surchamp

Av. Gallieni

Rue Thiers

Quai du Priourat

Rue des Quatre-Freres Robert

Square Joffre

Av. de Verdun

Rue de Montaudon

La Dordogne

Site of Chateau-Gaillard

N

Today, Libourne retains the distinctive atmosphere of a medieval *bastide* in the centre. The fortified township and port, completed in 1270, still reflect the exact site-plan conceived and executed in the thirteenth century. The most ancient parts have either been conserved or restored, particularly around the spacious arcaded central square, and in the suburb of Condat, at the junction of the Dordogne and Isle rivers. Although most of the defensive ramparts were destroyed during the Royalist uprisings of the nineteenth century, the tower bases of the Porte du Grand Port have survived, testifying to the massive dimensions of the walls which once surrounded the township. There is a fine distant view over the old town from the river bridge, and the machicolated clock-tower is the most distinctive, if isolated survivor of the quayside ramparts.

One of the most striking buildings of central Libourne is the fifteenth-century town hall in the Place Abel Surchamp, which was savaged and then left to fall into sad disrepair after the Revolution. It has now been restored to its former aspect; the interior has a grand staircase, wall tapestries and fine wood panelling. An elegant library room contains treasures of the past, including a manuscript of great heritage value, the *Livre Velu* (literally 'hairy book'), in which are compiled all the charters granted to the *bastide* town of Libourne by the kings of England. There is also an interesting archaeological museum and an art gallery, containing some of the works of René Princeteau, of whom Toulouse-Lautrec was once a pupil.

Some of the best-preserved ancient *bastide* buildings are in the Rue des Murs, the Rue du Port-Coiffe and the Rue des Chais, all near the Quai Souchet and the riverside Esplanade du 8 Mai. For a glimpse of military architecture of the *ancien régime*, see Les Casernes, just to the north of Place Joffre, the barracks built to the orders of Maréchal Richelieu over two centuries ago, part of an officer's academy opposite pleasant formal gardens known as the Square of the 15th Dragoons. These landmarks perpetuate the martial past of Libourne, and World War II is not forgotten either, with the Place des Martyrs de la Résistance.

The commercial heyday of Libourne was during the era of the Second Empire, when wine shipments were loaded aboard tall ships from a constantly bustling quayside, for this was the major embarkation point of Saint Emilion and many other Bordelais vineyards which were nearer to Libourne than to Bordeaux. The Atlantic is about 90km away, but the tidal flow is considerable at Libourne, so that it was possible for quite deep-draughted sailing ships to reach the port on the highest tides. The colourful maritime activity has long ceased, but the town remains a very important administrative centre of the wine trade, while the local town *caves* with their ultra-thick walls are almost tailor-made for storage of vintage wines.

Libourne is a nice place to consider as a touring base, with a genuine working town atmosphere and not too much tourist gloss. The people are friendly, and the urban urgency that affects so many sizeable towns is absent. There are a dozen hotels ranging from three-star luxury to unclassified adequate, plus many restaurants and

The arcades of Libourne

cafés, ranging from brasseries to American bars, English-style pubs and Italian trattorias. There is also a pleasant municipal camp ground 2km along the Saint Emilion road, which is level, tree-shaded and open from Easter to mid-October.

The indigenous population of Libourne is approximately 23,000, and this is not much increased by tourists, even in high summer, although there is always a steady flow of transit visitors interested in this wine-soaked region. Libourne is lively and interesting, yet it has its tranquil corners – tree-lined riverside walks where there were once mighty ramparts, a formal garden, quaintly old-fashioned with a bandstand, and some inner town strolls along historic, narrow streets, laid out with military precision by the Kentish Sir Roger. The tourist office (closed Monday) is in the Place Abel Surchamp, next to the town hall. Car parking is usually possible here, if you arrive early enough, except on market days which are Tuesday, Friday and Sunday morning.

Don't miss: Porte du Grand Pot; Rue du Port-Coiffe; Hôtel de Ville; Rue des Chais; Rue des Murs.

Libourne – Useful Information

Syndicat d'Initiative and tourist office: Place de l'Hotel de Ville Libourne, Tel: 57 51 15 04. (Immediately off Place Abel-Surchamp). There are ten hotel-restaurants, including one three-star, the Hotel Loubat in the Rue Chancy, close to the railway station, Tel: 57 51 17 58. There are more than two dozen restaurants and café-bars, including three brasseries, pizzerias, trattorias and a grill-Americain. The restaurant Le Chai, Place Decazes, specializes in wood-fire grills and *confit*. The restaurant Kim Dao, in the Rue President-Carnot, offers cuisine Franco-Vietnamienne, while Les Demons de Bacchus, 40 Rue Fonneuve, provides traditional specialities of the south-west of France.

The SNCF station is a mainline express stop between Bergerac and Bordeaux, with north lines to Périgueux, Angouleme etc. Off the Avenue Gallieni is the combined train and coach station and there is a regular local bus service. Cinemas (three screens), will be found in the Cours Tourny and the Rue Etienne Sabatié. The post office is in the Place Princeteau, while major banks will be found in and around Rue Gambetta. There are repair garages specializing in most makes and models, and there is a Hertz car-hire centre at 4 Place de la Gare, Tel: 57 51 26 15, plus a Europ-car office in Avenue Gallieni, Tel: 57 74 04 60.

Vayres

Excursions from Libourne From Libourne you will soon find Fronsac, on the right bank of the Dordogne, a couple of kilometres from the centre of the port town. There was formidable castle here long before Leybourne and his military engineers laid out the *bastide*, and centuries before that the caves dotting the south-facing limestone cliffs were occupied by Gallo-Roman people. Charlemagne, having completed his river port at *Condate*, had a bastion built upon Fronsac hill, above the Dordogne and Isle rivers, which was later modernized, strengthened and occupied by the English for most of the Hundred Years War. From the site of Fronsac's Romanesque church, there are some splendid views across the valley.

Fronsac, like neighbouring Pomerol, boast many ancient vineyards producing recognized fine vintages. These are mainly reds, of rich bouquet, and a long shelf-life of up to fifteen or even twenty years. The Fronsac vineyards cover some 300 hectares of stony limestone hill flanks, producing and retailing around a million bottles a year. Once again, a most enjoyable way of exploring this landscape is by bicycle, or on foot; it is within easy distance of Libourne town centre.

Railway buffs may be interested in a *ligne touristique*, with a terminus 16km north of Libourne, at the ancient village of Guitres. Where, steam and diesel engines pull traditional old *chemin de fer* carriages through Bordelais countryside along the banks of the Isle river, and you can recapture some of the atmosphere of earlier rail travel. The line extends to the outskirts of Marcenais village, 15km to the west and the journey takes an hour. An old watermill at the Guitres terminus has been converted to provide refreshments, and there is a P9-class steam engine, one of France's most powerful veteran locos, on display. Just to the east of Guitres there is a nice little municipal camping site at Coutras on the banks of the river Dronne, open from Easter to November. There are good facilities here and amenities include a heated swimming pool.

There are also interesting places to visit on the left bank of the Dordogne. One is probably the most famous and the most imposing of Libournais country estates, 8km south-west of Libourne off the N89 – the Château de Vayres. During the reign of Henry IV (the brave, popular, Protestant 'Henry the Great',

278

who was Lord of Guienne and only converted to Catholicism late in life), this was one of the most extensively fortified palaces in Guienne province, originally created as a royal estate. It was not destined to enjoy the king's patronage for long, for he was assassinated in 1610.

A wonderfully strategic location is enjoyed by Vayres, high above the waters of the wide Dordogne, and on the old military route between Bordeaux and what was then fortified Saint Emilion, so it was bound to suffer badly in times of trouble. The most damage was done during the *Fronde* Rebellion of 1648–53, when nobles fought collectively against the idea of central power being held exclusively by the crown, as instigated by Louix XIV, and again during the French Revolution. Today, its Italianate Renaissance style has been immaculately restored, and it epitomizes the grandeur of many sixteenth-century royal French palaces. The gardens are gracious and formal, and the *château*, on its raised and once-moated defensive mound, has steeply-pitched roofs (to deflect missiles), castellated walls and capped towers. Yet it is extraordinarily classical and unfussy of outline. The Château de Vayres is open to visitors every afternoon (3 to 5 pm) in July and August, and Sunday (afternoons only) at other times of year.

Bordeaux You will need at least one full day to see stylish and lively Bordeaux, Aquitain's capital city, and the major city of the Guienne province. It is not really within the Dordogne, but it is historically fascinating because it is the heart of old Aquitaine, the territory that saw the terrible Anglo-French contretemps of the Middle Ages and witnessed some of the most murderous episodes, and also some of the most civilizing advances in the development of the two countries. From the moment of the royal alliance in 1152 of Eleanor and Henry Plantagenet, future king of England, Aquitaine was guaranteed near-perpetual strike for the next 300 years. Bordeaux was to suffer from repeated wars and insurgences from the time of its creation as the major city of the Guienne province.

Worth a visit: Frousac; Guitres; Château de Vayres.

In the twelfth century Guienne and Gascony together formed the duchy of Aquitaine. After the French military successes against the English in the thirteenth century, the area of Guienne was restricted, and severed from Aquitaine, although it remained united with Gascony. The re-formed Guienne embraced part of Périgord, Limousin and Quercy, but its most important sector was

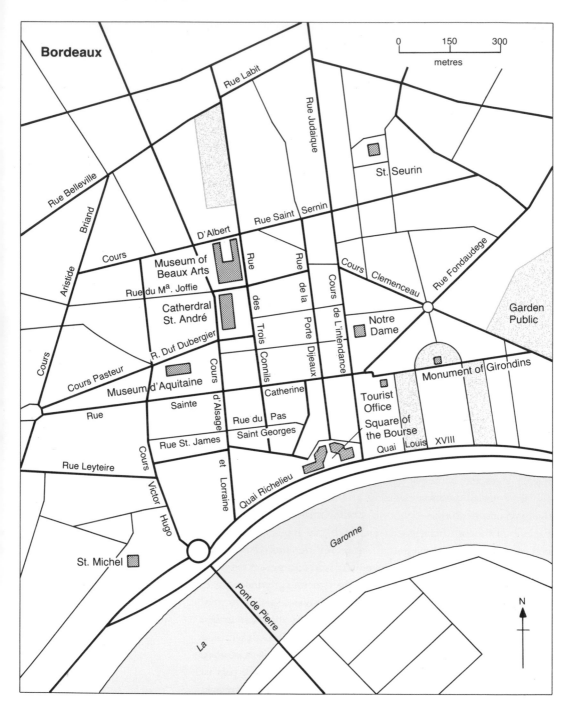

Bordeaux

0   150   300
metres

Rue Labit

Rue Judaique

St. Seurin

Rue Belleville

Briand

Rue Saint Sernin

Rue Fondaudege

D'Albert

Aristide

Cours

Museum of
Beaux Arts

Rue du Mª. Joffie

Catherdral
St. André

R. Duf Dubergier

Rue

des

Rue

de la

Porte

Cours

Cours Clemenceau

Cours de L'intendance

Garden
Public

Notre
Dame

Monument of Girondins

Cours

Cours Pasteur

Museum d'Aquitaine

Trois Connils

Dijeaux

Cours

Sainte

d'Alsage

Catherine

Tourist
Office

Rue

Rue du Pas

Square of
the Bourse

Rue St. James

Saint Georges

Quai Louis XVIII

Rue Leyteire

et

Lorraine

Quai Richelieu

Cours

Victor

Hugo

St. Michel

Garonne

Pont de Pierre

La

N

Bordelais, with the ancient countship and capital of Bordeaux at its heart. The political and commercial centre and seat of government of the combined Guienne-Gascony region endured until the end of the *ancien régime*; after the French Revolution the area was divided into the *départements* of today (under the *région* of Aquitaine), including Dordogne and Gironde.

Bordeaux's History *Burdigala*, as it was originally recorded, was founded in the third century BC, a Celtic settlement noted for its tin mining. The later Gallo-Roman town was raised approximately where the Cours de l'Intendance now runs westwards from the river. Among the principal Roman structures were aqueducts, temples and an amphitheatre. The Palais Gallien is one of the very few traces of Bordeaux's earliest era which remain, and is just to the south-west of the public gardens off the Rue Fondaudège.

Following the third-century invasion by Barbarians, the town was fortified for the first time; more sophisiticated ramparts were thrown up by the English when they took over the city in 1154, and these were extended in 1327, a decade before the start of the Hundred Years War. Finally, in 1453, with the French re-conquest, several fortresses were constructed around the city perimeter, to deter any revolt against the monarchy. Of all these massive defences, only traces remain.

Throughout its long history, Bordeaux posed awkward problems to rulers, both potential and actual. From the time it played host to the court of English kings at Château l'Ombriére, it was a contentious city and yet a port of immense commercial value, especially as an outlet for the thriving wine trade. Following the defeat of the English army in 1453 at Castillon-la-Bataille, Bordeaux was placed under siege, but it took three months to exact submission to Charles VII of France. The city was punished as a result, and a deep and lasting resentment against the crown was thus created. This resentment found its cause almost a century later when the citizens took up arms in protest at the imposition of a grossly unfair salt tax. This impelled every citizen over the age of eight to buy a fixed amount of salt weekly. In theory the tax was to be imposed uniformly nationwide but it happened that some provinces managed to get themselves exempted. Bordeaux was not one of them The subsequent revolt

The regal Pont de Pierre spans the Garonne at Bordeaux. To the left is the elegantly slim spire of Basilique St Michel

was put down with merciless ferocity by Anne, Duc (yes, *Duke*) de Montmonrency, Constable of France, a ruthless and bloodthirsty warlord who died by the sword in 1567.

As in many other towns in this region, there was a strong Huguenot following in Bordeaux, although the city was predominantly Catholic. After the Paris massacre of Protestants on St Bartholomew's day in 1572, some 300 people were slain in Bordeaux for their religious beliefs. Bordeaux played an even more important role in *La Fronde* in the seventeenth century, suffering much hardship since it was the principal stronghold of the movement. The *Frondistes* were nobles seeking to reverse the centralized government by royalty, instigated by Cardinal Richelieu and his successor Mazarin, in favour of the old provincial fiefdoms. The revolt escalated into a civil war which

raged across Guienne from 1648 to 1652, then exploded into a full-blown war with Spain. Two very serious uprisings took place in Bordeaux in 1653 and 1675.

Not until the eighteenth century did an enlightened governor of Guienne (the *Intendant* from whom the city-centre boulevard takes its name), the Marquis de Tourny, seek to heighten the quality of life in Bordeaux with a massive rebuilding and street-widening programme. City life improved, but Guienne and Bordeaux were to suffer again during the Reign of Terror after the Revolution, this time because they represented the main centre of Girondist activity.

The Girondists were a group of deputies, mainly from the *département* of Gironde, who were democratic revolutionaries, generally more intellectual than aggressive. Robespierre hated them as 'radicals who had become conservative'. Despite their patriotism they were repressively proscribed and most were eventually executed, murdered, or driven to suicide. Only when Robespierre himself was executed in 1794 were they acknowledged as martyrs of liberty. Today the Monument des Girondins remembers the esteem in which the gallant pioneer republicans were eventually held in Bordeaux and in the whole of France.

Seeing the Sights If you approach the centre of Bordeaux from the north, the experience is likely to put you off the city permanently. Take the short, straight approach from Libourne, on the N89. You will come into Bordeaux over Garonne via the Pont de Pierre, a magnificent multi-arched bridge over 500 metres long. The right bank offers a fine panorama of the left-bank quaysides of the town, and the impressive skyline punctuated by the spires of the great cathedral and the churches.

Pont de Pierre, built between 1811 and 1822, is a direct continuation of the N89, becoming, on approach to the river, Avenue Thiers. Cross it and immediately turn right along the Quai Louis XVIII, to reach the parking areas round the Place des Quinconces. There is an unmistakable landmark here, the tall Monument des Girondins, topped by a statue of liberty. The car parks are huge, and you should find a space. If you can squeeze in by the Allée d'Orléans, it is just a step to the tourist office, which is itself within easy strolling distance of the old town.

Most of the gems of historic Bordeaux are contained within a square-mile of wide, tree-lined avenues and beautifully-proportioned square. There were created when the ancient walled city was opened up and virtually rebuilt around the treasures considered worthy of preserving. Some gifted architects and sympathetic town planners of the eighteenth and nineteenth centuries including the classicist, Victor Louis, were responsible for ensuring that the best of the past was saved.

At the tourist office, in the Cours du XXX Juillet, you are adjacent to the spacious Place de la Comédie. Here, where splendidly wide eighteenth-century boulevards converge, is the Grand Theatre with majestic Corinthian columns, completed in 1783 by master architect Victor Louis. Close by is the massive Maison du Vin de Bordeaux, headquarters of the wine trade council; its location in the illustrious area of the city's architectural centre is evidence of a powerful public esteem.

Don't miss: Monument des Girondins; Cours de l'Intendance; Place Gambetta; Maison du XIV Siècle; Cathédrale Saint André; Saint Seurin church; public gardens.

Bordeaux

Place de la Comédie is the heart of Bordeaux

North from here, along the high-quality shopping street of the Cours de l'Intendance, Place Gambetta, perhaps the most impressive of all the city's meeting places. The square is dominated by the regal Porte Dijeaux arch, formerly a principal entry point to a fortified city that was once just a fraction of its present size. Another ancient gateway, representing the medieval English era of Bordeaux occupation, is the Porte de la Grosse Cloche, dating from the sixteenth century. This was the former belfry of the old town hall. Other legacies of the English era are the Tour des Anglais, close to the Palais de Justice off the Cours d'Albret, and the Porte Cailhau (Quai Richelieu), built at the end of the fifteenth century to commemorate the return of Bordeaux to the French. Here there are also fragmentary remains of a medieval *château*, L'Ombrière, the long-time residence of English overlords, including Edward the Black Prince.

Other sites of the preserved past are the house of Montaigne in the Rue de la Rousselle (Michel Montaigne was mayor of Bordeaux in 1580), and the Maison du XIV Siècle, in the Impasse Rue Neuve. This is the oldest house in the city, once the residence of a medieval noble, and a building with distinctive Gothic windows. Also, vestigial rampart fragments may be seen in the Impasse Bouquière.

The great religious gem of Bordeaux is the Cathedral of Saint André, begun in the eleventh century, completed almost five hundred years later, and only surpassed by Notre-Dame in Paris in overall dimensions. Incorporating both Romanesque and Gothic features, it is an awesome structure, with towering spires and a mass of medieval sculpture. The adjacent Pey-Berland tower, built in 1440, commemorates a medieval archbishop.

The most ancient of Bordeaux's churches is Saint Seurin in the Place des Martyrs de la Résistance, where, in an ancient crypt dating from the time of the Norman Conquest of England, there are burial tombs estimated to date from the sixth century.

From the Monument des Girondins in the Esplanade des Quinconces there is a marked-out pedestrian route of one or two hours' duration, which takes in the main attractions of the old riverside section of town, between the memorial and the church of Saint Michel to the south. And to the north-west of the monument is a popular picnic lunch area with locals and visitors, the 25-acre public gardens, just off the Cours de Verdun. Here there are lawns, flower beds and shrubs, as well as an orangerie, a boating lake, and a fine museum of natural history, containing many zoological specimens of Aquitaine, ancient and modern. The museum is open every afternoon from 2 to 5.30pm. (except Tuesdays).

The public gardens are not the only open space in Bordeaux. In the western part of the city the Parc Bordelais covers some 75 acres. The smallest park, and perhaps the nicest is the 1½-acre green patch in Place Gambetta, while the grandest is the Bois de Bordeaux to the north of the city centre. Here there are 350 acres of woodland, plus a 400-acre man-made lake, with footpaths, a cross-country circuit and golf links. Nine green open spaces altogether create some 1,000 acres of leisure terrain in the city.

One way of seeing all these sights is by bus. Pick up a brochure in the tourist office which lists four bus routes that take in most of the historic places of interest. Tickets (at reduced price, in booklets) may be bought from news-stands, or singly (at the standard rate) from the driver as you board.

Shopping The heart of Bordeaux has much allure for the discerning shopper, or the window-shopper. Most of the luxury stores and specialist shops are in the Cours de l'Intendance, the Allée de Tourny and the Cours Georges Clémenceau. The best antique shops are clustered in the older part of town, notably in the Rue des Remparts and Rue Notre-Dame.

For the most famous of all Bordeaux products, it will pay any potential buyer to call at the celebrated Maison du Vin de Bordeaux, just opposite the tourist office. Where, free advice and literature is available on everything you could wish to know about the range of world-famous wines which are available locally. Their address is 1 Cours du XXX Juillet, Tel: 56 52 82 82.

For old, cheap, intriguing or unusual souvenirs, visit the daily flea market at Place Saint-Michel. Also interesting is the 'ecological market', displaying organically-grown produce, held each Thursday at Place Saint-Pierre. (You might combine a visit to this area with seeing the colourful port and taking a boat trip – several launches operate trips along the Garonne and the Dordogne, varying from an hour to a whole day.) As well as the specialized and open markets there are five covered markets open

287

every morning (except Sundays), and two of the most popular are in the Place des Capuçins and the Cours Victor Hugo.

Museums Bordeaux has no fewer than eleven places of culture embracing every facet of past and present, from a Customs and Excise museum to the Centre National Jean Moulin, exhibiting memorabilia of the World War II Resistance movement. There is a marvellous Musée d'Aquitaine, covering the period from the reign of Louis XV to the present. The *Casa de Goya* in the Cours de l'Intendance, is the restored and preserved house where the Spanish portrait painter lived, and died (in 1828, aged 82).

After Dark For evening entertainment the choice is wide in a city of some 210,000 inhabitants, with over 600,000 within Greater Bordeaux. There are ten theatres, forty cinemas, seven theatre-workshops and fifteen café-theatres. For fun with youth-appeal, call at the Youth Information Centre, 5 Rue Duffour-Dubergier, where full details of all up-to-the-minute city activities and of less expensive accommodation may be obtained, Tel: 56 48 55 50.

If you want to dine out in style, there are numerous high-class restaurants, specializing in traditional or *nouvelle cuisine*, in and around the city centre, as well as many informal snack bars, cafés

The estuary of the lower Dordogne was once one of Europe's busiest commercial waterways, but is now devoted to leisure traffic

and pizzerias. If you like fish dishes, you will love Bordeaux, where the choice of seafood is superb – from lampreys to turbot, and from lobster to lemon sole, all served with a large selection of fine Bordeaux wines. All the classic dishes of Aquitaine are to be found in its capital, including *magret* (duck steak), *foi gras, confit*, oysters and the much-favoured *entrecôte à la Bordelaise* (beef steak served with a red-wine sauce and shallots).

The End of the Dordogne The north-western corner of Gironde *département*, along the right bank of the river, is markedly tranquil compared to the Entre-Deux-Mers left bank and the spreading influence of Bordeaux. Along the low landscape ridges to the north of the water, vineyards, fruit orchards and arable crops dominate, dotted occasionally by tiny hamlets. The sleepy atmosphere is shattered, however, as you make the flyover crossing of the A10 and negotiate St-André-de-Cubsac.

This town is not remarkable, although it has an imposing fifteenth century Romanesque church, and a huge number of retail outlets for wine but it provides a route, on the minor D669, to the intriguing and ancient riverside settlement of Bourg, about 30km from Libourne.

Bourg-sur-Gironde is an ancient and fascinating citadel, not overly patronized by holiday visitors

Despite its full name of Bourg-sur-Gironde, this town is on the Dordogne river – the Gironde appellation refers to the *département*, so it ought more correctly to be called Bourg-*en*-Gironde. Whatever, it is the substance that is the attraction – a cluster of medieval France, sun-baked almost to a Mediterranean degree, with a marvellous warmth embellishing the stone remnants of a fortified thirteenth-century citadel.

Bourg is situated on a natural limestone outcrop, and there was once a formidable fortress here. Evidence of the past survives in the extensive rampart walls, and in the old houses which line the steep and narrow streets winding upwards from the little harbour, once busy with commercial barges, and now almost exclusively a leisure-boat haven. This friendly working town, dominated by its architecture of the past, is devoted to viticulture, as it has been since the time when the nearby Château de la Citadel housed the eminent archbishops of Bordeaux during the seventeenth century.

Park at the port side, and wander, first around at picturesque waterside level, then up on the top town terraces, where you can see the advantage of the site to medieval builders who would have had defence and landscape domination in mind. The distant views

The confluence of the Dordogne and the Garonne rivers. A Roman watch-tower overlooks this strategic · stretch

are splendid. For a closer look at the massive rampart walls, walk along the lane past the municipal swimming pool to the camp ground, which centuries ago formed the first line of defence.

Beyond Bourg, and indeed *within* this compact little town, the vast width of the river dominates. This impression is accentuated a few kilometres westwards, along what is known locally as the Corniche de la Gironde. Climb the Pain de Sucre to see some wide and handsome sweeps of estuary water, made even more impressive now by the joining of the Dordogne with the Garonne. Far below the Château Tayac vineyards, where a Roman watch-tower still stands, the Dordogne and the Garonne become the mighty Gironde, which then rushes powerfully to the Atlantic. If you have traced the whole of the Dordogne watercourse, from its source in the Auvergne mountains, it is an impressive final view.

There is one more waterside town that is fascinating enough to be included. Blaye lies some 12km downriver along an estuary edge minor road, where the islet-dotted waters of the Gironde exceed 3km in width. It is a charming estuary port, largely sustained by the wine trade and a degree of light industry, and, apart from a scenic waterside location opposite the Médoc

vineyards (accessible by ferry boat), it is worth visiting because of its connections with two of the most illustrious figures of French history – Roland and Vauban. Roland is said to be buried here, while Vauban has left to posterity a mighty citadel fortress, one of an incredible total of more than 160 thrown up or rebuilt around France's frontiers during the reign of Louis XIV. The structure at Blaye is the only one lying alongside the Dordogne watercourse.

Roland is to the French what King Arthur is to the English – a valiant hero, half real, half legend, a tantalizing figure of mystery shrouded in the mists of time. The facts are that Charlemagne's army, returning to France after campaigning in Spain in 778, was ambushed by Basque tribes in the Roncevaux Pass (south of St-Jean-Pied-de-Port) where a rearguard legion was wiped out. The medieval romance (much embroidered by troubadours), has heroic Roland, the rearguard commander, battling stubbornly and refusing to enlist Charlemagne's aid (despite the pleas of his dwindling kinsmen), until the last desperate moments. Only then, with his dying breath, did he warn his liege with a blast on his hunting horn. In the legend, the Basque band (who actually melted away unharmed into their familiar mountains), become a Saracen horde of some 400,000, which Charlemagne, returning promptly to the pass with his main army, proceeded to annihilate. This stirring stuff was related in the famous poem of chivalry, knightly valour and treacherous betrayal, *La Chanson de Roland*.

It is claimed that beneath the Blaye fortifications, built in the seventeenth century when the port was known as Blaye-et-St-Luce, is a far more ancient basilica of a settlement named Blavia, where the body of Roland was laid to rest in 778. If this is true, the knight has royal company, for a century later Charibert, King of Toulouse, was buried in the same place.

The citadel of Blaye is really significant as a standing memorial to Vauban, a man with an amazing life story. Born in 1633, this impoverished orphan rose to become Marshal of France and the greatest military engineer in the history of Royalist France. As a young man he sympathized with the anti-Royalist *Fronde*, fighting with conspicuous gallantry and exhibiting a flair for siege warfare. He eventually gave his allegiance to Louis XIV, and fought for him in many battles and sieges.

Vauban's knowledge of military engineering was brilliant, and during his service with the Sun King he created a ring of impregnable bastions right around France. The citadel at Blaye has all the hallmarks of the master-builder's projects – massive scale, inherent strength and incredible durability.

Sebastien Le Prestre de Vauban was an innovative genius and equal credit is due to Louis XIV for realizing the potential of his military engineer. In later years Vauban, also a prolific writer, became increasingly uneasy about national poverty and reverted to the politics of his youth. He was prophetic in foreseeing the French Revolution, and died, virtually out of royal favour, in 1707. Wherever you go in the Republic, a Vauban colossus of stone will not be far away. The bastion at Blaye epitomizes the permanence of all Vauban's structures, and is an intriguing seventeenth-century creation at the end of the Dordogne.

Part Six: **Further Information**

Souillac

Further Information

Sport The Dordogne can offer a comprehensive range of leisure activities, from downhill or cross-country skiing in deep winter to windsurfing in high summer. Rock-scrambling, rambling, canoeing and pony-trekking all have a wide scope, while there are high-standard heated pools, tennis courts and, increasingly, golf courses, within easy distance of nearly all the main towns. In addition, the Dordogne caters particularly for potholers, anglers, cyclists and walkers.

Hiking and Rambling Leisure walking is much the most popular pursuit in the region, especially day-walking and backpacking. The whole area is networked by long-distance trails and a wealth of circuit rambles of short or medium duration.

Hiking and rambling enjoy many advantages in France, and especially in the Dordogne, not least the semi-Mediterranean climate and the favourable geography. Heavy walking boots and thick socks will not be necessary here in the summer, except perhaps in the Parc des Volvans high mountains. Training shoes, preferably of a design giving good angle support, are perfectly adequate for short- or medium-distance forays, and even for long-distance trekking, provided your rucksack is only light. (Heavy footwear may be needed to offset the carried weight of camping gear.) Similarly, light clothing will generally suffice, since heat, not cold, and dehydration, not drenching, are the hazards in high-summer France. In the southern region shorts and vests are seen far more along footpaths and trails than anoraks and over-trousers. Carrry a wool pullover, though, and waterproofs. Consider a wide-brimmed linen or cotton floppy hat as a shield against a Dordogne sun that can shine surprisingly fiercely.

Remember, too, that distances between watering holes can be great. On long-distance trails road-walking can be fatiguing over unshaded terrain, so be reasonable when setting personal distance targets. And for any pedestrian venture more ambitious than a local stroll, take a large scale map and a compass. For detailed information about all the major hiking trails, contact the Comité Départemental des Sentiers de Grande Randonnée, 7 Impasse Vesone, 24000 Périgueaux, Dordogne.

The most spectacular walking is at the north-eastern end of the region, while the Corrèze area of Limousin is also delightful, richly wooded and thinly populated, and easier on the legs. There are a number of scenic pockets and marked footpath routes west of Bergerac too, notably north of the river Dordogne within the adjacent forests.

Angling There *are* trout to be had along the narrow mountain streams and in the catchment lakes, but the best fishing is found where the Dordogne widens; anywhere the Dordogne widens; anywhere west of Argentat should prove fruitful. In France fishing is the main participant sport of the indigenous population, and along almost every reach of the Dordogne and its neighbouring rivers you will see fishermen casting hopefully. It is worth packing your own rod and tackle; take the longest rod you can for those wide-water French rivers, plus a selection of floats to deal with widely differing depths and current flow. Float fishing is top favourite in France, while ledgering and spinning have fewer adherents. In hill country the fly fishermean comes into his own among the fast-flowing white-water streams, domain of the brown trout.

Because angling is so popular you will find tackle and bait shops in nearly every town, while many *Syndicat d'Initiative* offices dispense anglers maps freely, or for a modest charge. These maps show many first-category trout streams to the south-west of Souillac, and many more to the south-east of Bretenoux along the Cantal boundary. For detailed information on the various river and lake waters (and the necessary visitor permits), Périgueux is the best source. Enquire at the Association de Peche, 31 Rue Wilson, 24000 Périgueux Tel: 53 53 44 21. Camping sites are often well informed about angling potential in the immediate locality, especially those situated along the barrage lakes, and many of them are authorized to issue day tickets, advise on the hire of rowing boats and so on. Waterside hotels will offer the same services, and guests may even have access to private water. In the *département* of Corrèze alone, there are no less than 2,500 acres of natural and man-made lakes (many of which are south of Brive and Ussel and thus within the Dordogne area). For those who prefer river fishing, Corrèze is also the natural overflow region of the Millevache Plateau (source of a thousand springs), which results in numerous swift-flowing waters.

Equestrian Sport Horse-riding centres are located, in the main, in the central and north-eastern *départements* notably Dordogne, Corrèze, Cantel and Puy de Dôme. The tourist office or the *Syndicat d'Initiative* of the principal town in your area will give information on the kind of riding you prefer. Some stables specialize in tuition for the whole family (where hunters and half-pint ponies are kept together), others concentrate on hourly or half-day excursions, and others are involved with the fast-growing pursuit of long-distance trekking (*randonnée*). Some stables cater for experienced riders only, some for novices only, some for both.

The *randonnées* are organized from centres which tour the lakes and volcanoes of Puy de Dôme. There are all-inclusive guided treks, with meals and *gîte* accommodation, which may extend to five, six or seven days of horseback exploration, for parties of up to ten people. Zanières Stables at Ardes sur Couze south-west of Issoire Tel: 73 71 84 30 offer this type of trek. There is another high-country stables at Besse, the Centre Equestre de Berthaire, which is open from mid June to the end of August Tel: 73 79 55 21. Horses and ponies are available, as is tuition, and short rides or distant treks through the surrounding hills.

On a similar theme, the horse-drawn waggon is becoming an increasingly popular method of holiday transport in certain areas of the Dordogne. There are now a number of stables which specialize in this delightful pursuit in the company of a willing draught horse. Routes are carefully selected, along back lanes and farm tracks, and often in the most beautiful and uncrowded countryside. Further details from the Association Départementale du Tourisme Equestre, BP28, 33025 Bordeaux Tel: 56 88 02 68, or write to Hobby Voyages, 8 Rue de Milan, 75009 Paris.

Canoeing and Canoe-Camping The Dordogne river holds much appeal for those who like to paddle their own canoe,

and no watercourse in France has better provision for the enthusiast. At all the riverside towns, and at many of the smaller villages too, you can hire not only the craft, but camping gear to go with it, and a list of transit bases where you can haul out and pitch your tent at the end of each day's travel.

The kayak and the canoe (especially those containing all the gear to allow for self-contained independence), are one of the best ways of seeing the river valley from water level. The canoeist, enjoys really breathtaking views of towering limestone cliffs and fairy-tale *châteaux*. And if you don't want just to drift lazily with the current, you can relish the shooting white-water rapids on the neighbouring river Vézère.

There are half a dozen canoe/kayak centres in Dordogne *département*, as follows:

Copeyre at Martel	Tel: 65 37 33 51;
Safaraid at Luzech	Tel: 63 56 23 54;
Circal at Creysse	Tel: 65 32 20 40;
Canoe-Raid at Siorac	Tel: 53 31 64 11;
Canoe-Loisirs at Vitrac	Tel: 53 59 10 71;
Roye at Vitrac	Tel: 53 28 33 05.

Horse riding is one of The Dordogne's fastest growing pursuits, with outdoor enjoyment for the most part well away from roads and traffic

Gregarious water sport is available on many lakes

Canoe centres will provide all the necessities for a canoe tour. For example, Safaraid suggest a tour between Argentat and Beynac, a distance of about 120km. You pick up your canoe and kit (including safety gear, like flotation jackets, river notes and maps), and set off. You may choose to start and finish your trip anywhere between the limit centres – perhaps Beaulieu or Souillac – and you can take your time according to your aptitude and inclination. A company bus service operates along the entire river route (calling at each base at regular times each day), so you can return to a chosen set base each night if you prefer. Hire a craft and additional gear can be by the day, week, or even hourly at certain periods during the season. All overnight camping pitches are reserved for you and expert tuition is available you need it.

Other Sports If you enjoy (or want to try) the exciting and increasingly popular sports of hang-gliding and parascending, there are several recognized places along the central and upper Dordogne valley where you can leap off and enjoy eagle-eye views of the landscape. One popular base will be found just south-west of Argentat, where the richly wooded hills to either side of the wide river valley are lofty without being too intimidating for newcomers to the sport. For information, between Easter and the end of October, contact Camping Au Soleil d'Oc, at Monceaux Tel: 55 28 05 97.

Also gaining enthusiasts at a rapid pace is the sport of archery (*tir a l'arc*). You will find it available at Monceaux and at other long-stay touring sites along the river.

Visitors and locals alike seem to be inspired to take part in sports, and there is not shortage of facilities for them. Bordeaux has no fewer than six swimming pools, indoor and out, heated and natural, with one of Olympic standard, and rock-climbing to squash, golf to ten-pin bowling, windsurfing to potholing, every preference is catered for.

As well as participant sports, there are many spectator sports, including rowing club competitions at Bergerac (one of the oldest rowing clubs in France), horse-racing at Le Bugue in July, motor racing at Clermont, and car hill-climb events at Le Mont Dore. Motorcycle scrambles are keenly followed at many weekend meetings, and, at the other end of the scale, you can watch the gentle art of *boules* at just about every village in the Dordogne region.

The Dordogne for Children Most smaller children need simple and straightforward sea, sand and sunshine on holiday. Although there is no sea along the great Dordogne valley, there is no shortage of fresh water, and the number of inland *plages* is quite surprising. There are beaches at many, if not most, of the barrage lakes, including Bort-les-Orgues and Servières (Lac Feyt), and at countless designated reaches along the Dordogne, Vézère and other rivers in the region. The beaches may be narrow and quite tiny, but they will keep countless kids happy for most of the day.

One word of caution: regarding small children all the watercourses in the Dordogne area have reaches where the current is fast (and not always obviously so), or where the depths

Camp grounds for children take some beating for informal fun and easy living. The French are masters of the outdoor life

are deceptive. Release small children only at designated stretches of water, preferably under proper supervision.

At river or lakeside *plages* it is usually possible to hire inflatable boats or pedalo craft for use in specific, marked stretches of water. These stretches of water are often adjacent to long-stay caravan and camping parks, and Château du Gibanel near Argentat is a good example. This funsport provides every kind of water sport and pastime, and they may be enjoyed from your own caravan or tent, or from hired studio flats or mobile homes in a scenic wooded valley setting. Open from May to September Tel: 55 28 10 11.

For older children the Dordogne offers the natural world. There are interesting aquariums at riverside towns, including Sarlat and Le Bugue (the latter claims to be the biggest private aquatic enterprise in western Europe), exhibiting a wide variety of indigenous and migratory species. For mammal enthusiasts, there are a large number of wildlife parks in this part of France.

Visit the popular Forest of Monkeys at L'Hospitalet, near Rocamadour, where many species, from marmosets to Barbary Apes, roam more or less freely within some 10 hectares of attractive woodland. Also good is the Parc de Vision, at Gramat, where there is a scenic combination of flora and fauna, including botanical specimens to be found on the wild *causses*, and many wild animals of European origin. A third popular venue is the Tropicorama Zoo at Padirac, close to the cavernous *Gouffre*, which contains a colourful collection of tropical birds, a selection of mammals and rare species of plants.

Visits to some of the spectacular *grottes* of Dordogne, such as Padirac or Proumeyssac, near La Bugue, will always find favour with children, as will entry to the Féénedu Rail (world in miniature exhibition), at l'Hospitalet near Rocamadour. They will also be fascinated by the Prehisto Parc de Tursac, near Les Eyzies, a prehistoric theme park to stimulate any imaginative young mind and perhaps awaken a lasting interest in the ancient past. Here there are scenes of daily life as it is presumed to have been lived thousands of years ago in the Dordogne river valley, with Neanderthal hunters and replica mammoths pose in tableaux of frozen action. A visit here might well be followed up by a trip to a genuine prehistoric settlement and archaeological site, such as Castel-Merle, near Sergeac, where there are also troglodyte medieval cave dwellings, and expert flint-knapping demonstrations. Both Tursac and Sergeac lie a few kilometres north-west of Sarlat, in the secluded heart of the Vézère valley.

There is not doubt, however, that the area neat to the source of the Dordogne river is the best choice for the young. Le Mont Dore and La Bourboule offer a wealth of amusements, and a variety of child accommodation (accompanied or otherwise) that could not be wider. They will appreciate the leisure park of Le-Mont Dore, while the popular Lac Chambon at Murol, covering about 60 hectares, is something of a kids' paradise in July and August. Here they can swim from supervised shallow bathing beaches, fish, learn to sail, or splash about in small boats. As an alternative, the lake of Bort is not far from Bourboule; it has a massive 1,600 hectares of water, supervised bathing beaches, and sophisticated water sports, like water-skiing, for older children.

Wildlife and Nature As the French coasts became more and more crowded and polluted, nature lovers look inland for their leisure pursuits. The Dordogne is doubly blessed – far enough from the seaboard to avoid the overcrowding suffered by the Riviera and other coastal regions, and still unspoilt so that wildlife can live unharmed. There *are* pockets of urban bustle, but the area is still a haven, both geographically and climatically, for many species of European animals and birds.

The natural vegetation thrives in the Dordogne region is part Mediterranean and part sub-Alpine, with deciduous forest prevalent, and coniferous trees and sub-Alpine tundra gradually dominating the north-eastern sector. Within a relatively small span of countryside, you can see heat-loving lizards along with pine martens, more associated with the conifer forests of the Scottish Highlands.

Massive city sprawl does not exist anywhere in this area; even Périgueux, the Dordogne *préfecture,* is quite compact and ecologically inoffensive. The dominant feature of this great landscape tract, apart, the Bordelais vineyards and the Auvergnat green mountains, is forest. Geologically, the region is influenced primarily by the *massif central,* the largest area of elevated terrain in France. This plateau was thrust upwards from the Earth's crust around 250 million years ago, and today it includes two of the best wild areas of the country – the Parc des Volcans of Cantal, and the *causses* of the Lot and Dordogne *départements.* Among the

The Upper Dordogne particularly is a riot of colour at times – a happy hunting ground for wild-flower enthusiasts

splintered gorges is a richly diverse range of wild flowers, bird life and animals not dependent on forest cover (eagles, buzzards, hawks and the rock-dwelling, sun-loving mammals and reptiles which are their life-support prey).

In the rest of the terrain, woodland predominates; in fact, almost a quarter of the total land-mass of France is forested. Some

304

of the more secluded woodland supports quite large species such as roe deer, red deer and wild boar. The first are common, the second rare, and the third more widespread than you might think, and there is a chance (albeit a slim one) of seeing any of these once common game species in the semi-open mixed woodlands between Bergerac and Périgueaux or in the area to the north-east of Argentat.

Medium-sized mammals like the red fox, badger or otter, will be more easily spotted, although bager and otters are now very shy of man along the Dordogne. To observe the species good local knowledge is essential, and chances for the casual visitor are inevitably reduced. You need to find evidence of occupation (usually in an isolated location), then make regular and frequent dawn or dusk forays in the hope of success. The prize is immense, but the pursuit requires infinite patience. Impromptu sightings of wildlife are probably the best the transient traveller can expect.

The Dordogne area is further enhanced for animals, since between the great forest swathes there are mini-plains created by agricultural activity. Here the farms are small, not too concentrated, one adjoining the other, and the arable land is not worked to the point of exhaustion. Fields are often allowed to rest as meadow for years rather than months and the result is an undisturbed habitat for hares, rabbits, field voles and woodmice, which in turn attract the hunters like the stoat, weasel, polecat and pine marten.

The forest clearings and woodland margins which separate the scattered farmsteads are home to a healthy population of red squirrels, and the red foxes which catch them when they can. (The urban fox, a common sight in Britain, is rare in the Dordogne.

Bird life is prolific throughout the area, and you will often see common buzzards, or the less common red or black kites (distinguished from the buzzard by a forked tail). If you are lucky you may also spot a golden eagle, whose smaller predatory brethren – the harrier, sparrowhawk, hobby and kestrel – all thrive healthily here too, because of the light pressure of man upon the landscape and the abundance of the food supply.

You will also see all the common smaller species, as well as the more rare shrike, crested skylark, golden oriole, tawny pipit, great reed warbler, short-toed creeper and rock sparrow. Noisy

Nature lovers will find a host of species among the foxgloves and broom

305

woodpeckers can often be heard too; there is a large population, including two rare species, the grey-headed and the middle-spotted woodpeckers. Night-hunting owls also abound, most often heard by the camping enthusiast.

Every stretch of water supports a heron population, while waders like the bittern, although not often seen, can be identified by their booming call, especially among reed beds at dusk, or long after dark. Shelduck, teal, tufted ducks, pochard and shoveller can all be found where the water of the rivers have been barraged and then left more or less undisturbed, while the estuaries of both the Dordogne and the Garonne, before they join the Gironde, are much-favoured haunts of duck, especially the ubiquitous mallard. On the faster-flowing upper reaches of the rivers, particularly the Vézère, the little dipper and the flashing kingfisher are frequently sighted by the observant visitor, and just occasionally there may be the visual treat of an exotic hoopoe with its impressive head crest.

Along the water courses, especially in the sun-warmed shallows rich with reed-bed insect life, all the familiar reptile species thrive, including the common frog, common toad, natterjack toad and common newt. You will also see the lizard species (more frequently seen in the drier, scrubland of the *causses*) – the little common lizard, the wall lizard, the sand lizard, the colourful green lizard, which can grow to nearly 40cm in length, and the snakelike slow worm, which inhabits woodland areas where there is plenty of water.

The non-poisonous grass snake likes water too, and enjoys swimming in areas where there is a big frog population. The smooth snake looks like an adder but it also harmless. There are two poisonous native snakes, the common adder and the asp viper. The former is found almost anywhere throughout the Dordogne, while the latter favours the drier domain of the stonier, more open country uplands the bite of either is painful, although rarely fatal. Any naturalist deliberately seeking snake habitats should carry a snake-bite antidote kit, just in case.

If you want to take nature study seriously, choose dun-coloured clothing or even a camouflage jacket and bush-hat; if the hat has a veil attached, this will tone down the potentially alarming flash of the face. It will also keep midges and mosquitoes at bay during any long vigil. Carry a pair of standard naturalist

The truly quiet Dordogne country, so often sought by British visitors. A scene between Bort-les Orgues and Argentat

binoculars (approximately 8 x 30 magnification), and perhaps a stout walking-stick, which can be used as a steadying unipod, to help you negotiate rough ground, and to ward off strange dogs. Don't wear strong aftershave or perfume, and make sure the wind is towards you when approaching any wild creature habitat.

Learn as much about your preferred species before going into the field. What are their preferred habitats? What tell-tale signs are they likely to leave? At what hour and seasons of the year are they likely to be most active? Dawn and dusk are the feeding times of most wild creatures. Dawn is likely to be best for the watcher, since this is the time of least human activity; of course dusk is good if badgers or owl are your quarry. Bird watchers should be armed with a good pocket-sized identification guide, preferably with coloured illustrations of species to be found in Europe.

The butterfly population of the Dordogne is interesting, particularly in the north-east of the region where colourful species will be found from late spring to early autumn. The swallowtail, Camberwell beauty, red admiral and peacock are just a few of the more sizeable and dramatically marked to be seen basking where there are banks of wild flowers and plants such as fennel, clover, nettles or thistles, along forest margins and at sheltered higher altitudes. There are some handsome moths too, including the death's head and the Emperor, usually common in south-western France in early summer, in lowland open woodland. A good variety can always be attracted after dark with the aid of a paraffin pressure lantern.

The trees, shrubs and plants of the south-west region which provide the natural habitat for all this wildlife are so variegated that it would take an entire book to list them. There is a wealth of wild flowers, including the striking Yellow Gentian which flourishes in the high mountains of the Auvergne, and the riverside red campion. There is also a wonderful world of trees, ranging from the deciduous hornbeam, walnut, sweet chestnut and beech, to the poplar, both black and white, the distinctive plane tree, the pyramidal cypress and the feathery silver birch. Such is the variety of soil and climate that the visitor may also see tall silver firs, Mediterranean cork-oaks and the majestic English oak.

Language Guide This list contains enough words and phrases to cover most practical travel eventualities. Such a woefully brief lexicon can only contain absolute essentials, especially in view of the language, which is one of the richest in the world. There are, of course, countless omissions, which even the most elementary student of French will quickly detect. The following can claim to be nothing more than a building block of the most rudimentary kind.

There is no illustration of grammar, nothing about the all-important masculine and feminine genders, nothing about sentence construction, and no attempt to accompany the word with phonetic spelling. In short, this is a language guide to stimulate further learning through specialized books, tapes, TV; preferably all three, then practising in the best way possible, within the country of origin!

Words that are closely akin to English are omitted; such as 'pork' and 'porc', together with the most elementary of courtesy words and phrases like 'thank you' and 'good day'. Lastly, simplicity, plus brevity of the real world is acknowledged; i.e. 'plein' for a tankful of petrol, not a wordy if more grammatical alternative.

On the Road

Left	à Gauche	Poor surface	Chaussée Déformée
Right	à Droite		
Straight on	Toutdroit	Give Way (to traffic from right)	Priorité à droite
Bends	Virages		
Remember reminder (speed limit)	Rappel	Truck route	Poids Lourds
		Lorry	Camion
Slow	Lent	No Parking	Interdit de Stationner
Slow down	Ralentir		
One-Way Street	Voie Unique or Sens Unique	No through road	Toute Barrée
		Repair	Reparation
Forbidden	Interdit	Windscreen	Pare Brise
Speed	Vitesse	Punctured	Crevé
Pedestrians	Piétons	Brakes	Les Freins
Toll	Péage	Petrol (low grade)	Essence
Cul de Sac	Voie Sans Issue	Petrol (high grade)	Super
Road Works	Travaux	Full (tank)	Plein

308

Broken	Cassé	Indoors	Dans la maison
Breakdown (of vehicle)	En Panne	Outdoors	Dehors
		Dinner	Diner
Slippery road surface	Glissante	Eat	Manger
Tyres	Pneus	Drink	Boisson
Safe journey	Bonne route	Drinking water	Eau potable
Help	Assistance	Meal	Repas
Help me! (emergency)	Au Secours	Food	Aliment
		Meat	Viande
Headlights	Les phares	Bread	Pain
Traffic lights	Les feux	Bread roll	Petit pain
Pretty route	Bison Futé usually signposted simply as route 'Bis'	Cheese	Fromage
		Ham	Jambon
		Fish	Poisson
Low bridge etc	Hauteur limitée	Cod	Cabillaud
Look out	Prendre garde	Haddock	Aiglefin
Hurry	Presse	Lamb	Agneau
Give way at roundabout	Vous n'avon pas priorité	Oysters	Huîtres
		Lobster	Langouste
Give way at junction	Cedez le passage	Head waiter	Maître d'Hôtel
Starter (motor)	Demarreur	Cake	Gâteau
Gear box	Boit-de-Vitesse	Seafood	Fruits de mer
Spark plug	Bougie	Grapefruit	Pamplemousse
Tow-rope	Corde	Peach	Pêche
Jack	Cric	Veal	Veau
Injured	Blessé	Sugar	Sucre
Anti-freeze	Antigel	Vegetables	Legumes
Seat belt (or fan belt)	Ceinture	Yoghurt	Yaourt
Boil	Bouiller	All in price	Tout compris
Driver	Pilote	Mushrooms	Champignons or Cepes
I'm lost	Je suis perdu		
Found	Trouve	Jam	Confiture
Screwdriver	Tournevis	Sweets	Bonbons
Hammer	Marteau	Clear soup	Consommé
My car	Ma voiture	Soup of the day	Potage de jour
Mechanic	Mechanicien	Chicken	Poulet
Food & Eating		Wholemeal bread	Pain complet
Breakfast	Petit Déjeuner	Sausage	Saucisson
Lunch	Déjeuner	Self-service (restaurant)	Libre service

Apple tart	Tarte aux pommes	**Out of Doors**	
Plate	Assiette	Earth	Terre
(also cold-meat selection)		Sky	Ciel
Cup	Tasse	Wind	Vent
Knife	Couteau	Breeze	Brise
Fork	Fourche	Good weather	Beau temps
Spoon	Cuillère	Bad weather	Mauvais Temps
Cook	Cuire	Rain	Pluis
Bill please	l'Addition s'il vous plaît	Fog	Brouillard
		Changeable	Variable
Raw green salad mix	Crudité	Cloudy	Nuageux
Milk	Lait	Sun	Soleil
Fat	Graisse	Hot	Chaud
Eggs	Oeufs	Cold	Froid
Bottle	Bouteille	Chill	Frisson
Water (or wine) bottle	Carafe	River	Fleuve
Waiter	Garçon	River bank	Rive
Turkey	Dinde	Stream	Courant
Rye bread	Pain de seigle	Rivulet	Ruisseau
Melon	Canteloupe	Fields	Champs
Tuna fish	Thon	Hill	Colline
Nuts	Noix	Woods	Bois
Water ice	Sorbet	Rock	Roche
Ice cream	Glacé	Games	Jeux
Beer (from the pump)	Bière pression	Play ground	Terrain de Jeux
Glass	Verre	Stroll	Promenade
Toasted cheese sandwich	Croque Monsieur	Hiker	Randonneur
Lemon squash	Citron pressé	Hunter	Chasseur
Lemonade	Limonade	Fisherman	Pecheur
Hunger	Faim	Traveller	Voyageur
Thirst	Soif	Vineyard	Vignoble
Very good	Très bon	Wild	Sauvage
Bad	Mauvais	Footpath	Sentier
Vintage (wine)	Cru	Rucksack	Sac à Dos
Bun	Brioche	Sleeping bag	Sac de Couchage
Garlic	Ail	Return	Retour
Pineapple	Ananas	Starting point	Point de Départ
		Suntan oil	Huile solaire
		On foot	à Pied

Countryside	Campagne	Marsh	Marais
Country	Pay	Snowstorm	Tempéte de neige

Accommodation

Leisure	Loisir	Bed	Lit
Tree	Arbre	Room	Chambre
Star	Étoile	With bath	Avec bain
Dawn	Aube	With shower	Avec douche
Shelter	Abri	Dining room	Salle à manger
Riverside	Bord de la Rivière	Twin beds	Lits jumeaux
Spring	Printemps	Shade	Ombrage
Summer	Été	Quiet	Tranquil
Autumn	Automne	Clean	Prop
Winter	Hiver	Home	Maison
Bathe	Baigner	Holiday camp	Camp de vacances
No entry	Défense d'entrer	First floor	Premier étage
Upstream	En amont	Second floor	Deuxiéme étage
Downstream	En aval	Opposite	En face
Bird	Oiseau	Behind	Derrière
Rainbow	Arc-en-ciel	Bed & Breakfast	Lit et petit
Thunder-storm	Orage		déjeuner
Thunder	Tonnerre		
Lawn grass	Pelouse	Full board	Pension complète
Pond	Étang	Stairs	Escalier
Forest	Forêt	Dormitory	Dortoir
Dark	Obscur	Welcome (reception)	Accueil
Deep	Profond	Reading room	Salle de lecture
Study	Étude	Bell	Cloche
Cliff	Falaise	Ring	Sonner
Tired	Fatigué	Rest	Repos
Farm	Ferme	Rent	Louer
Leaf	Feuille	Roadhouse	Auberge
Search	Fouille	What is the	Quel est le prix
Cool	Frais	nightly charge?	pour nuit?
Frost	Gel	Front	Face
Stone	Pierre	Rear	Arriàre
Sun-stroke	Insolation	To leave	Quitter
Flood	Inondation	Key	Clé
Savage dog	Chien méchant	Full	Complet
Butterfly	Papillon	Upstairs	En haut
Bull	Taureau	Downstairs	En bas

Shopping

Shops	Magasins	Manufacturer	Fabricant
Chemist	Pharmacie	Closed for holidays	Fermeture Annuelle
Bakery	Boulangerie		
Butchers	Boucherie	Charge card	Carte de credit
Food store	Alimentation	Buy	Acheter
Grocery	Épicerie	Sell	Vendre
Cooked meat shop	Charcuterie	Money	Argent
Cake shop	Patisserie	Closing down sale	Liquidation totale
Bank	Banque		

General

Clothes	Vêtements	Agreed	d'accord
Jeweller	Bijoutier	Belongings	Affaires
Watch maker	Horloger	Round trip	Aller-retour
Shoe shop	Magasin de Chaussures	Quick	Vite
		Now	Actuel
Shopping area	Centre Commercial	Understand	Comprendre
		Friend	Ami
Film	Pelicule	Much	Beaucoup
Colour slide	Diapositif	Little	Petit
Paper shop	Magasin de la Presse	Need	Besoin
		Well	Bien
Closing time	Heure de Fermeture	Soon	Bientôt
		Free	Gratuit
Opening time	Heure de Ouverture	Ticket	Billet
		Information	Renseignements
Wine cellar	Cave	Each	Chaque
Hairdresser	Coiffeur	Have	Avoir
Furniture store	Meubles	Notice	Avis
Fish shop	Poissonnerie	Before	Avant
Book shop	Libraire	Other	Autre
How much?	Combien	Workshop	Atelier
Expensive	Cher	Repair	Reparation
Cheap	Pas Cher	Light	Allume
Presents (souvenirs)	Cadeaux	Count	Compter
Travellers cheques	Chèques de voyage	Phone book	Annuaire
		Discover	Decouvrir
Cheque book	Carnet de chèques	Ask	Demander
Cash till	Caisse	Difficult	Difficile
Stamp (postage)	Timbre	Easy	Simple
		Available	Disponible

312

Entertainment	Divertissement	This year	Cette Année
Give	Donner	Half	Demi
Listen	Écouter	Approximately	A peu prés
Equal	Égal	Illness	Malade
Delighted	Enchanté	Pottery	Faience
At last	Enfin	Trust	Confiance
Strange	Bizarre	Fact	Fait
Later	Plus tard	Happy	Heureux
At once	Immédiatement	History	Histoire
Child	Enfant	Century	Siecle
Wife	Epouse	Timetable	Horaire
Husband	Mari	Town Hall	Hotel de Ville
Today	Aujourd'hui	Here	Ici
Yesterday	Hier	Even	Même
Tomorrow	Demain	Odd	Impair
Day	Jour	Hospital	Hôpital
Week	Semaine	Perfect	Parfait
Month	Mois	Waterproof	Imperméable
Year	Année	Incredible	Incroyablc
Daily	Quotidien	Interesting	Intéressant
Weekly	Hebdomadaire	Head	Tête
Monthly	Mensuel	Hand	Main
Yearly	Annuel	Foot	Pied
Next Year	Prochain an	Never	Jamais

Further Reading

Michelin Motoring Atlas of France (Hamlyn)

The French, Francois Nourissier (translated by Adrienne Foulke) (Hutchinson)

Guide des Logis et Auberges de France (current edition)

Concise History of France, Marshall Davidson (Cassell)

Cycle Touring in France, Rob Hunter (Frederick Muller Ltd.)

Footpaths of France, Michael Marriott (The Crowood Press)

Michelin Camping Caravanning France, (current edition)

The Holiday Naturalist in France, Christopher O'Toole & Linda Losito (Christopher Helm)

Birds of Britain and Europe Bertel Bruun (Hamlyn)

Michelin Red Guide (hotels) (current edition)

The Dordogne Index

Note

Page references in *italics* indicate illustrations.
Page references followed by m indicate maps.